Also by Jeannette Ferrary and Louise Fiszer

The California-American Cookbook

SEASON TO TASTE

Jeannette Ferrary

Louise Fiszer

Illustrated by Lauren Jarrett

SIMON AND SCHUSTER
New York London Toronto Sydney Tokyo

PUBLISHED BY SIMON AND SCHUSTER
A DIVISION OF SIMON & SCHUSTER INC.
SIMON & SCHUSTER BUILDING
ROCKEFELLER CENTER
1230 AVENUE OF THE AMERICAS
NEW YORK, NEW YORK 10020

SIMON AND SCHUSTER AND COLOPHON ARE
REGISTERED TRADEMARKS OF SIMON & SCHUSTER INC.

DESIGNED BY LEVAVI & LEVAVI, INC.
MANUFACTURED IN THE UNITED STATES OF AMERICA

1 3 5 7 9 10 8 6 4 2

LIBRARY OF CONGRESS CATALOGING-IN-PUBLICATION DATA
FERRARY, JEANNETTE, DATE
SEASON TO TASTE.

BIBLIOGRAPHY: P.
INCLUDES INDEX.
1. COOKERY (HERBS). 2. COOKERY, AMERICAN.
I. FISZER, LOUISE. II. TITLE.
TX819.H4F47 1988 641.3'57 88-4484
ISBN 0-671-62132-7

FOR PETER, MATT AND NATASHA
AND FOR MY PARENTS, FERD AND
LORETTA FERRARY. J.F.
FOR MAX, MICHAEL AND MITCHELL,
MY OWN PRIVATE SPICE BLEND. L.F.

Acknowledgments

For their endurance, sense of the absurd, and spirit of adventure, we are most grateful to Max Fiszer and Peter Carroll. During the two and a half years of writing this book, they have eaten more experiments than meals, proofread more recipes than they've tasted. In addition to their role as culinary victims, they have also, during times of crisis, jiggled the computer, straightened out tangles of ideas and filled in every kind of blank.

We thank our friends who lent us their cherished old cookbooks and precious recipe collections, and who have probably been wondering if they would ever see them again. It was these dusty pages that so often gave us a feel for an era, a community or a way of living that we could glean in no other way. Our gratitude to Phyllis Browning, Rebecca and Bob Cherney, Leslie Hsu, Toni Illick, Evelyn Larsen, Frances Mayes and especially to M. F. K. Fisher, who so generously shared not only her library but her time.

This is our second book with our editor, Carole Lalli, whose most appreciated *modus operandi* we have finally figured out. Whether she's making "just a tiny suggestion" or unravelling the insoluble, she manages to do so leaving all relevant egos intact. Her authors are thus reinforced in the delusion that they have done everything themselves (even though, when they think about it, they know better).

Fred Hill, our literary agent, has once again taken care of those things which utterly befuddle, and has embraced several of these recipes with an enthusiasm beyond the call of duty. We're glad and grateful.

We thank Matthew Carroll who was invaluable in imposing alphabetical order on file folders, bibliography cards and miscellaneous scraps of data. And we thank Natasha Carroll-Ferrary, just seven years old, whose willingness to pick the herbs from the garden for recipe testing was always appreciated, even before she learned the difference between the rosemary bush and the Douglas fir.

Foreword

One reason I know that *Season to Taste* is good is that it reminds me of another old and true friend in my long life of reading about herbs and spices in America: *Herbs in the Kitchen* by Irma Goodrich Mazza. She wrote it as an experienced home economist who rather surprisingly found herself married to an Italian named Mazza. This astonishing fact showed in her own naive amazement at using some of the herbs and spices that had not been a part of her early American training. There is a distinct astonishment evident in the prose of this prim and proper deputy from an American school for home cooking and living.

I've always suspected that Mrs. Mazza wrote such a delightful book because she was so amazed at her unsuspected sensuality as a Latin lady. Of course, in *Season to Taste,* almost half-a-century later, marjoram and rosemary are less exotic, and at least one of the writers, Jeannette Ferrary who is half Spanish, is innocent of any such ethnical naiveté. The subtleties of nutmeg and peppercorns are familiar to her, as they surely are to her collaborator, Louise Fiszer, and no worldly sophistication can hide the fact that they are Americans writing about spices and flavors. They know and tell more skillfully even than Mrs. Mazza the story of flavorings in America, and with her same honest curiosity and enjoyment, but the fact remains that this subject will always be mixed with sensuality and a strange foreignness to our basically Puritanical history. That these two books are so alike in their innate approach is proof positive of their goodness.

M.F.K. Fisher

Contents

Season to Taste: Why We Wrote This Book

This is the era of the herb. Restaurant menus boast of their herbal ingredients; supermarkets are adding flowery bouquets of basil and dill to the familiar clumps of parsley and watercress; and aficionados are cultivating kitchen gardens to keep the freshest flavors close at hand. These interests are not exactly new. In its original forms, American cooking has always emphasized the role of herbs, but the mass production of food during the past century or so has diminished the importance of fresh ingredients and thoughtful cooking. Today's reawakening of interest in herbs and spices undeniably reflects the emphasis on simple cooking and the preference for natural ingredients with their intrinsic flavors intact.

So Americans are again learning to appreciate a variety of herbs, throwing them boldly into numerous dishes even without the sanction of a recipe. There is, in fact, something of the pioneer spirit about the current herb movement, a feeling that this natural resource has too long been ignored and now it's time to catch up.

So we knew there was room on the shelf for a cookbook about herbs. In this book, we offer more than two hundred new, richly flavored recipes, based on American herb and spice traditions and tailored to today's emphasis on lighter fare and healthful eating. Most of the ingredients we use are generally available to the home cook in all parts of the country. Though fresh herbs are always recommended for their fuller taste, directions are given for using dried herbs successfully. Procedures and cooking techniques are straightforward and clearly explained. And, most important, these recipes take full advantage of the flavors of herbs and spices and their ability to bring out the best in the ingredients they accompany.

In addition to the culinary herbs, we also include several spices with an important place in America's culinary past. In a sense, spices can be viewed as herbs, anyway, since they are most often the seeds or roots of an herb, and often in dried form. There are many complicated ways to define spices which would have excluded them; but we chose to consider them herbs and include them in this collection.

We also found that herbs and spices illuminate many little-known aspects of everyday life. In tracking down the development of regional specialties—how, for instance, a fennel-studded breadstick from the hill towns of Italy became an over-the-counter snack on the streets of San Francisco—we discovered some wonderful American stories about chives and sage, mustard and saffron; and we tell them again here. As much as possible, we report some of the lore, folkways, and home uses of herbs and spices in America. We do this because, oddly enough, it is still easier to find information about the ancient Greeks using oregano than the New England Portuguese or the Brooklyn Sicilians.

The American experience with herbs and spices is not just beginning; on the contrary, this country's culinary heritage encompasses a broader variety of herbs and spices than does any other country in the world. American cookery has benefited from the sheer diversity of contributors: hundreds of Amerindian cultures with their own, distinct food ways; colonists and settlers everywhere on the continent; the succession of nationalities and ethnic influences that continues to this day. As heirs to this splendid tradition, we all now have a new opportunity to share in its delicious wisdom.

Herbs and Spices: An American Adventure

The taste of herbs and spices is like the whistle of a train. It jogs the memory, it reminds you of a time when. . . . Like the whistle, the remembered tastes are invisible but powerful, fleeting, and eternal. They mean something beyond the moment: the soup in Barcelona when you were on vacation; the attempted Christmas goose that wasn't what you expected but had the stuffing that dreams are made of; the movies and pizza, pizza and the movies, with pepperoni only on special occasions.

In a sense, this book is about those occasions. It's about herbs and spices in this country—their American past, their continuing presence. The kind of cooking people brought to this country changed when they got here, partly because the available foods were different, but also because the people themselves changed. Much depended on where they settled and when. The Jews who came to South Carolina in 1694 have different food-styles from the Jews who settled in New York in the 1900s. Greeks in Tarpon Springs, Florida, cook differently and live differently from Greeks in Gloucester, Massachusetts.

In the kitchen, this meant adapting, intermingling, substituting, and omitting: one spice for another, two "new" herbs instead of one old favorite. Old Country dishes evolved to become the underpinnings of American regional cooking, different here from back in the homeland, different in Florida from that in Massachusetts.

Those who think American cooking is bland and devoid of seasonings will see that in its origins it is distinguished by herbs and redolent of spices. In the cooking of Native Americans, of early settlers, of every incoming ethnic group, herbs and spices were basic. They were a signature, an identity. This is why Colonial Americans planted culinary and medicinal herbs with equal urgency. To keep the character of their beloved food, Germans nursed the delicate saffron crocus to fruition in the wilds of Pennsylvania; midwestern Czechs cultivated poppies in their front yards; and urban Italians grew basil on their fire escapes.

In this book we try to recapture the spirit of this cooking in a way that appeals to current tastes and needs. Often this meant putting *back* some of the seasonings that have somehow disappeared over the years. These recipes are simpler and easier to prepare than the dishes that inspired them. They are often lighter, achieving a richness of flavor through the mingling of fresh ingredients with herbs and spices. In researching the history and food-styles of our American herb and spice heritage, we hope to celebrate what we've forgotten as well as what we remember.

• • •

Like most good stories, that of herbs in America begins before anyone started taking notes. In the wake of the European explorers, however, came the first journal writers who were anxious to report such things as the botanical goings-on across the seas. From them we know, or at least have been told, that the North American Indians used about fifty-nine different herbs, either as raw salads or boiled greens. In the western part of this continent, some Indian women were viewed as gourmets by the early explorers, who marveled at their sensitive use of herbs similar to basil, oregano, and various sages and cresses in their stews and soups. But they had many plants for cooking, such as gromwell root and *yerba del buey,* which had no counterparts among the herbs preferred by the early colonists. American Indian women are considered the inventors of the vegetable "casserole," actually an animal bladder stuffed with vegetables and seasonings. They were also pioneers in at least one borderline culinary application: chewing gum, in this case, chicory roots and salsify. From the Indians, colonists learned to boil game with peppergrass, dandelions, and cress. Those who survived also learned about other Indian herbal practices which transcended both the medical and culinary. Among these was the dramatic recovery of three shiploads of scurvy-ridden settlers, led by Jacques Cartier in 1535, after being fed a mixture of hemlock and black spruce. It was two hundred years before surgeon James Lind realized that the underyling cure was vitamin C. The Indian use of foxglove as a heart stimulant preceded by centuries its discovery, as *Digitalis purpurea,* by William Withering in England.

Generally speaking, native American herbs were not of culinary interest to incoming Europeans. Bergamot, used as a tea by the Indians, who extracted an oil from its leaves, was a rare exception. Its seeds were even brought back to England in 1744 from Oswego, on Lake Ontario, and a tea made from it was called Oswego tea. It was also Oswego tea that the American patriots drank after they had thrown the product of the British East India Company into Boston Harbor.

Except for a few native American species similar to their familiar homeland herbs, settlers grew their own plants as soon as possible. There is no mystery about which herbs these were. This information was carefully chronicled by such people as John Josselyn, whose *New England Rarities* (1672) is a list "Of such Garden herbs [amongst us] as do thrive there and of such as do not." They included sorrel, parsley, rosemary, sage, and "time." He also mentions what Indians did with them and even, in a second book (*Two Voyages to New England*), includes cooking directions, such as an "eel receipt." In seventeenth-century Virginia, Alexander Whitaker reported on the prevalence of thyme, hyssop, and marjoram; in the following century, John Randolph of Williamsburg described the progress there in *A Treatise on Gardening by a Citizen of Virginia* (ca. 1770). There were detailed pictures in Adriaen van der Donck's *A Description of the New Netherlands* (1653) in which he mentions "dill, sorrel, radishes, cresses, leeks . . . rosemary, lavender, holy onions," adding that "cummin seed . . . and the like succeed well but are not sought after." Because of Holland's powerful spice trade, the Dutch in New Netherland also had access to great quantities and varieties of spices until the English took New Amsterdam in 1664. We know that Swedes and Hollanders were growing parsley, peppergrass, and more or less the same things as their English neighbors in 1759, according to Dr. Israel Acrelius's *History of New Sweden.*

We also know which seeds were available through newspaper ads, such as the one that appeared in Williamsburg's *Virginia Gazette,* September 9, 1675: "To be sold at Mr. Miles Taylor's in the Town of Richmond, the following seeds, lately imported from Italy, viz. Sweet Basil, citron ditto, Chervil, Poppy, sweet Fennil [*sic*]"; and in the *South Carolina Gazette* in 1735: "Just imported from London to be sold by John Watson . . . mustard seed." We also know which herbs were best-sellers from seed catalogs published by nurseries, such as Bartram's in Philadelphia and Prince's in Flushing, New York. Most of the early herb gardens were of the most practical sort, but the finest of them have been simulated, under the auspices of the Metropolitan Museum of Art, in the medieval gardens at the Cloisters in New York's Fort Tryon Park.

In the early settlements, decisions about what to plant were based on culinary and medicinal considerations. The herbals that provided this valuable information on the properties of herbs often accompanied colonists to the New World. Among the most popular of these were the classics like Dioscorides's *De Materia Medica,* Pliny's *Naturalis Historia,* and *The Herbal of Apuleius.* More relevant was the sixteenth-century *Dos Libros,* in which Nicolas Monardes described the drug plants in the New World; and the ever-popular and still-used John Gerard's *Herball* (1597). Although herbals were not famous for their gourmet recipes, some did contain cooking instructions as well as directions for love potions and aphrodisiacs. Whatever the reason, three seventeenth-century herbals remained particularly popular among American colonists: William Coles's *The Art of Simpling* (1657), Nicholas Culpeper's *The English Physician* (1652), and John Parkinson's *Paradise in Sole Paradisus Terrestris* (1629).

The line between culinary and medicinal uses of herbs was, obviously, very thin. Paradoxically—at least from a twentieth-century viewpoint—one of the connections between them is the invention of candy! This is because herbal medicines were often accompanied by honey or sugar to disguise their bitterness. In fact, the anonymous author of the Hippocratic treatise on medicine (4000 B.C.) says that most medical concoctions began with the cook.

Decisions about planting were also based on the Doctrine of Signatures, the theory, explained in Culpeper, that the physical structure of a plant is a clue to its properties. Plants with heart-shaped leaves have coronary benefits; sharp thorns alleviate bites; dandelions and buttercups cure jaundice. Herbs that attracted bees were also important, especially before sugar was generally available. And some herbs were planted because of what might be called the natural human need for magic, in the kitchen and everywhere else.

In the kitchen, choices about which herbs and spices to use were based on personal experience and the products on hand. Although cookbooks contained recipes for herbal tonics and poultices, the food recipes often mentioned no herbs at all. This is not because they weren't used, but because it was assumed the cook would know enough to add them. Directions said simply, "put the same herbs and spices as if for soup," or "a thin broth made of suitable herbs," or "as much mace as needed." Recipes referred vaguely to sweet herbs, potherbs, or salad herbs, but these terms did have very specific meanings. Sweet or culinary herbs have an aromatic flavor or fragrance because of volatile oils or chemicals in their leaves, seeds, roots, or flowers. Potherbs are succulent plants like kale and cabbage, eaten as vegetables; the same plants eaten raw are called salad herbs. As for spices, they were always precious commodities since they were not, of course, grown in the garden. Their presence in the menu depended on the vicissitudes of the spice trade. Old favorites, like ginger, nutmeg, cinnamon, and mace, were more available in the port cities than elsewhere in the new country.

Colonial women had to import their cookbooks from England. One early favorite was *The English Huswife . . .* (1615) by Gervase Markham, in which the author postulates that the first step in acquiring cooking skills is "knowledge of all sorts of herbes." Hannah Glasse's *The Art of Cookery, Made Plain and Easy* (1747), the most popular cookbook in the colonies and in England, contained several recipes from India, many with ginger, curry mixes, and turmeric. Also a favorite of the times was the first cookbook published in America, which was also English: *The Compleat Housewife* (1742), edited by William Parks of Williamsburg from a work by Eliza Smith.

It wasn't until 1796 that anyone published an American cookbook by an American author using American ingredients, all packaged under one of the longest titles in the annals of American publishing. This was Amelia Simmons's *American Cookery, or the Art of Dressing Viands, Fish, Poultry and Vegetables, and the Best Modes of Making Pastes, Puffs, Pies, Tarts, Puddings, Custards and Preserves, and All Kinds of Cakes, from the Imperial Plumb to Plain Cake. Adapted to this Country, and All Grades of Life. By Amelia Simmons, an American Orphan.* Published according to Act of Congress in Hartford, Connecticut. Naturally this American collection was essentially a compendium of the New England cookery with which Simmons was familiar. Herein one finds for the first time the fine points of making spiced watermelon pickles, slapjacks, pumpkin pudding, coriander-seed cookies, as well as a list of "herbs, useful in Cookery." Five years later the American lexicon of herbs was given full treatment in Samuel Stearns's *The American Herbal.*

But books weren't the only source of herbal information. Along with his seedlings, Johnny Appleseed often brought an herb lore and information to the frontier families of Indiana and Ohio. And the Shaker religious communities, founded in 1774, printed useful herbal suggestions on the seed packets in which they sold their herbs. They also published the Shaker *Manifesto,* a periodical containing herb recipes and urgent exhortations like "Cucumbers want herbs!" They printed leaflets to advertise how their herbs could "add charm" to common, everyday fare. At their parent community in New Lebanon, New York, and in many of their settlements throughout the East, the Shakers planted an extraordinary variety of herbs, originally for their own use. Eventually they marketed their high-quality seeds, herbs, and herb products, including ointments and cough drops, from Australia to India.

Around this time, the interest in regional cooking, with its "exotic" mixes of herbs and spices, led to the publication of Lucy Emerson's *The New-England Cookery* (1808), often touted as this country's first regional cookbook. Actually it was largely a reprint of the Simmons recipes, repackaged under a homier and much shorter title. It was followed in 1824 by Mary Randolph's *The Virginia Housewife,* which offered various dishes to be cooked "in the Virginia style" as well as instructions for "Gaspacho-Spanish" and "To Make an Ollo-a Spanish dish." Lydia Maria Child's *The American Frugal Housewife* (1832) strongly reflects the New England preferences of its author (baked beans and chowders abound); but Eliza Leslie's *Directions for Cookery* (1837), published in Philadelphia, breaks away from specific regions to qualify as the first general American collection (complete with sandwiches and lots of white potatoes).

By 1857, Catherine Beecher's *Domestic Receipt Book* contains a recipe for "Southern Gumbo," which she describes as a favorite dish from the South and West. Peppers from New Mexico were often used in nineteenth-century recipes as one of the "new herbs." Indeed, the use of herbs and spices became a little too widespread for culinary "reformers" like Sylvester Graham, who cautioned that pepper, mustard, and catsup could cause insanity!

Immigration from abroad during the nineteenth century added a variety of flavors to the American melting pot—literally. Germans brought marjoram to their Texas sausages; Chinese imported fresh coriander and ginger for pork and vegetable dishes; Hungarians contributed paprika everywhere; Scandinavians created a fad for dill. Cookbooks of the era mirrored this interest in "foreign" culinary practices by presenting recipes for the "Portuguese method of Dressing a Loin" and "Sauce Italienne with white wine, sweet herbs," as well as Flemish soup (with a faggot of sweet herbs). Then, at the end of the century, a wave of "new" immigrants from southern and eastern Europe—Italians, Czechs, Greeks, Poles, Ukrainians, Jews, Slavs, and others—introduced a wealth of traditional dishes, many of them strikingly similar. Italian *gnocchi* weren't very different from Czech *noky* and Austro-Hungarian *Nockerln.* Turkish *shish kabob* resembled Greek *souvlaki,* Serbian *raznjici,* Russian *shashlik.*

Middle-class cookbooks such as *Miss Parloa's New Cook Book* (1880) reflected the broadening of tastes. Recipes included references to their ethnic origins as well as a variety of herbs and spices: leg of lamb à la Française, fillet of beef à l'Allemand, *zigaras* à la Russe, *gnocchi* à la Romaine, German toast, and even English monkey. Turn-of-the-century cookbooks, such as Fannie Farmer's first edition, offered eggs à la Finnoise, à la Suisse, and à la Caracas, plus a whole chapter of recipes for the chafing dish, a utensil that could be "traced to the time of Louis XIV." (The French influence was so pervasive that many newfangled dishes were dignified with French or ersatz French names.)

In the kitchen, instructs Miss Parloa, one needs a variety of fresh herbs on hand which "you can get . . . for five cents each at the vegetable market; . . . for a quarter of a dollar [you can get] herbs enough to last a large family a year." Urbanization and improving transportation meant that, ironically, "the housekeeper in large cities has no difficulty in finding all the herbs she may want, but this is not so in small towns and villages." Meanwhile, the *New Cook Book* (1898), by Sarah Tyson Rorer, domestic science editor of the *Ladies Home Journal,* included chapters on Mexican, Creole, Hawaiian, and Jewish cooking influences.

Whatever the names of these dishes, by the time they got into American cookbooks, they had, in essence, become regional American specialties showing the effect of adaptations and substitutions. There were always collections of regional recipes, assiduously compiled by ladies' church groups; handed out at state fairs; scribbled into private journals and diaries.

But in this century American cooking and regional cookbooks began attracting the attention of people outside the region in and for which they were written. *The Picayune's Creole Cook Book,* published in 1901, is still popular today, as are many of the early Pennsylvania Dutch collections and southern cookery books. The mix of influences, reflecting the nation's varying ethnic backgrounds, could be seen in such eclectic dishes as Taos salmon corn cakes; Valencia tamale pie; Murray County cornmeal dodgers and potlikker; and New England succotash from Kansas, Kentucky, and

Massachusetts, which are as different from each other as their points of origin. And of course we also find recipes for American vichyssoise, a shortcut made with a can of cream of chicken soup.

Most recently the influence of Asian and Eastern cooking has added the tang of hitherto unknown herbs like curry leaves, lemon grass, greater galingale (Laos root), and lesser galingale (*kentjur*). Familiarity with Chinese regional cuisines has brought us into contact with such flavorings as lotus seeds, tiger lily buds, various seaweeds, dried chrysanthemum, and five-spice powder (anise, fennel, clove, Sichuan pepper, cinnamon). From Indian curries and stews we're learning to distinguish the spicy tastes of tamarind, fenugreek, asafetida, and *kalongi* (nigella). We're not surprised to hear the waiters, in many restaurants today, refer to herb ingredients like yarrow, arugula, *epazote* (lamb's quarters). And we've almost come to expect salads and soups garnished with aromatic and brightly colored flowers, from thyme, rosemary, or nasturtium to chives or even garlic. The emphasis on herbs and spices keeps restaurant owners busy not only in the kitchen but in the garden, growing an unprecedented abundance and variety of fresh flavorings. The counterpoint of Eastern and Western cuisines is one of the most interesting of today's culinary trends, an inspiration to eclectic-minded chefs in their never-ending battle to provide surprises for their serious and demanding eaters.

As we congratulate ourselves on this new-found willingness to taste and experiment, to cross-fertilize in a discriminating manner, we should be aware that it is nothing new. In *A Kitchen Manual* (1941), Sheila Hibben describes the early 1930s as just such a time. Urged on by food writers, "Ladies who had secretly longed to add a bit of shredded coconut to their Tartar sauce straightway did so with assurance. . . . Everywhere cooks with literary tastes not only experimented with startling conceits of flavor, but wrote about them with naive enthusiasm." Hibben reminds us wisely that "although surprise is a desirable element in a meal, shock is stimulating neither to the palate nor to the gastric fluids."

Then as now, however, some good comes of these attempts to dissolve the gastronomic bands that have connected rosemary with lamb, sage with pork, and all the other traditional alliances. In fact, this penchant for fomenting little culinary revolutions is part of the American character, a salutary restlessness with the code as it has been handed down. We know what there is; we know what we're supposed to do. But, we also know about the spirit of adventure. And it prevails.

How to Use This Book

The chapters are arranged alphabetically, first herbs and then spices. Each chapter opens with the lore and lineage of the herb or spice, an inviting chronicle of its use and adventures in the American kitchen. The Vintage recipes and Signature dishes found along the way will fix the herb or spice in our culinary history. Next is the Consumer Guide, a handy reference chart of names and aliases of the herb or spice, the varieties available, what to look for on the produce shelves, how to store and care for, if and when to substitute dried for fresh, and which other herbs and spices make compatible companions.

Recipes are not categorized into courses within each chapter. Many people these days like to decide those things for themselves; one person's appetizer is often another person's main dish, and so forth. However, we also succumbed to the suspicion that a little conventional organization never hurt anyone—especially if it's optional. Therefore in the back of the book we provide a List of Recipes by Courses, a separate section in which all recipes are grouped by course (for example, "Salads") or by type ("Pizzas, Pastas, and Grains," and so on). Some recipes (for example, pasta salads) are listed under more than one category.

A separate chapter, Herb and Spice Vinegars and Mustards, contains some unique combinations and suggestions for mixtures useful as condiments, dressings, sauces, and flavorings. Herb Bundles and Spice Blends is a collection of interesting and useful arrangements of herbs and/or spices, wrapped up, tied together, or beautifully bundled. The chapter Suggested Seasonal Menus is meant to help in planning everything from the most intimate tête-à-tête to the most informal forkless feasts, all keyed to seasonal foods and events. The Basics and Methods chapters explain terms and techniques indicated throughout.

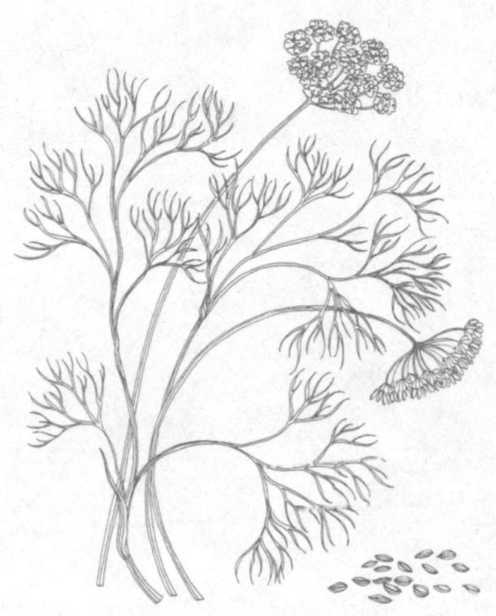

THE HERBS

Basil

LORE AND LINEAGE

We use it to remind ourselves that there is yet something in life that is sweet and spicy.

—ANGELO PELLEGRINI
The Food-Lover's Garden, 1970

If there were no such thing as pesto, basil may still have become popular in this country. But at the moment, basil seems assured certain immortality and even a bit of notoriety, thanks to its importance in the making of pesto. In Parma, Michigan, for example, the annual Pesto Challenge has become the major event of the Fox Hill Farm Basil Festival.

It's hard to believe that the few ingredients required for pesto—basil, garlic, oil, plus or minus a very few other ingredients—could generate the endless numbers of recipes that have come from this one festival alone. Each of the winners, and even the losers, insists that his or her recipe is the only way to reproduce authentic *pesto Genovese.* Warfare seemed imminent when the first pesto award was given to a member of the Piemontese Social Club, whose families came originally from Italy's Piedmont. This area is close to Genoa but, as one disgruntled Genovese put it, "not close enough."

Even the experts can't agree on *pesto correcto.* Edward Giobbi, author of several Italian cookbooks, who traveled to Genoa in search of the true version, announced solemnly that, "There is no such thing." In some recipes, cream is added or pancetta used in place of butter, or walnuts or almonds instead of pine nuts. Today's irrepressibly inventive chefs have even added American regional touches such as pecans, hot chile peppers, and various cheeses; some have borrowed from the French interpretation, called *pistou.*

But there is another dilemma even more basic to the great pesto debates: which type of basil is the absolute best for pesto? There are over 150 species of basil throughout the world. And the one called Genovese Basil, with both green and purple leaves and a distinctly sweet taste, is not considered the finest for pesto. Neither is Lettuce Leaf Basil, which has wonderful, big leaves that can be wrapped around food, as are grape leaves. *Tulasi* "Holy" Basil, sacred to Hindu and Muslim sects and the Hare Krishna, may be a spicy addition to sweet yeast breads, preserves, and jams, but is not right for pesto. The dark Opal Basil, with its deep purple leaves, makes a glorious garnet-colored pesto, but is hardly the classic pesto basil. In fact, Opal Basil is an American variety, produced in the late 1950s by scientists at the University of Connecticut.

Also disqualified for serious pesto consideration are the tropical Licorice Basil, with a tarragon taste that is welcome with fruits; Cinnamon Basil, with its undertones of clove and cinnamon; and Lemon Basil, both sweet and tart, popular in Thai cooking. Camphor Basil, a nonculinary herb named for its fragrance, is altogether out of the running. For people who know their basils, the winner and still champion is Piccolo Verde Fino, which has flutelike leaves and a bright, melodic flavor: flowery, sweet, immediate.

One of the world's oldest herbs, sweet basil is the only member of the mint family that is not from the Mediterranean area. Supposedly it originated in Thailand or India and was brought west by early traders. By the sixteenth century, basil was a full-fledged member of the English herb garden and figured prominently in the herbals and general cookbooks that accompanied the American colonists to the New World. By 1775 its availability was advertised in the *Virginia Gazette*. A variety called Dittany was popular with American Indians of the Far West as an aromatic flavoring. Basil was essential to rabbit soup, mock turtle soup, and a number of the other soups that fill the pages of nineteenth-century American cookbooks. One cookbook of that era advises the use of basil vinegar to "impregnate a tureen of soup with basil and acid flavors at very small cost, when fresh basil and lemons are extravagantly dear."

SIGNATURE DISH: PASTA WITH PESTO

Although the essence of this dish—garlic, basil, and enormous enthusiasm—may seem uncomplicated, pesto contests in this country have become almost as competitive as traditional, all-American chili cook-offs.

Descendants of Germans who settled in Texas in the mid-1800s still prepare traditional dishes like hot German potato salad with sprigs of basil, evidence of strong local influence from Mexico and the Old South. Corn and squash dishes of the area reveal a mixture of many heritages by pairing basil with cumin, oregano, and thyme. Around Puget Sound,

Washington, Yugoslav fishing communities, which were settled around Grig Harbor over a hundred years ago, celebrate their annual feast days with the basil-scented Slavonian pasta called *mostaccioli,* possibly followed by *tchorba,* the Yugoslav national chicken soup, fragrant with basil. In Massachusetts, Portuguese fish soup is rich in basil and ground almonds. Lebanese Americans use the herb with garlic, lemon juice, and mint to flavor their lentil lemon soup (*adass bi hamod*). But the little storefront restaurants of Greektown in Chicago, always redolent of basil, seldom use it in their cooking. Though basil appears in poems and in windowbox gardens, and is given as a token of friendship, many Greeks never use it in cooking. Perhaps this is because, according to various Greek traditions, basil symbolizes everything from royalty to misfortune.

Deep-fried purple basil leaves characterize *pad Thai,* a noodle dish ubiquitous in Thai cuisine and now familiar to Americans who frequent the expanding number of Thai restaurants. Also on the menu might be a dipping sauce of lime, chiles, and basil used for shrimp dumplings and squid salad in ginger-basil-garlic dressing. At other Southeast Asian restaurants, Cambodian spring rolls are served with baskets of fresh basil to be wrapped in lettuce leaves; and Vietnamese beef noodle soup (*pho*) is sprinkled with sprigs of the fresh herb.

"I use basil almost everywhere in cooking," admits the author of *Minnie Muenscher's Herb Cookbook* (1978), "except in desserts. Some day," she fantasizes, "I will make a chocolate basil ice cream." This fondness for basil has led otherwise level-headed folks to devise all sorts of uses for the herb, culinary and otherwise. Colonists fond of snuff used a mixture of many herbs, but only the formula made from dried basil was credited with the ability to cure nervous headaches. Dried mint, pounded cloves, and basil stuffed into a small pillow could "induce sleep and fragrant dreams," according to an early cookbook, the *Compleat American Housewife* (1776). According to legend, basil is to be hung in doorways to protect the family or simply to keep out flies; it is a welcome symbol of love as well as a dreaded prognosticator of death. According to Jewish lore, a few sprigs of basil provide strength if held in the hand when fasting.

Most people trace basil's regal nature to its etymological beginnings as *basilikon,* meaning "king" in Greek (indeed, the French call it *l'herb royale*); but its name may just as well derive from the Latin *basilicus,* or fire-breathing dragon. In either case, it seems to have settled down to more or less domestic activities in the last millennium or so. There are recipes for basil hot packs for the hair, body rubs, after-shave lotions, and summer facials. Basil is an important ingredient in the 130-herb, four-century-old liqueur Chartreuse. Basil brew is a tea, and even the odd-sounding basil-pepper jelly might be worth a try.

Basil mania has fostered quite a bit of creativity in preserving the beloved herb for the off-season: packing it in salt, freezing it in ice, covering it in oil, steeping it in vinegar, and smothering it in Parmesan. To various degrees, they are all successful methods for ensuring that, when winter comes, at least some form of pesto—or any of the following recipes—will not be far behind.

VINTAGE RECIPE

The following early basil recipe is from *The Kitchen Directory, and American Housewife: Containing the Most Valuable and Original Receipts, in All the Various Branches of Cookery; Together with a Collection of Miscellaneous Receipts, and Directions Relative to Housewifery. Also the Whole Art of Carving, Illustrated by Sixteen Engravings* (New York: Mark H. Newman and Company, 1844 and 1846).

Sauce for Turtle, or Calf's Head

To half a pint of hot melted butter, or beef gravy, put the juice and grated rined [sic] of half a lemon, a little sage, basil, or sweet marjorum, a little cayenne, or black pepper, and salt. Add a wine glass of white wine just before you take it up.

Consumer Guide

Also known as: sweet basil; French—basilic; Italian—basilico; German—Basilienkraut; Spanish—albahaca.

LATIN: *Ocimum basilicum*

Common varieties: French Fine Leaf Basil, Opal Basil, Lemon Basil, Cinnamon Basil.

Selection: Bright green color or, for Opal, deep purple; unbruised leaves, aromatic.

Storage: Place bunch of basil in plastic bag, leaving some air space. Seal tightly. Do not store in refrigerator. Will keep reasonably well for about 6 days. To freeze, wrap each stalk in plastic wrap, place in plastic bag, and freeze. (When defrosted, color might be dulled and texture limp, but flavor will be good.) Another method of freezing is to remove leaves from stem, place in freezer container, pour a layer of oil over leaves, seal tightly, and freeze. We do not recommend pureeing for freezing because it turns the leaves black.

Fresh vs. dried: Even a very high quality dried basil makes a poor substitute for fresh. Fragrance is the most reliable indicator of quality.

Compatible herbs and spices: Parsley, thyme, oregano, garlic.

RECIPE LIST

Basil Cheese Spread
Basil Cheese Toasts
Eggs Basildict
Cream of Cauliflower Soup with Broccoli–Basil Puree
Parsnip Soup with Basil Cream
Pasta with Two Pestos
Savory Green Tart
Pizza Primavera
Basil and Potato Torte
Warm Yellow Squash in Tomato–Basil Vinaigrette
Carrot and Zucchini Salad with Basil and Walnuts
Two Lettuces with Basil Vinaigrette
Basil Burgers
Springtime Chicken Sauté with Asparagus and Basil
Scallops of Veal in Basil
"Sauce for Turtle or Calf's Head" (Modern Version)

Basil Cheese Spread

½ pound cream cheese, room temperature
½ pound mild goat cheese, room temperature
1 pound (4 sticks) butter, room temperature
1 recipe Pesto (page 356)
Basil sprigs
¼ cup toasted pine nuts (page 360)
Crackers and baguette slices

In a mixer or food processor, blend cream cheese, goat cheese, and butter until very smooth. Line 1-quart soufflé dish with damp cheesecloth, allowing it to overhang the sides. Spread about one-quarter of the cheese mixture in the soufflé dish, followed by one-third of the pesto. Continue until cheese mixture and pesto are used up, ending with cheese. Fold ends of cheesecloth over top and smooth with fingers. Chill about 3 hours, or until mixture feels firm. Unfold cheesecloth, unmold onto serving dish, and gently remove cheesecloth. Press pine nuts around sides and garnish with basil leaves. Serve with bread and crackers.

Serves 12–16

Basil Cheese Toasts

1 thin baguette, cut into ½-inch-thick slices
Olive oil
6 ounces Italian fontina cheese, shredded
32 large basil leaves
8 sun-dried tomatoes (packed in oil), quartered

Preheat oven to 400 degrees. Brush both sides of each slice of bread with olive oil. (The oil from the tomatoes is wonderful.) Place on baking sheet and bake about 8 minutes, or until very lightly toasted. Sprinkle with cheese, covering the surface of each slice well. Top with a basil leaf and a tomato quarter. Return to oven and bake about 5 minutes, or until cheese is melted. Serve immediately.

Serves 12–16 as an appetizer

Eggs Basildict

3 tablespoons olive oil
2 cloves garlic, chopped
2 pounds ripe tomatoes, peeled and chopped
½ cup heavy cream
½ cup chopped fresh basil tightly packed plus 6 whole leaves for garnish
Salt and pepper
8 eggs
8 slices good French bread, lightly toasted

In a large skillet, heat the oil. Sauté garlic about 3 minutes, and add tomatoes. Cook over medium heat about 10 minutes; add cream and cook another 3 minutes, or until thickened. Add chopped basil and salt and pepper to taste.

Make 8 wells in the sauce. Carefully break an egg into each well, cover skillet, and poach about 5 minutes. Place 2 pieces of bread on each plate, put an egg on each piece of bread, and cover with sauce. Garnish with whole basil leaves.

Serves 4

Cream of Cauliflower Soup with Broccoli–Basil Puree

1 quart Chicken Stock (page 352)
1 small head cauliflower, cut into flowerets
3 cloves garlic, peeled
1 small shallot, peeled
1 stalk broccoli, peeled and cut into small pieces
½ cup heavy cream
¼ cup fresh basil leaves, tightly packed, or ¼ cup fresh parsley plus 1 teaspoon dried basil
Salt and pepper

In a medium saucepan, bring 3 cups stock to a boil. Add cauliflower, garlic, and shallot and simmer about 10 minutes, or until cauliflower is tender. Set aside. In a small saucepan, bring remaining 1 cup stock to a boil. Add broccoli and simmer about 10 minutes, or until tender. Place broccoli mixture in food processor with ¼ cup cream and the basil. Puree until smooth. Taste for salt and pepper. Place cauliflower mixture in food processor with remaining ¼ cup cream and puree until smooth. Reheat if necessary and divide among 6 soup bowls. Reheat the broccoli-basil puree if necessary and swirl into cauliflower soup.

Serves 6

Parsnip Soup with Basil Cream

3 tablespoons butter
1 small onion, chopped
5 cups Chicken Stock (page 352)
1 pound parsnips, scraped and sliced
½ cup white long-grain rice
Salt and pepper
1 cup basil leaves, tightly packed
2 cloves garlic, peeled
2 tablespoons oil
½ cup heavy cream

In a medium saucepan, heat butter. Sauté onion until wilted. Add stock, bring to a boil, and add parsnips and rice. Reduce heat, cover, and simmer 20 minutes. Puree soup in blender or processor until smooth. Taste for salt and pepper and return to saucepan.

To make basil cream, puree basil, garlic, and oil in processor or blender. Add cream slowly until a smooth mixture is formed. To serve, place soup in bowls and swirl basil cream into each portion.

Serves 6

Pasta with Two Pestos

½ recipe Pesto (page 356) plus ½ recipe Pesto, substituting purple basil for green
½ cup heavy cream
1 pound linguine, fresh or dried
Green and purple basil leaves for garnish

Mix green pesto with cream until smooth. In a large pot of boiling salted water, cook linguine until tender: fresh, 3 minutes; dried, 10 minutes (approximately). Drain and mix with green pesto mixture in large bowl. Ribbon the purple pesto on top, sprinkle with basil leaves, and serve immediately.

Serves 6–8

Savory Green Tart

1 recipe Pâte Brisée (page 354), fitted into a 10-inch tart shell and partially baked
3 tablespoons olive oil
1 bunch fresh spinach leaves, washed and coarsely chopped
2 cloves garlic, chopped
1/2 teaspoon salt
1/4 teaspoon freshly ground black pepper
1 cup coarsely chopped fresh basil, tightly packed
1/2 cup chopped fresh parsley
8 ounces whole milk ricotta cheese
3 eggs
1/2 cup grated asiago cheese
Freshly grated nutmeg

Preheat oven to 375 degrees. Have tart shell ready to be filled.

In a medium skillet, heat oil. Sauté spinach and garlic just until wilted. Remove from heat and drain off most of the liquid accumulated during cooking. Stir in salt, pepper, basil, and parsley. In a separate bowl, mix remaining ingredients until well blended. Add spinach mixture and mix again. Fill tart shell. Bake about 35 minutes, or until a knife inserted into the center comes out clean; do not overcook.

Serves 6–8

Pizza Primavera

Cornmeal for dusting
1 recipe Herbed Pizza Dough (page 355)
8 ounces whole-milk ricotta cheese
¼ teaspoon salt
2 cloves garlic, minced
½ cup chopped fresh basil, tightly packed
¼ cup grated Parmesan cheese
1 egg
8 sun-dried tomatoes (packed in oil), cut into strips
½ pound asparagus, peeled and cooked until tender-crisp
½ cup shredded Italian fontina cheese

Preheat oven to 475 degrees. Sprinkle a 15-inch pizza pan with cornmeal.

Roll out dough to fit pan. Combine ricotta with salt, garlic, basil, Parmesan, and egg. Spread on dough. Sprinkle with sun-dried tomatoes and top with asparagus in a spokelike pattern. Sprinkle with cheese. Bake for 12–15 minutes.

Serves 8

Basil and Potato Torte

3 cloves garlic
6 tablespoons (¾ stick) butter
1½ pounds red potatoes, sliced and cooked 10 minutes
1 cup chopped fresh basil, tightly packed
Salt and pepper
2 eggs
1 cup heavy cream or half-and-half

Preheat oven to 350 degrees. Chop 2 cloves of garlic and halve remaining one. Rub a 10-inch baking dish with the halved garlic and grease with 1 tablespoon of butter. Layer the potatoes, basil, and chopped garlic in a round baking dish. Sprinkle with salt and pepper. Beat eggs and cream until blended and pour over potato mixture. Dot with remaining butter. Bake 45 minutes, or until top is golden brown. Allow to rest about 10 minutes before serving.

Serves 6

Warm Yellow Squash in Tomato–Basil Vinaigrette

8 yellow summer squash, cut into julienne
2 carrots, coarsely shredded

VINAIGRETTE
2 ripe tomatoes, peeled, seeded, and coarsely chopped
1 clove garlic, minced
1 small shallot, minced
¼ cup chopped fresh basil, tightly packed
3 tablespoons white wine vinegar
Pinch of sugar
Salt and pepper to taste
⅓ cup olive oil

In a large pot, bring 2 quarts salted water to a boil. Add squash and carrots and blanch (page 361) for 1 minute. Drain under cold water and place in serving bowl. Mix vinaigrette ingredients, pour over vegetables in bowl, and toss. Serve immediately.

Serves 6

Carrot and Zucchini Salad with Basil and Walnuts

¾ pound carrots, shredded
¾ pound zucchini, shredded
½ cup chopped fresh basil, tightly packed
1 cup toasted and coarsely chopped walnuts (page 360)
2 tablespoons capers, rinsed and drained
½ cup olive oil
¼ cup lemon juice
1 teaspoon Dijon mustard
1 teaspoon honey
1 clove garlic, chopped
Salt and pepper to taste

In a large salad bowl, combine carrots, zucchini, basil, walnuts, and capers. Mix remaining ingredients, pour over salad, and toss well.

Serves 8

Two Lettuces with Basil Vinaigrette

½ large head romaine lettuce, shredded
½ head iceberg lettuce, shredded
¼ cup grated Parmesan cheese
¼ cup toasted pine nuts (page 360)

VINAIGRETTE
2 cloves garlic, peeled and blanched (page 361) for 2 minutes
½ cup chopped fresh basil, tightly packed
1 teaspoon Dijon mustard
Pinch of salt
¼ teaspoon freshly ground black pepper
3 tablespoons lemon juice
½ cup olive oil

Prepare vinaigrette. Mince garlic and combine with rest of dressing ingredients until blended. In a large bowl, toss vinaigrette with lettuces and sprinkle salad with cheese and pine nuts.

Serves 6

Basil Burgers

1½ pounds ground beef round, or 1 pound ground beef and ½ pound ground veal
1 teaspoon salt
½ teaspoon freshly ground black pepper
1 egg, lightly beaten
½ cup whole-milk ricotta cheese
2 tablespoons grated Parmesan cheese
1 clove garlic, minced
½ cup chopped fresh basil, tightly packed
Salt and pepper to taste

In a large bowl, mix ground meat with salt, pepper, and egg. Divide into 6 portions. Mix remaining ingredients and divide into 6 portions also. Form each portion of meat around a portion of basil mixture. Preheat grill, broiler, or skillet and cook each burger to desired taste—5 minutes per side for rare, 7 for medium, 8 for well done.

Serves 6

Springtime Chicken Sauté with Asparagus and Basil

3 whole chicken breasts, boned, skinned, and cut into strips
Salt and pepper
¼ cup (½ stick) butter
2 leeks (white part only), sliced
4 red potatoes, diced
6 cloves garlic, minced

1 cup dry white wine
1 tablespoon good-quality Dijon-type mustard
½ pound fresh asparagus, peeled and cut into 1-inch pieces
4 sun-dried tomatoes packed in oil, coarsely chopped
¼ cup heavy cream
½ cup chopped fresh basil, tightly packed

Season the chicken with salt and pepper. In a large skillet, heat butter and sauté chicken on both sides, just until it turns white, about 3 minutes. Remove and reserve. Add additional butter if needed and, in same skillet, sauté leeks, potatoes, and garlic until barely tender, about 5 minutes. Add wine and mustard and bring to a boil; cook about 5 minutes. Return chicken to skillet, along with asparagus and tomatoes. Cover and simmer about 5 minutes. Add cream, stir, and cook another 2 minutes. Sprinkle with basil and serve.

Serves 6

Scallops of Veal in Basil

12 veal scallops, ¼ inch thick (about 2 ounces each)
⅓ cup plus 3 tablespoons grated Parmesan cheese
⅓ cup all-purpose flour
¼ cup (½ stick) butter
¼ cup dry white wine
¼ cup Veal or Chicken Stock (pages 352, 353)
¼ cup heavy cream
½ cup chopped fresh basil, tightly packed

Blot veal dry. Mix ⅓ cup cheese with flour and dredge veal in mixture. Chill for about 30 minutes.

Preheat oven to 350 degrees. In a large skillet, heat butter. Sauté veal about 1 minute on each side. Transfer to a baking dish large enough to hold veal in single layer. Into same skillet, pour wine, stock, and cream.

Cook over medium-high heat, scraping bottom of pan, about 2 minutes, or until slightly thickened. Stir in basil and pour over veal. Sprinkle with remaining cheese. Cover loosely with foil and bake about 10 minutes.

Serves 6

"Sauce for Turtle or Calf's Head" (Modern Version)

¾ cup (1½ sticks) butter
1 shallot, chopped
1 clove garlic, minced
1 cup chopped fresh basil, tightly packed
½ cup dry white wine
½ cup heavy cream
2 tablespoons Dijon-type mustard
Salt and pepper

In a small skillet or sauté pan, heat ¼ cup (½ stick) butter. Add shallot, garlic, and basil and cook just until wilted. Deglaze (page 361) pan with wine. Add cream and reduce the sauce until it coats the back of a spoon. Cut remaining ½ cup (1 stick) butter into small pieces and stir in one piece at a time until sauce appears smooth and slightly thickened. Add mustard and stir until blended. Add salt and pepper to taste. Serve hot or at room temperature with fish, shellfish, or chicken.

Serves 6

Chives

LORE AND LINEAGE

In this country, chives have inspired at least three famous recipes. The story of each provides a nice chunk of herbal Americana.

SISTER ABIGAIL'S BLUE CHIVE OMELET (CIRCA 1800)

Sister Abigail was a member of the Shaking Quakers, an eighteenth-century spin-off of the Society of Friends (Quakers). They were a celibate group whose rituals centered on the wild dervish dancing from which they got their name. Shakers were organized into families of Brothers and Sisters. In 1774, under the leadership of Mother Ann Lee, Shaker communities formed in the Northeast, Ohio, and Indiana. Within ten years, they established eleven thriving centers, including their parent community at New Lebanon, New York. The self-sufficient Shakers operated their farms and herb gardens very efficiently, providing for all their needs and producing a generous surplus as well. Celebrated for the excellent quality of their produce, they could sell herbs and seeds for good prices.

In their own kitchens, the Shaker Sisters used their fresh, flavorful herbs to create many original dishes for which we still have recipes. When Sister Abigail made her famous chive omelet, for example, she enhanced both its taste and its beauty by mixing in a handful of lovely lavender chive flowers. Shaker breads like the Rutland loaf, Sister Lottie's Shaker gems, Sister Jennie's potato bread, and Sister Lisset's tea loaf were full of chives and other herbs. A Shaker soup of chopped chives, sorrel, chervil, tarragon, nutmeg, and celery in chicken stock is still served at restored Shaker villages in Pleasant Hill, Kentucky, Hancock Shaker Village in the Berkshires of Massachusetts, and the active Shaker community at Sabbathday Lake, Maine. In Ohio, near the Union Village community, local restaurants like the Golden Lamb, in Lebanon, offer on their regular menus Shaker dishes distinctively flavored with herbs.

SIGNATURE DISH: BAKED POTATOES WITH SOUR CREAM AND CHIVES

Purists will anoint the sacrosanct baked potato with few embellishments; among them, chives are the only herb that has achieved permissibility.

LOUIS DIAT'S VICHYSSOISE (1910)

When New York's Ritz-Carlton Hotel opened its rooftop garden restaurant on Madison Avenue and 46th Street in 1910, chef Louis Diat created a special soup to commemorate the occasion. Made with pureed leeks and potatoes and strewn with chopped fresh chives, it was served chilled to such honored and presumably appreciative guests as Charles Schwab, the steel magnate. Chef Diat named his soup after its inspiration: the leek and potato soup his mother used to make back home in Vichy, France.

Several French chive-based dishes were always popular in this country, including *sauces verte, rémoulade,* and *ravigote.* Anything "*aux fines herbes*" includes chives, as does the French goat cheese, Cervelle de Canut. Helen Morgenthau Fox, who wrote extensively about herbs in America, commented that you could tell a French gardener because he always had, among his household possessions, a flat of fresh chives.

GREEN GODDESS DRESSING (EARLY 1920s)

Not to be outdone in the area of commemorative dishes, San Francisco's Palace Hotel created a chive-laden salad dressing with dramatic connotations. The occasion was a long-running play called *The Green Goddess,* starring George Arliss; the dressing it inspired starred anchovies, tarragon, and lots of chives.

The spirited onionlike taste of chives makes them popular in American kitchens throughout the country. Their long, delicate spears are an attractive garnish, as are their blue pompom flowers floating on a clear soup. Rumanians in Cleveland top their leek soup, called *ciorba de praz,* with both chives and parsley. Members of New York's Ukrainian community roll fish filets around a stuffing of chive-and-tarragon–spiced croutons and make a similar filling for their traditional pork *kotley.* German-descended families in the Pedernales region of Texas bake quail with white wine and chives; and Swiss Americans make *Kalbsleber*—calves liver in chive cream. Composed butters laced with chives are a versatile spread for grilled meats and fish, hot cooked beets, potato dishes, and other vegetables. Chives also work well with cheeses and in egg dishes and salads where, as Irma Goodrich Mazza (*Herbs for the Kitchen,* 1939) puts it, "they never fight with their associates." Beautiful vaselike bottles of chive vinegar, which include the frilly blue flowers, have been made since colonial days. Chives were important members of the "sweet hearbs" included in such dishes as "To Make a Frykacy of Shikin, Lamb, Ueale or Rabbits" from *Martha Washington's Booke of Cookery.*

Some believe that because chives originated in Siberia and spread southward, North America may very likely have had chives before Europe. Certainly they have been grown in this country since 1653, according to Adriaen van der Donck's *Description of the New Netherlands.* A clue to their popularity may be found in John Randolph's *Treatise on Gardening by a Citizen of Virginia* (circa 1770), in which he contends that chives provide the taste of onion without the usual legacy of onion breath. On the other hand, chives are called the "orchids of the lily family" because of their blossoms, not their perfume!

Chives, in some form, have always been close at hand. Early settlers along Lakes Superior and Huron found Wild Chives, called Rush Garlic, growing in abundance. Today in California, one of the world's largest chive farms, run by the Armanino family, supplies a large portion of the nation's freeze-dried chives. Also gaining in popularity are Garlic Chives, or Cuchay, also called Chinese Chives; these are a long-leaf variety with a more pronounced, garlicky taste. The word *chives* has some interesting relatives as well, being derived from the same root as *civet,* a kind of stew in which chives and other members of the onion family are a central flavoring. Old cookbooks refer to the herb as "cives," deriving from the Latin word for onions.

Modern science confirms the old herbals' advice that chives are a natural antibiotic, an antidote for various poisons, and an effective antiseptic. Their high nutritional content makes them especially valuable: they are rich in vitamins A and C, calcium, phosphorus, and sulfur. One tablespoon of chopped chives, for example, has as much vitamin A as two cups of chopped cabbage. However, to get the same amount of vitamin A as is in one carrot you would have to eat *fifty tablespoons* of chives! With these nutritional benefits firmly in mind, we have included such pleasures as the forthcoming Salubrious Soup (page 49) or the Warm Carrot Salad (page 51), made with a full cup of the herb.

VINTAGE RECIPE

Sister Abigail's Blue Chive Omelet

4 eggs
¼ cup milk
Salt and freshly ground black pepper
1 tablespoon each chopped chives and parsley
2 tablespoons (¼ stick) butter
12 chive blossoms

Whip eggs with milk and seasonings. In a heavy skillet, melt butter, pour in eggs, and cook until omelet begins to set. Arrange chive blossoms over the omelet, roll omelet over on itself, and tip out of skillet. Serve immediately.

Serves 4

Consumer Guide

Also known as: Arabic—basal; Dutch—bieslook; French—ciboulette; German—Schnittlauch; Italian—erba cipollina; Spanish—cebolleta.

LATIN: *Allium schoenoprasum*

Common varieties: The most common variety of chives is the long, thin shoot type. Oriental markets offer another variety that has thicker shoots, called Chinese Chives or Garlic Chives; this type is redolent of garlic and has a stronger flavor.

Selection: Fresh chives should be a vibrant green and unwilted. Freeze-dried chives should have a fresh aroma.

Storage: Wrap fresh chives in paper towels and seal in plastic bag; store in refrigerator for up to 1 week. To freeze, wrap airtight in plastic.

Compatible herbs and spices: Almost every herb and spice.

48 Season to Taste

RECIPE LIST

Sunchoke Vichyssoise
Salubrious Soup
Cream of Beet Soup with Chives
Chive Omelet Wheels
Warm Carrot Salad with Cinnamon and Chives
Potato Pancakes with Chive Sauce
Shrimp and Cucumber Rémoulade
Chicken Breasts with Chived Cauliflower
Glazed Carrots and Brussels Sprouts with Chives and Toasted Almonds

Sunchoke Vichyssoise

3 tablespoons butter
1 leek (white part only), chopped
1 carrot, chopped
2 cups Chicken Stock (page 352)
1 pound sunchokes, cleaned and sliced
Salt
1 teaspoon freshly ground black pepper
1½ cups heavy cream
1 cup half-and-half
¾ cup chopped chives

In a medium saucepan, heat butter. Sauté leek and carrot about 6 minutes, or until soft. Add stock, bring to a boil, and add sunchokes. Simmer, partially covered, for about 12 minutes, or until sunchokes are tender. Puree mixture until smooth and return to saucepan. Add salt to taste, pepper, 1 cup cream, half-and-half, and ¼ cup chives. Stir well over low heat for about 1 minute. Remove from heat and allow to come to room temperature or chill.

Whip remaining ½ cup cream. Serve soup at room temperature or chilled, with a dollop of whipped cream sprinkled with chives.

Serves 4–6

Note: Sunchokes are also known as Jerusalem artichokes, and sometimes, simply as "chokes."

Salubrious Soup

2 tablespoons vegetable oil
1 head Boston lettuce, shredded
2 zucchini, chopped
1 parsnip, peeled and sliced
1 quart Chicken Stock (page 352)
1 10-ounce package frozen peas
¾ cup chopped chives
½ cup plain yogurt
Salt and pepper

In a medium saucepan, heat oil. Cook lettuce, zucchini, and parsnip about 3 minutes, or until soft. Add stock, bring to a boil, and then add peas. Simmer, partially covered, for 10 minutes. Puree mixture until smooth, then stir in chives and yogurt. Taste for salt and pepper. Serve warm, at room temperature, or chilled. If reheating soup, do not bring to a boil or yogurt will curdle.

Serves 6

Cream of Beet Soup with Chives

1 quart water
1 pound small beets, peeled and diced
2 tablespoons lime juice
1 tablespoon honey
½ cup half-and-half or plain yogurt
Salt and pepper
½ cup chopped chives

In a medium pot, bring water to a boil. Add beets, cover, and simmer about 10 minutes, or until beets are tender. Puree mixture with lime juice, honey, and half-and-half. Taste for salt and pepper and stir in chives. Delicious hot or cold.

Serves 6

Chive Omelet Wheels

4 eggs, separated
Pinch of salt
1 teaspoon sugar
⅓ cup all-purpose flour
¼ cup grated Parmesan cheese
¼ cup finely chopped chives

FILLING
6 ounces cream cheese
3 tablespoons dairy sour cream
1 cup chopped chives, plus additional for garnish
2 ripe tomatoes, peeled, seeded, and coarsely chopped

Preheat oven to 400 degrees. Line a jelly-roll pan with parchment. Beat egg whites with salt until thickened. Add sugar and beat whites until stiff-peak stage. In a separate bowl, break up yolks. Stir in about 1 cup of the beaten whites and then pour blended mixture over whites. Sprinkle with flour, cheese, and chives and gently fold all ingredients together, just until no large pieces of white show. Spread mixture in prepared pan and bake about 10 minutes, or until golden brown. Allow to cool about 3 minutes and then turn out omelet onto a cooling rack.

Mix cream cheese and sour cream for filling until smooth. Cut dried edges from omelet and discard. Spread omelet surface with cream cheese mixture, then sprinkle with chives and tomatoes. Starting at short end, roll up like a jelly roll. Slice 1-inch-thick "wheels," and place 2 wheels on each plate, sprinkled with additional chives.

Serves 4–6

Warm Carrot Salad with Cinnamon and Chives

2 pounds carrots, peeled and sliced 1/4 inch thick
1 cup chopped chives
1/4 cup parsley
1/4 cup lemon juice
2 tablespoons white wine vinegar
1 1/2 teaspoons ground cinnamon
1 teaspoon honey
1/2 cup olive oil
Salt and pepper to taste

Cook carrots in boiling water for about 2 minutes, or until barely tender; keep warm. Mix in chives and parsley, then combine remaining ingredients and pour over warm carrot mixture. May be served immediately or at room temperature.

Serves 6–8

Potato Pancakes with Chive Sauce

3 baking potatoes, finely shredded
2 eggs
2 tablespoons all-purpose flour
¼ cup finely chopped chives
Salt and pepper
Oil for frying

SAUCE
½ cup chopped chives
2 tablespoons chopped parsley
1 tablespoon lemon juice
Dash of Tabasco
¼ cup mayonnaise
½ cup dairy sour cream

In a medium bowl, mix shredded potatoes with egg, flour, chives, and salt and pepper to taste. In a large skillet, heat oil until almost smoking. Drop 1 tablespoon of batter into hot oil to form a pancake. Cook on each side until brown and crisp, then drain on paper towels and keep warm while you make remaining pancakes.

To make sauce, puree ingredients until smooth. Top each pancake with sauce or pass sauce separately.

Serves 4 as light lunch or 8 as an appetizer

Shrimp and Cucumber Rémoulade

¼ cup parsley
1 clove garlic
2 tablespoons basil leaves
½ cup chives
1 egg yolk
1 teaspoon grainy mustard

1/3 cup red wine vinegar
1 cup vegetable oil
Salt and pepper
2 tablespoons capers, rinsed and drained
1 English cucumber, peeled, halved lengthwise, seeded, and thinly sliced
1 pound cooked bay or smallest shrimp

In the bowl of a food processor, put parsley, garlic, basil, chives, egg yolk, mustard, and vinegar. Process until smooth and slightly thickened. With machine running, add oil very slowly until dressing emulsifies, much like preparing a mayonnaise. Add salt and pepper to taste and stir in capers by hand.

Toss cucumber slices and shrimp in a medium bowl. Pour dressing over salad and toss well to combine. Chill and serve.

Serves 6 as a first course

Chicken Breasts with Chived Cauliflower

1 cup cooked cauliflower
Salt and pepper
1/4 teaspoon ground red pepper
1 egg
1/4 cup grated Swiss cheese
1/4 cup heavy cream
1/4 cup (1/2 stick) butter
1/4 cup finely chopped chives
2 whole chicken breasts, boned, halved, and skinned

Puree the cooked cauliflower with salt and pepper, red pepper, egg, cheese, and cream. Stir in chives and set aside. Preheat broiler.

In a medium skillet, heat butter. Salt and pepper the chicken breasts and sauté about 4 to 6 minutes on each side, or until juices run clear when meat is pricked with a fork. Place chicken breasts in broiler pan and spread with cauliflower mixture. Place pan about 3 inches from heat and cook about 6 minutes, or until golden and slightly puffed.

Serves 4

Glazed Carrots and Brussels Sprouts with Chives and Toasted Almonds

1 pound Brussels sprouts, outer leaves removed
½ pound carrots, cleaned and sliced ⅛ inch thick
6 tablespoons (¾ stick) butter
1 tablespoon light-brown sugar
1 tablespoon lemon juice
Salt and pepper
½ cup chopped chives
½ cup toasted sliced almonds (page 360)

In a large pot, cook sprouts in boiling water for 10 minutes. Add carrots and cook for another 4 minutes. Drain. In a large skillet, heat butter with brown sugar and lemon juice. Add sprouts and carrots and cook, stirring, about 5 minutes, or until vegetables are glazed. Taste for salt and pepper and toss with chives and almonds.

Serves 6

Coriander (Fresh)

LORE AND LINEAGE

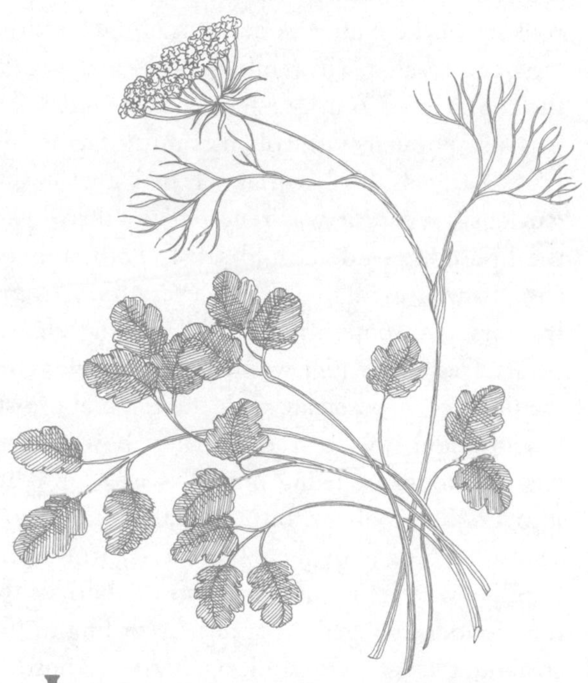

"It looks like parsley, doesn't it?" asked a friend planning a Mexican meal of three coriander-sprinkled dishes.

Three! One after the other: an appetizer, a soup, and a main course. We told our friend there was something she should know about coriander right away. Some people don't instantly love it. Fresh coriander, or cilantro as it is also called, is a zesty little herb with a highly distinctive taste. Even in the smallest quantities, it makes its presence felt. No one ever asks, "What is that subtle flavor?" When it's there, it's obvious. The guests who didn't acquire a taste for it in the appetizer or the soup probably won't be looking forward to more of it in the main course. On the other hand, some people—we here include ourselves—can't get enough of it.

Americans, it seems, have always been passionate about fresh coriander. The Spaniards brought it to South America, where it became a permanent success. Its popularity spread northward through Mexico and into the cookery of the Native Americans of the Southwest. The Zunis ate the herb fresh, as a salad with chile peppers and vegetables, an influence basic to the character of southwestern cookery today. Surprisingly, fresh coriander was also popular with colonists much farther north.

As early as 1672, coriander had a place in New England's "kitchen gardens," where it was reported to "thrive exceedingly." Grown close to the house, coriander could satisfy both culinary and medicinal emergencies. It was used to prevent everything from nosebleeds to gout, heart tremors, and something called "creeping ulcers." When mixed with violet petals, fresh coriander was part of a popular cure for hangovers, something we don't often associate with the colonial life-style.

Coriander's place in the kitchen, however, was even more venerable. It has the honor of being one of the first Mediterranean herbs introduced into English cookery, brought 2,000 years ago by the Romans, who were accustomed to it in their bouquets garni. American colonists were quite familiar with its reputation from the herbals they consulted, which makes it a wonder they grew it at all! According to John Gerard's *Herball (1597),* coriander is a "very stinking herbe" whose "leaves are unwholesome"; nevertheless he does like the seeds. Others have also waxed nasty about coriander. Dorothy Childs Hogner (*Herbs: From the Garden to the Table,* 1953) counsels that it is "not fit to grow in a flower or herb garden except in a remote corner" because of its buglike fragrance. Irma Goodrich Mazza (*Herbs for the Kitchen,* 1939) is even more ominous, warning "always use it with caution." Maud Grieve (*Culinary Herbs and Condiments,* 1971) complains that the liberal use of coriander makes Peruvian dishes "objectionable to any but a native." Some have compared its smell to rubber and even bedbugs, from which it gets its name: *koris,* the Greek word for insect. Kinder souls liken it to honey, or fresh oranges, or a mixture of cumin and caraway. Its proponents point out its highly nutritious nature. A mere quarter cup of chopped fresh coriander provides more vitamin A and C, iron, calcium, and phosphorus than an equivalent quantity of green beans, for example. It is also high in potassium.

Although coriander mixed with vinegar was an early preservative for meat, we have inherited few specific recipes from early America. There are none in the first American cookbook, Amelia Simmons's 1796 *American Cookery.* In fact, the herb seems to have disappeared from New England gardens by the 1800s.

Nevertheless, the country seemed destined to become acquainted with coriander eventually, since it is the world's most widely used culinary herb. In the first pages of Exodus, coriander is praised like manna. Readers of *The Thousand and One Nights,* which extols coriander's powers as an aphrodisiac, may have experimented with its nonculinary applications. Coriander enlivens everything from English steak-and-kidney puddings, Moroccan *chermoula,* South American seviches, and Indian chutneys and curries to Chinese dumplings. It is often called Chinese parsley, perhaps because it has been used by the Chinese since 1500 B.C. and is the one herb clearly discernible in Chinese cooking. A member of the parsley family, coriander has appeared in many disguises in this country. The Portuguese whalers who settled in New Bedford, Massachusetts, and their relatives who took up dairying in California, grew coriander to flavor their green soup (*caldo verde*), meat stew, chicken-rice dishes (*arroz de galinha*), and basic sauces like *strugido.* For Jews in some parts of the world it is also one of the herbs of Passover. Germany is almost unique in shunning fresh coriander; yet in eastern Texas, where many German families settled, fresh coriander is customary in German potato salad, cactus (*nopales*) dishes, jicama *en escabeche,* and other now-traditional Tex-Bavarian dishes.

At the moment, coriander seems to be the culinary world's most fashionable herb. Certainly it is the essence of popular Southwest-inspired fare: chile-rich dishes, guacamole, fillings and stuffings, and uncooked salsas. It is wonderful in marinades for fish; as cilantro butter; in newfangled hollandaises; in Oriental-style salads; as a garnish for avocado soup, with rice, beans, or pasta. In fact, for the willing cook—and guest—there seems to be no end to its possibilities.

SIGNATURE DISH: SOUTHWESTERN SALSA

Uncooked salsa, made with ripe tomatoes, chile peppers, and toasted freshly ground cumin, plus or minus other aromatics, is a fast food that requires no rationalization; it doesn't even require a microwave oven.

VINTAGE RECIPE

This recipe is adapted from Marcia Keegan's *Pueblo and Navajo Cookery* (Dobbs Ferry, N.Y.: Earth Books, 1977), page 89.

Popcorn Oxtail Stew

2 pounds oxtails
½ small green cabbage, shredded
4 celery stalks, chopped
4 carrots, chopped
3 tomatoes, coarsely chopped
1 onion, chopped
¼ cup chopped fresh coriander
4 potatoes, cut in small cubes
4 cups popped corn

Place oxtails in large pot, cover with water, and bring to the boil. Simmer for 3 hours, remove oxtails, and set aside. Place remaining ingredients in pot and cook slowly for 1 hour. Return oxtails to pot and simmer 15 minutes. Serve in large bowls and sprinkle with popcorn.

Consumer Guide

Also known as: cilantro, Chinese parsley; Arabic—kuzbara; French—coriandre; German—Koriander or Krapfenkorner, Schwindelkraut; Indian—dhania, kotimli; Italian—coriandolo; Singapore—ketumbar; Spanish—coriandro, cilantro.

LATIN: *Coriandrum sativum*

Selection: Bright green color, flat leaves, pungent smell.

Storage: Place entire bunch in a small jar with a bit of water touching the root ends. Place plastic bag over jar and refrigerate. Remove any yellowing leaves. Keeps well for about 1 week. Before using, remove grit and sand from leaves by holding bunch of coriander by root ends and swishing leaves in acidulated water. Shake or blot dry.

Fresh vs. dried: Do not substitute dried; it is unacceptable.

Compatible herbs and spices: Fresh mint, whole and ground coriander seed, cumin seed.

RECIPE LIST

Coriander-cured Salmon with Tortilla Wedges
Coriander Sunchoke Soup
Red Lentil and Potato Salad
Marinated Swordfish with Chile–Coriander Pesto
Toasted Almond Coriander Chicken
Ribs in Spicy Orange–Coriander Sauce
Julienned Golden Squash in Coriander Cream
Sweet Potato Pancake with Apples and Coriander
Coriander Corn Pudding
Ported Pineapple with Papaya Puree

Coriander-cured Salmon with Tortilla Wedges

2 fresh salmon filets (about 1¼ pounds each)
⅓ cup coarse salt
2 tablespoons sugar
½ teaspoon white pepper
½ cup fresh coriander leaves, loosely packed
8 corn tortillas
1 large, ripe tomato, seeded and chopped
1 small cucumber, peeled, seeded, and chopped

Blot salmon dry with paper towels. Combine salt, sugar, and white pepper and rub into both sides of filets. Place 1 filet on a large piece of foil. Sprinkle with coriander. Place second filet over first. Wrap securely in foil and place on a plate. Put another plate on top and weight down with a 2-pound weight. Refrigerate for 3 days, turning every 12 hours.

To serve, stack tortillas and wrap them in foil. Heat in a 350-degree oven for about 8 minutes. Remove coriander leaves from salmon and thinly slice filets on the diagonal. Cut tortillas into quarters. Place 2 slices of salmon on each tortilla wedge and garnish with tomato and cucumber.

Serves 6 as a first course

Coriander Sunchoke Soup

3 tablespoons butter
1 leek (white part only), sliced
½ small fennel bulb, sliced
5 cups Chicken Stock (page 352)
½ pound sunchokes, cleaned and sliced (See Note, page 49)
¼ teaspoon grated nutmeg
1 cup fresh coriander leaves, loosely packed
Salt and pepper

In a 4 quart saucepan, heat butter. Add leek and fennel and cook about 5 minutes, or until wilted. Add stock, bring to a boil, and add sunchokes and nutmeg. Simmer, covered, for about 15 minutes, or until sunchokes are tender. Place soup and coriander leaves in a blender or food processor and puree. Taste for salt and pepper.

Serves 6

Red Lentil and Potato Salad

1 cup cooked red (or brown) lentils, cooled
2 pounds Yukon gold or red potatoes, cooked, cooled, and diced
½ red onion, diced
¾ cup coarsely chopped fresh coriander, loosely packed
2 tablespoons white wine vinegar
2 tablespoons lime juice
6 tablespoons olive oil
2 cloves garlic, finely minced
½ teaspoon ground cumin
¼ teaspoon ground coriander
½ teaspoon ground allspice
Salt and pepper to taste

Toss lentils, potatoes, onion, and fresh coriander in a bowl. Mix remaining ingredients until well combined and pour over potato mixture. Toss well and serve.

Serves 6

Marinated Swordfish with Chile–Coriander Pesto

6 pieces swordfish steak, 1 inch thick (½ pound each)
¼ cup lime juice
¼ cup dry white wine
¼ cup olive oil
½ teaspoon ground cumin
½ teaspoon paprika
½ teaspoon salt

CHILE–CORIANDER PESTO
1 cup fresh coriander leaves, loosely packed
¼ cup chopped parsley, loosely packed
1–2 jalapeño peppers, deveined and seeded (page 361)
3 green onions
¼ cup fresh bread crumbs
1 cup vegetable oil
Salt and pepper to taste

Blot steaks dry with paper towels. Mix marinade ingredients, then brush on both sides. Place fish in a noncorrosive dish (glass, porcelain, or stainless steel) and pour remaining marinade over. Cover and refrigerate 30 minutes to 1 hour.

Meanwhile, combine pesto ingredients in a food processor or blender. Do not overblend. Set aside. Preheat grill or broiler.

Remove fish from marinade and grill or broil for 4 minutes on each side, brushing once or twice with marinade. Remove to serving platter and place a dollop of pesto on each fish steak.

Serves 6

Toasted Almond Coriander Chicken

3 large skinned and boned whole chicken breasts, cut into ½-inch cubes
½ cup all-purpose flour
¼ teaspoon ground red pepper
¼ cup (½ stick) butter
½ cup dry white wine
½ cup Chicken Stock (page 352)
2 cloves garlic, finely chopped
½ cup chopped fresh coriander, loosely packed
4 green onions, sliced
¾ cup toasted and chopped almonds (page 360)
1–2 jalapeño peppers, chopped (page 361)
6 tablespoons (¾ stick) butter, melted
Juice of 1 lime
Salt and pepper

Lightly dust chicken with mixture of flour and red pepper. In a large skillet, heat the butter. Sauté chicken breasts just until golden on all sides. Remove chicken with slotted spoon to a 10-inch round or oval baking dish. Preheat oven to 375 degrees.

Add wine and stock to skillet and deglaze (page 361) over medium-high heat. Reduce sauce for about 5 minutes, or until lightly syrupy.

Pour sauce over chicken. Combine garlic, coriander, green onions, almonds, and jalapeños and sprinkle over chicken. Combine melted butter and lime juice and pour over almond mixture. Cover with foil and bake for 15 minutes. Remove foil and bake another 5 minutes. Taste for salt and pepper and serve.

Serves 6

Ribs in Spicy Orange–Coriander Sauce

2 tablespoons vegetable oil
4 pounds beef ribs or pork spareribs
2 onions, chopped
2 cloves garlic, minced
1 small dried red chile pepper, crushed
1–2 jalapeño peppers, seeded, deveined, and cut into strips (page 361)
1 teaspoon ground cinnamon
1½ cups tomato puree
½ cup fresh orange juice
¼ cup dry red wine
2 tablespoons honey
2 tablespoons grated orange zest (page 363)
2 tablespoons sherry wine vinegar
1 cup fresh coriander leaves
Salt and pepper
Orange slices for garnish

In a large Dutch oven, heat oil. Brown ribs on all sides for about 15 to 20 minutes. This may have to be done in 2 batches in order not to crowd pan. Remove to a plate and reserve.

Discard all but 2 tablespoons of fat from pan. Add onions and garlic and sauté over medium heat for about 3 minutes. Add chile and jalapeño peppers; add cinnamon and cook about 1 minute. Add tomato puree, orange juice, wine, honey, and zest. Bring to a boil, then add ribs and reduce heat to a bare simmer. Cook, covered, until ribs are tender, about 1½ hours. Remove ribs to a serving plate. Skim fat from sauce and stir in vinegar and half the coriander. Taste for salt and pepper, then spoon sauce over ribs. Serve garnished with remaining coriander and surrounded by orange slices.

Serves 6

Julienned Golden Squash in Coriander Cream

1½ pounds yellow summer squash, cut into julienne (page 362)
2 tablespoons (¼ stick) butter
½ onion, chopped
½ teaspoon salt
½ teaspoon freshly ground black pepper
¼ teaspoon freshly grated nutmeg
½ cup coriander leaves, loosely packed.
¾ cup heavy cream

Place squash in a kitchen towel and squeeze out excess moisture. In a large skillet, melt butter. Sauté onion until soft, then add squash. Add salt, pepper, and nutmeg, and cook over medium heat for about 3 minutes. Meanwhile, make a puree of the coriander leaves and cream. Pour over squash, raise heat to medium-high, and cook about 3 minutes, until thickened.

Serves 6

Sweet Potato Pancake with Apples and Coriander

3 large sweet potatoes, cooked until barely tender and cooled
6 tablespoons (¾ stick) butter
3 large tart green apples, peeled, cored, and sliced ⅛ inch thick
1–2 jalapeño peppers, seeded, deveined, and chopped (page 361)
½ cup coarsely chopped fresh coriander, loosely packed
Salt and pepper
½ cup Chicken Stock (page 352)
2 tablespoons light-brown sugar

Preheat oven to 350 degrees. Slice potatoes ⅛ inch thick. Set aside.

In a medium skillet, heat 3 tablespoons butter and sauté apples about 2 minutes, until barely tender. In a 10-inch round baking dish, arrange apples, potatoes, jalapeños, and coriander in alternating layers, ending with a layer of potaotes. Pour stock over all, sprinkle with brown sugar, and dot with remaining butter. Bake about 30 minutes, or until top is browned.

Serves 6

Coriander Corn Pudding

1 cup milk
1 cup heavy cream
½ cup grated Monterey Jack cheese
¼ cup (½ stick) butter, melted
2 tablespoons yellow cornmeal
1 tablespoon sugar
½ teaspoon salt
½ teaspoon ground coriander
4 cups uncooked corn kernels, cut from about 8 fresh or frozen ears
½ cup chopped fresh coriander, loosely packed

Preheat oven to 325 degrees. Mix first 8 ingredients until well combined. Add corn and fresh coriander and mix again. Pour into a well-buttered 2-quart baking dish. Place dish in a larger pan half filled with warm water and bake about 1 hour, 15 minutes, or until a knife inserted in the center of the pudding comes out clean. May be served hot, warm, or at room temperature.

Serves 6–8

Ported Pineapple with Papaya Puree

1 large pineapple, cut into cubes
1–2 tablespoons light-brown sugar
¼ cup port wine
¼ cup fresh coriander leaves, loosely packed, plus leaves for garnish
1 large papaya, peeled and seeded
1 tablespoon fresh lemon juice
2 tablespoons honey
½ cup heavy cream, whipped

In a large bowl, toss pineapple with brown sugar, port, and coriander. Cover and refrigerate at least 1 hour.

In a food processor or blender, puree papaya with lemon juice and honey. Fold into whipped cream. Remove pineapple from refrigerator and stir well. Place in serving dishes and spoon papaya puree over fruit. Garnish with additional coriander leaves, if desired.

Serves 4

Dill

LORE AND LINEAGE

Witch gardens are no longer as common as they once were, but they have contributed at least one plant to our herb repertoire. In these special gardens, early New England settlers who could afford the space grew the special plants that reputedly were effective against evil spells and other unsociable activities of witches. The colonists knew just which herbs would do the trick, thanks to a book called *The Art of Simpling* (1657) by William Coles, a best-seller in its time. Among the most effective of the antiwitch herbs were mugwort, vervain, and dill.

So it is perhaps no coincidence that one of the earliest American recipes using dill comes from old Salem, where a Mrs. Frances R. Williams of Winchester authored a dill-infused cure for mosquito bites. Massachusetts must have been overpopulated with mosquitos at the time, considering that one recipe fills half a dozen wine bottles. Where to get the wine bottles is a question that Mrs. Williams leaves to the imagination.

Except for its curative attributes, dill makes no appearance in the colonial kitchen, even though it was being cultivated successfully by the seventeenth century in New England, New Netherlands, and Delaware's New Sweden. Martha Washington's cookbook refers to it without apologies as "common in Europe but absent from our manuscript." The national passion for pickles generated hundreds of different recipes for brines, cures, piccalillies, and chow-chows made with everything from cucumbers to Mrs. Child's mysterious martinoes. ("Martinoes are prepared in nearly the same way as other pickles," is her cryptic advice in *The American Frugal Housewife,* 1833.) Even more mysterious than martinoes, however, is the virtual absence of dill in any of these pickling recipes. It is not until the last half of the nineteenth century that dill makes a comeback.

This time dills starts out in the middle of the country, introduced there by its most lavish users. Responding to the offers of free or cheap land made by American railroad companies, many Scandinavians began leaving their homelands in the 1850s to settle in such midwestern centers as Iowa, Wisconsin, Minnesota, Nebraska, and the Dakotas. There they found the climate, the agricultural conditions, and even the fish, like lake herring, similar to their native lands. Swedish *gravlaks* (dill-marinated salmon), *gos med dill sas* (baked pike with dill sauce), Eple Kake (Norwegian Apple Cake), Danska wienerbröd (Danish pastries), and Finnish *kurkkusalaatti* (cucumber-dill salad) soon became part of the emerging cuisine known as Midwestern Scandinavian. Even today, Norwegians in Minnesota have their traditional *torsk* (cod) and *lutefisk* (lye-cured fish) on Syttende Mai, or May 17, to commemorate Norway's independence from Sweden in 1814!

A new surge of dill made its way into the country's kitchens with another wave of immigration in the 1880s. This included Lithuanians, Rumanians, Ukrainians, and especially the dill-loving Poles, who came to work in the mining towns of Pennsylvania, in industrial areas like South Bend, Indiana, and most of all in Chicago. Stores and bake shops all along

Chicago's Noble Street clearly reflect the Polish character; in herbal terms that means dill, the most popular herb in Polish cookery. Dill is the zestful taste in *krupnik,* a traditional vegetable barley soup; in *pierogi,* little potato and pot-cheese dumplings; and in *kotlety z grzbow,* the dill-flavored mushroom cutlets by which homesick Poles reminded themselves, through their tastebuds, of their native mushrooms.

Dill also made its way south with the Poles, Germans, and Hungarians who went to work in the coal mines after the Civil War. And Greek sponge fishermen delivered it to Florida, through the media of dill-rubbed snapper and *lahanika psita.* For this dish—a traditional dill and green vegetable casserole—these transplanted Greeks adapted the regional collard and mustard greens, and even okra.

Agrarian Swedes planted the herb in Texas in the latter half of the nineteenth century, founding there the town of New Sweden. Swedish and Finnish lumberjacks brought dill to the Northwest, and it came to Colorado with Scandinavians and Slavs working in the mines there. In Watertown, Massachusetts, also known as Little Armenia, dill appears by the cupful in *yalanchi sarma*—stuffed grape leaves.

By World War I, dill was in, reinforced by the lure of borscht, with its "dillful" dollops of sour cream. This hard-to-pin-down soup, made with beets and/or vegetables and/or meat, is always served cold unless, of course, it is served hot. Its myriad variations in the United States appeared coast to coast, made by Russians at California's Fort Ross, by Jews from the Lower East Side of Manhattan, and by New York's Hungarian community, who claim to have invented it in the first place.

But what made dill eternal in this country's heart was its close association with pickles. They came in all ethnicities: Hungarian summer pickles, Russian *malossols,* kosher half-sours, Polish gherkins. In Vermont, pickles, doughnuts, and coffee formed the unlikely menu at Vermont sugar suppers after a main course of "sugar on snow," or boiling maple syrup trickled onto a cup of fresh snow. Elsewhere in New England, "pickle love" led to such colorful possibilities as these Sail Boats: "Cut large dill pickles in half, lengthwise. Make a lengthwise slit in each dill pickle, and insert a piece of salami sausage cut into sail shape. Flute edges of sail with cream cheese pressed through a pastry tube, if desired."

Dill has more to offer than its inviting and distinctively tart taste. It has potassium, sodium, sulphur, and phosphorus. According to herbal lore, burning sprigs of dill have been known to clear the air and drive away impending rainstorms. For centuries, brides have put salt and dill seeds in their wedding shoes for good luck, even though it meant a rather crunchy walk down the aisle. As the sole important herb of Jewish chicken soup, dill may deserve all the credit for the soup's reputed curative powers. The astringent flavor of fresh dill can perk the appetite and enliven the monotony of root vegetables; it should be added to the cooking pot just before removing from the heat.

Dill seed, by contrast, is a spice, often used in Asian dishes, Indian curries, and Scandinavian breads. American Indians made dill tea in order to benefit from its long-respected powers as a digestive aid. The word *dill,* by the way, comes from *dilla,* the ancient Norse word for "lull." No surprise, then, that insomniacs have been using dill seeds for centuries, hopefully stirring up soporific concoctions in the wee hours.

SIGNATURE DISH: DILL PICKLES

Though pickles can be flavored with any number of seasonings, dill works effectively with all sorts—from sweet gherkins to sour pickle chips and everything in between.

But the first real dill appreciators in this country were probably the children of colonial America. They were often given handfuls of dill seeds, called "meeting house seeds," to chew on during church services and community gatherings. Dill's sleep-inducing properties may have kept the children quiet. But even more intriguing, it makes dill a kind of colonial chewing gum with all its modern attributes: harmless, nutritious, flavorful, and even sugarless.

VINTAGE RECIPE

The following Native American recipe is adapted from *Native Harvests: Recipes and Botanicals of the American Indian* by Barrie Kavasch (New York: Random House, 1977), page 48.

Marinated Milkweed Pods

1 quart tender milkweed pods
1 cup milkweed flowers and blossoms
2 cups small onions, peeled
½ cup maple syrup

MARINADE
2 cups chopped pimentos
1 cup chopped fresh dill
1 quart cider vinegar
½ quart corn oil

Make marinade and set aside.

In a large, noncorrosive pot, put all above ingredients and bring to a boil. Cover and simmer 25 minutes, stirring occasionally. Drain in colander and run cold water over all to stop cooking. Place all ingredients in 2-quart jar or crock, pour marinade over, and stir to combine. Refrigerate, covered, at least 12 hours before serving.

Consumer Guide

Also known as: Arabic—shibith; French—aneth; German—Dill; Italian—aneto; Polish—koper; Russian—ukrop; Spanish—eneldo.

LATIN: *Anethum graveolens*

Selection: The feathery leaves of dill should have a good green color and fresh aroma.

Storage: Fresh dill should be wrapped in paper towels and sealed in a plastic bag. It will keep well in refrigerator for about 1 week. Dill leaves may be chopped, sealed airtight, and stored in the freezer for up to 6 months.

Fresh vs. dried: Fresh dill is available in many supermarkets during most of the year. Dried dill (dillweed) is available in the spice section of every supermarket. When fresh dill is not available, use only very small amounts of dried dill as a substitute.

Compatible herbs and spices: Mint, parsley, oregano, chives.

RECIPE LIST

Dilled Pickle and Dried Mushroom Soup

1 ounce dried mushrooms, soaked 1 hour in hot water to cover
2 cups water
3 cups Beef or Chicken Stock (pages 353, 352)
2 onions, chopped
2 cloves garlic, minced
1 bay leaf
1 carrot, peeled and sliced
3 potatoes, peeled and diced
Salt and pepper
2 dill pickles, chopped
2 tablespoons chopped parsley
2 tablespoons chopped fresh dill, or 1 teaspoon dried

Drain mushrooms and rinse, making sure they are free of sand. Chop coarsely.

In a 4-quart saucepan, bring water and stock to a boil. Add mushrooms, onions, garlic, bay leaf, and carrot. Cover and cook 1 hour over low heat. Discard bay leaf and puree soup. Return to saucepan and add potatoes, salt and pepper to taste, and pickles. Cook over low heat about 15 minutes. Add parsley and dill and serve.

Serves 6–8

Cold Cucumber and Beet Soup with New Potatoes

1 quart buttermilk
2 cups dairy sour cream or plain yogurt
2 large beets, cooked, peeled, and diced
2 cucumbers, peeled, seeded, and diced
3 green onions, sliced
1½ teaspoons salt
¼ teaspoon freshly ground black pepper
¼ cup chopped fresh dill, or 1 teaspoon dried
12 new potatoes, halved and cooked

In a large bowl, blend buttermilk and sour cream until smooth. Add remaining ingredients except potatoes and mix well. Allow to chill at least 2 hours, but not more than 4. Place potatoes in each bowl and pour soup over them.

Serves 6–8

Note: Freshly cooked, warm potatoes make this delicious soup even better.

Dilled Red Onion Relish

¼ cup olive oil
6 large red onions, thinly sliced
¼ cup balsamic vinegar
¾ cup Chicken Stock (page 352)
2 tablespoons honey
Salt and pepper
¼ cup chopped fresh dill, or 1 tablespoon dried

In a large skillet, heat oil. Sauté onions about 15 minutes, or until soft but not browned. Add vinegar and simmer about 10 minutes, or until half the liquid is reduced. Add stock and cook until the liquid is again reduced by half. Add honey, taste for salt and pepper, and stir in dill. Relish may be served warm, cold, or at room temperature. It will keep for several weeks if refrigerated in a tightly sealed glass jar.

Yield: 6 cups

Veal Stew with Carrots and Dill

2 pounds veal stew meat, cut into 1½-inch cubes
Salt and pepper
2 tablespoons all-purpose flour
¼ cup olive or vegetable oil, approximately
1 leek (white part only), sliced into thin rings
2 large carrots, peeled and sliced ¼ inch thick
¼ pound green beans, cut into 2-inch pieces
1 cup dry white wine
1½ cups Chicken or Veal Stock (pages 352, 353)
½ cup heavy cream
2 tablespoons dairy sour cream
1 tablespoon Dijon-type mustard
½ cup fresh chopped dill, or 2 teaspoons dried

Blot meat dry. Mix salt, pepper, and flour and toss with veal. In a large skillet, heat oil. Sauté veal over medium-high heat until golden on all sides. Remove and reserve. Add more oil if necessary, sauté leek, carrots, and green beans about 2 minutes, or until barely tender. Remove and reserve. To same skillet, add wine and stock and bring to a boil while scraping bottom of pan. Reduce heat to a simmer and cook liquid about 5 minutes, until somewhat reduced and slightly syrupy. Return veal to skillet, cover, and cook about 1 hour, or until veal is tender.

Return reserved vegetables to skillet and cook another 5 minutes, covered. In a small bowl, mix cream, sour cream, and mustard. Pour over veal and vegetables and simmer 5 minutes. Add dill, stir, and serve.

Serves 6

Note: This stew is delicious with Fried Polenta (page 322).

Halibut Ragout with Pine Nuts and Dill

6 halibut filets or any firm white fish (about 6 ounces each), cut into 2-inch strips
Salt and pepper
½ cup all-purpose flour
1 tablespoon finely chopped fresh dill, or 1 teaspoon dried
½ cup (1 stick) butter
½ cup pine nuts
4 small zucchini, sliced
½ pound small fresh mushrooms, quartered
1 clove garlic, minced
1 small onion, chopped
½ red or yellow bell pepper, cut into strips
3 ripe tomatoes, seeded and coarsely chopped
½ cup chopped fresh dill, or 1 tablespoon dried for garnish

Blot fish dry. Mix salt, pepper, flour, and dill. Dredge fish in flour mixture. In a large skillet, heat half the butter. Cook fish about 2 minutes on each side, then remove and reserve. Add remaining butter to skillet and heat. Add remaining ingredients except tomatoes and dill garnish. Sauté about 3 minutes, or until tender but still crisp. Add tomatoes and cook another minute. Return fish to skillet and heat through briefly. Sprinkle with dill and serve.

Serves 6

Barley Pilaf with Pecans and Dill

3 tablespoons olive oil
2 shallots, chopped
1 tablespoon dill seed
½ teaspoon grated nutmeg
1½ cups pearl barley
3 cups water or Chicken Stock (page 352), approximately
Salt and pepper
½ cup toasted pecans (page 361)
3 tablespoons chopped fresh dill, or 1 teaspoon dried

In a medium saucepan, heat oil. Sauté shallots until tender. Add dill seed, nutmeg, and barley and cook, stirring, until barley becomes shiny and slightly translucent. Add stock or water, bring to a boil, and simmer, covered, about 40 minutes, or until liquid is absorbed and barley is tender; add additional water or stock if necessary and continue to cook—barley should be tender, but not mushy. Taste for salt and pepper, stir in pecans and dill, and serve.

Serves 6

Mushroom Cakes with Lemon–Dill Sauce

6 tablespoons oil
1½ pounds fresh mushrooms, chopped
1 small onion, chopped
½ cup cooked long-grain white rice
Salt and pepper
Dash of Tabasco
2 tablespoons chopped fresh dill, or 1 teaspoon dried
2 eggs
¼ cup heavy cream
Flour for dusting

SAUCE
1 cup Chicken Stock (page 352)
2 tablespoons lemon juice
¼ cup dairy sour cream or Crème Fraîche (page 359)
¼ cup chopped fresh dill, or 2 teaspoons dried, plus additional dill for garnish

In a medium skillet, heat 3 tablespoons oil. Sauté mushrooms and onion until tender and liquid has evaporated from skillet. Remove to a mixing bowl and allow to cool about 10 minutes. Mix well with salt and pepper to taste, Tabasco, dill, eggs, and cream. With floured hands form mixture into 6 patties, dredging each side in flour. Chill for about 30 minutes before cooking.

In a medium skillet, heat remaining oil. Cook mushroom cakes about 5 minutes on each side. Remove and keep warm. For sauce, add stock and lemon juice to skillet and bring to a boil, deglazing (page 361) the pan and stirring about 5 minutes until syrupy. Add sour cream and dill and heat through. Serve each mushroom cake with a dollop of sauce and an additional sprinkling of dill.

Serves 6

Savory Cabbage–Apple Strudel

¼ cup (½ stick) butter
4 cups finely grated green cabbage
2 Red Delicious apples, cored and chopped
1 large onion, chopped
2 tablespoons balsamic vinegar
1 tablespoon sugar
1 teaspoon salt
1 teaspoon freshly ground black pepper
½ cup dairy sour cream
¼ cup chopped fresh dill, or 2 teaspoons dried
8 sheets filo dough
½ cup (1 stick) butter, melted
½ cup dry bread crumbs

In a large skillet, heat butter. Sauté cabbage, apples, and onion about 10 minutes, or until tender. Add vinegar and sugar and continue cooking until liquid is almost evaporated. Stir in salt, pepper, and sour cream and cook until thickened. Sprinkle with dill, mix, and allow to cool.

Preheat oven to 350 degrees.

Brush a filo sheet with some of the melted butter and sprinkle with ⅛ of the bread crumbs. Repeat with a second sheet of filo and continue until you have used 4 sheets. Place half the cabbage mixture in a log shape along the short edge of the filo sheets, leaving a 1-inch margin. Fold 1 inch of the long ends over the filling and roll up jelly-roll fashion. Place seam side down on a buttered baking sheet. Repeat with remaining filo and filling to make a second strudel. Brush each strudel well with butter. Cut 4 diagonal steam vents on tops of strudels and bake 25 minutes, or until golden brown. Allow to cool 10 minutes before cutting.

Serves 8 as a first course or 16 as an accompaniment

Braised Lentils and Leeks

¼ cup olive oil
3 leeks (white part only), sliced
2 small carrots, diced
1 clove garlic, minced
1 large ripe tomato, seeded and chopped
1 tablespoon tomato paste
2 cups Chicken or Beef Stock (pages 352, 353)
1 cup lentils, washed
1 tablespoon red wine vinegar
Salt and pepper
¼ cup chopped parsley
¼ cup chopped fresh dill, or 1 tablespoon dried

In a medium saucepan, heat oil. Sauté leeks, carrots, garlic, and tomato about 10 minutes, or until tender. Add tomato paste and stock and bring to a boil. Add lentils and simmer about 25 minutes, until tender. Remove one-fourth of the vegetables and lentils with a slotted spoon and transfer to a blender or food processor. Add vinegar and puree. Return pureed mixture to saucepan, taste for salt and pepper, and stir in parsley and dill. Cook gently to reheat and serve hot or warm.

Serves 6–8

Fennel

LORE AND LINEAGE

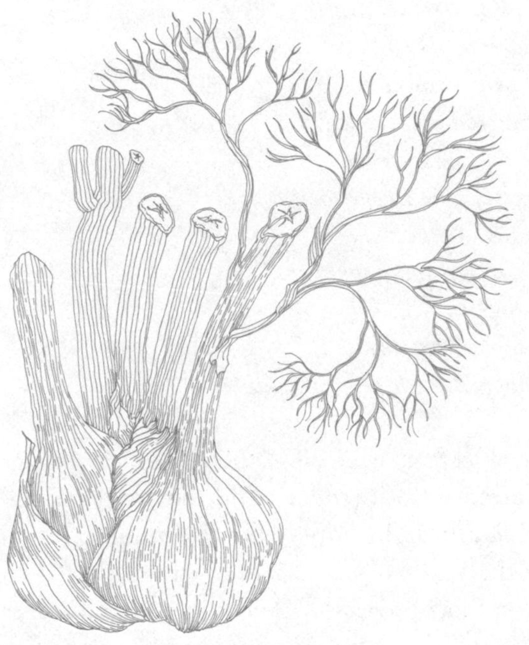

Fennel blades, when "grated into green salads . . . prove the delight and bewilderment of guests."

—IRMA GOODRICH MAZZA
Herbs for the Kitchen, 1939

As we know from *Who's Afraid of Virginia Woolf*, dinner parties provide hosts with all sorts of opportunities to bewilder their guests. Thanks to fennel, the jesting can commence with the first course as we slyly slip the fennel blades into Mrs. Mazza's salad. Its crisp white stalks look like—and even crunch like—celery; but the unexpected, licoricelike taste registers immediately in each guest's appreciative smile.

Fennel is capable of even greater bewilderments. In addition to its role as a vegetable, it can serve as an herb, a spice, and even a fragrant floor covering, depending on how and where you look at it. Peering down its stalks, we see that fennel opens into a spray of frilly leaves similar to dill in appearance though not in taste. Its seeds resemble anise, though they are plumper, lighter colored, and more delicately flavored; the seeds also look like caraway, though their taste, as Elizabeth David puts it, is "less brutal than caraway"; and the seeds resemble cumin, too. This last confusion is further reinforced by the French word for fennel, *cumin des pres*, and by its English nickname "sweet cumin." Similarities in taste are ascribed to the presence of anethole, a component of one of the essential oils in anise, fennel, licorice, and the botanically unrelated star anise. The word *fennel* means "fragrant hay."

There are two main types of fennel: Florentine Fennel—or *finocchio* or Italian Celery (*Foeniculum dulce*)—is cultivated for its stalks, stems, leaves, and flowers. Sweet Fennel (*F. vulgare*), or Herb Fennel, is favored for its leaves and seeds.

American Indians along the Laramie River and elsewhere ate fennel leaves, roots, and stalks like celery and used the seeds to flavor barley water and other foods. The early colonists used fennel, along with lavender and chamomile, as a "strewing herb" to cover floors and fill the air with its captive fragrance. Outside of that, nobody used very much of it. One eighteenth-century recipe for fennel vinegar requires a mere "half a dozen walms" of fennel, which doesn't seem like a lot of walms. *Martha Washington's Booke of Cookery*, calls for "annyseeds & fennell seeds, of each halfe an ounce" in its Sirrup of Liquorish. Yet the English settlers probably brought over sweet memories of the herb from their traditional Confection Boxes, assortments of twelve different seeds and herbs sweetened with honey and eaten like candy. Less abstemious colonists may have retained a fondness for fennel from nipping sack, a mead-based drink popular at the time. Fenouillette and the Spanish Hierbas are other liqueurs based on fennel.

Thomas Jefferson obviously knew something of fennel's beguiling attributes because he requested the American consul to send two varieties of fennel directly from Italy for cultivation at Monticello. Johnny Appleseed was fond enough of the herb to plant it among his hedgerows right along with his more famous crop all across the country.

But it was the Scandinavians who really brought fennel to America's table. Fennel was the alluring and unique taste in the soups, game dishes, meats, and desserts on the Danish *smørrebrød*, the Swedish smörgasbord, the Finnish *voileipäpöytä*, and the Norwegian *koldtbord*, all of which began appearing in the mid-nineteenth century. In Fargo, North Dakota, where Norwegians soon became and still remain the predominating population, fennel was used for pickling fish and for traditional pastries like *goro*, *krumkaken*, and the majestic, pyramid-shaped *kranskake*. Fennel traveled farther west with the 17,000 Mormon Danes whose emigration to Utah made them that state's largest nationality, except for the English.

Swedish *limpa*, an orange- and fennel-flavored holiday bread, began winning converts when the Swedes started baking it in Minnesota over a hundred years ago. Today at the American Swedish Institute in Minneapolis, the buttery smells that warm the frigid air at holiday times might include *sandbakkels* (almond cookies), *fattigmannbakels* (poor man's cookies), *bollers* (Shrovetide buns), and the two fennel-rye breads, *ragbröd* and the beery *vortbröd*. All relocated Swedes—in New Sweden, Maine, and Chandler Valley, Pennsylvania; rural Swedes in Kingsburg, California; and the Boxholm Swedes near Des Moines, Iowa—had at least one custom in common: whatever their work, they stopped it twice a day to have coffee with some fennel-flecked crullers, almond cakes, and/or spice cookies. It's no wonder that Scandinavians are often credited with inventing the all-American coffee break. It is also no wonder that Montana's Olson Creek and Olson Mountain were named in honor of Swedish-born Charley Olson who was, as one might guess, a cook. At any rate, by 1910, one-fifth of the world's Swede's were living in America, and the flavor of fennel was all through the land.

It was, nevertheless, the Italians who introduced fennel to the general community. By the 1920s and 1930s, Italians were not only the country's vegetable growers and greengrocers, they were also running the most popular restaurants. And so fennel, which was seldom found in home kitchens, became endeared to many through its restaurant appearances. Who could resist slices of fennel sautéed and then grilled under showers of Parmesan cheese and presented under the name *finocchio Siciliana*? In San Francisco's North Beach, where the walls of the old Italian family restaurants are vertical photograph albums of baseball players, local politicos, and other gourmets, fennel-sweetened bowls of *minestrone Milanese* are ladled from apparently bottomless tureens. Italian breads from nearby Columbus Avenue are often baked in fennel-lined pans; or there might be fennel-seed breadsticks to be dipped, along with raw, fresh stalks of fennel, into *pinzimonio*, the traditional olive oil sauce. The menu is likely to feature *finocchiona*, the pork and fennel salami originating in Tuscany. Opera-singing waiters have been known to deliver a few arias along with such fenneled fare as *porchetta umbri ar girarosto* (spit-roasted suckling pig), *arista perugina* (roast pork), fennel-sprinkled veal scaloppine, and *fegatelli* (deep-fried pork liver spiced and speared with a sprig of fennel). One great recipe for this last dish has traveled down from the state of Washington, where Angelo Pelligrini's family introduced it into the melting pot (at least according to Angelo Pelligrini). To end the meal, the Italian dessert of lightly roasted figs stuffed with fennel and almonds makes a magnificent fennel finale.

In San Francisco and in Chinatowns everywhere, fennel seed flavors the five-spice powder sold in Asian groceries and rubbed into rows of marinated cooked ducks strung across butcher-shop storefronts. French brasseries with open fireplaces lay grilled sea bass on sun-dried fennel stalks and flame the whole arrangement with brandy to fuse the flavors. A side dish of boiled chestnuts—or of pickled olives, cucumbers, or capers—is often tempered with fennel flowers. More eclectic restaurants toast and grind fennel seeds for curries and chutneys. Included in bouquets garnis or fines herbes mixes, fennel adds depth to anybody's restaurant stew or bouillabaisse, goulash, or even borscht.

Known as the "fish herb," fennel stalks are often wrapped around oily fish, which is then marinated in a fennel-flavored mixture before it finally is cooked in a fennel-scented court bouillon. And oily fish is often served with fennel mayonnaise or sauce. These culinary customs are related to the plant's interesting chemistry which, in effect, predigests food by breaking down its oils and fats. For this reason, fennel is credited with slenderizing qualities, a long-held reputation, judging from the Greek word for fennel—*marathon*, meaning "to grow thin." Our grandparents' generation called it the "slimming herb" and chewed fennel seeds to allay hunger pangs and quiet rumbling tummies during church sermons. Fennel is also supposed to aid digestion, alleviate earaches, and even cure serpent bites. Italian Americans fold fennel into the bouquets given young couples moving into a new home; there its mission is to promote fertility and protect against various evils. Fennel is fed to dairy cattle to increase milk yield and to nursing mothers for the same reason. Its doubtful reputation as a cure for failing eyesight and chronic toothaches may cause frustration in ambitious ophthalmologists and dentists. But its effectiveness as a flea repellent has endeared it to dog lovers, not to mention dogs, and won it a place among the world's most minor poetic achievements, to wit: "Plant fennel near the kennel."

SIGNATURE DISH: FENNEL AND FISH

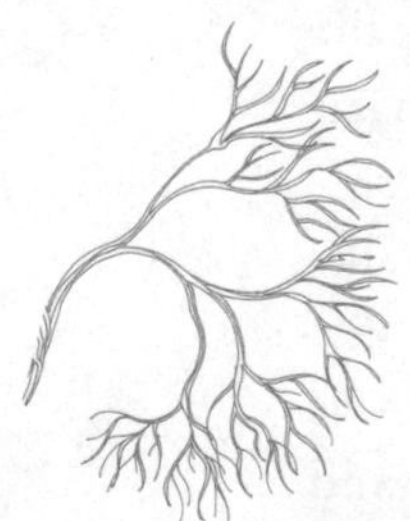

This popular couple makes its appearance in many forms. Their association may begin with a fennel marinade for the raw fish followed by a fennel wrap before the fish is lowered into a fennel court bouillon. Emerging from the oven, fish is often served with fennel sauce or mayonnaise.

Better yet, plant it in a bowl of fresh raspberries and figs, or in any of the following recipes.

VINTAGE RECIPE

From *The Art of Confectionery: Collected from the best New York, Philadelphia, and Boston Confectioners, and including a large number from the French and other foreign nations* (Boston: E. Tilton & Co., 1866).

Seed Ratafia

Take one ounce each of dill, angelica, fennel, caraway, carrot, coriander, and green anise seed; pound them, and steep them for a month in six quarts of alcohol; strain, and add a syrup of eight pounds of sugar with one quart of water; then filter.

Consumer Guide

Also known as: Arabic—shamār; French—fenouil; German—Fenchel; Italian—finocchio; Spanish—fankal.

LATIN: *Foeniculum dulce (for stalks, stems, leaves)*
F. vulgare (for leaves, seeds)

Common variety: Florence Fennel is the most available type.

Selection: Bulbs should be firm and light green in color without any brown spots; this part is used as a vegetable. The feathery leaves should be a darker green and fresh looking; this is used as the herb. The seed is found on spice shelves.

Storage: The bulb and leaves should be wrapped in paper toweling and stored in a plastic bag in the refrigerator for up to 1 week. The seeds may be stored in airtight containers on a shelf.

Compatible herbs and spices: Garlic, parsley, oregano, thyme.

RECIPE LIST

Shrimp in Fennel Mustard
Cream of Fennel and Zucchini Soup
Fennel and Wild Mushroom Soup
Caesar Salad with Raw Fennel and Red Pepper
Shrimp and Fennel Gratin
Baked Sea Bass with Mushrooms And Fennel
Grilled Chicken with Fennel Puree
Grilled Fennel with Sun-dried-Tomato Butter
Fennel Fricassée
Fennel and Honey Rye Muffins
Lemon Fennel Pound Cake
Fenneled Figs and Fresh Raspberries

Shrimp in Fennel Mustard

1 pound bay or smallest available shrimp, cooked and shelled
½ fennel bulb, coarsely chopped
2 teaspoons fennel seed, crushed
¼ cup hot sweet mustard
1 tablespoon lemon juice
½ cup plain yogurt
Salt and pepper

Place shrimp and fennel bulb in a bowl. Mix remaining ingredients until well blended and pour over shrimp. Serve with toothpicks for hors d'oeuvre or on lettuce leaves as a first course.

Serves 6–8

Cream of Fennel and Zucchini Soup

¼ cup olive oil
2 fennel bulbs, thinly sliced, tops reserved
2 leeks (white part only), thinly sliced
2 zucchini, sliced
½ teaspoon dried oregano
6 cups Chicken Stock (page 352)
1 large potato, peeled and diced
1 cup heavy cream
Salt and pepper

In a medium saucepan, heat oil. Sauté fennel slices, leeks, and zucchini until tender. Add oregano and stock, bring to a boil, and add potato. Simmer, covered, for 30 minutes. Puree soup with cream, taste for salt and pepper, and heat through. Garnish with chopped fennel tops.

Serves 6

Fennel and Wild Mushroom Soup

2 ounces dried porcini
¼ cup (½ stick) butter
1 small shallot, minced
½ pound fresh mushrooms, sliced
1 small fennel bulb, chopped
Pinch of dried red pepper flakes
5 cups Chicken Stock (page 352)
2 ounces angel's hair pasta, broken up
Salt and pepper

In a medium bowl, pour at least ¾ cup boiling water over porcini to cover. Allow to soak at least 30 minutes. Drain, reserving the soaking liquid.

Strain the liquid through fine mesh or cheesecloth to remove all sand. Coarsely chop porcini.

In a 4-quart saucepan, melt butter. Add shallot, mushrooms, fennel, porcini, and red pepper flakes. Sauté over medium heat until all vegetables are soft. Add chicken stock and ¾ cup porcini soaking liquid. Bring to a boil and simmer 15 minutes. Add pasta and cook 5 minutes more. Taste for salt and pepper and serve.

Serves 6

Caesar Salad with Raw Fennel and Red Pepper

1 small head romaine lettuce, leaves torn into bite-size pieces
2 small fennel bulbs, thinly sliced
1 red bell pepper, seeded, deveined, and thinly sliced
¾ cup coarsely chopped toasted walnuts (page 361)
2 tablespoons fresh lemon juice
2 cloves garlic, minced
4 anchovy filets, rinsed, dried, and minced
1 egg, lightly beaten
½ cup olive oil
½ teaspoon freshly ground black pepper
⅓ cup grated Parmesan cheese

In a large salad bowl, combine lettuce, fennel, red pepper, and walnuts. In a small bowl, mix remaining ingredients until well blended. Pour over salad and toss well.

Serves 6

Shrimp and Fennel Gratin

1/4 cup olive oil
1 onion, sliced
3 cloves garlic, minced
3 fennel bulbs, halved lengthwise and julienned (page 362)
3 large ripe tomatoes, or 1 12-ounce can tomatoes, seeded and coarsely chopped
Salt and pepper
1 1/2 pounds large shrimp, shelled and deveined
1 cup fresh bread crumbs
2 tablespoons chopped parsley
4 ounces goat cheese, crumbled

Preheat oven to 425 degrees. In a large skillet, heat oil. Sauté onion, 2 cloves garlic, and fennel until tender. Add tomatoes and simmer for about 10 minutes. Add salt and pepper to taste.

Place shrimp in a 10-inch baking dish. Pour tomato sauce over shrimp. Combine bread crumbs, remaining garlic, parsley, and cheese and sprinkle over sauce. Bake about 10 minutes, or until topping is golden.

Serves 6

Baked Sea Bass with Mushrooms and Fennel

2 tablespoons olive oil
6 tablespoons (3/4 stick) butter
3/4 pound fresh mushrooms, sliced
1/2 fennel bulb, thinly sliced, feathery leaves reserved
6 sun-dried tomatoes packed in oil, halved
1 cup dry white wine
1/2 cup water
6 sea bass filets, 6 ounces each
Salt and pepper

Preheat the oven to 400 degrees. In a medium skillet, heat oil and 2 tablespoons butter. Sauté mushrooms, fennel slices, and tomatoes until soft. Add wine and water and bring to a boil. Cook over high heat about 5 minutes, until sauce becomes slightly syrupy. Pour about 3 tablespoons of the sauce on the bottom of an ovenproof dish just large enough to hold the sea bass. Sprinkle each side of the filets with salt and pepper and place in dish. Pour remaining sauce over fish, cover with aluminum foil, and bake in oven for 20 minutes. Remove fish to serving plate and keep warm. Pour sauce into a small saucepan and boil 3 minutes while gradually swirling in small pieces of remaining butter. Pour over fish and garnish with fennel leaves.

Serves 6

Grilled Chicken with Fennel Puree

3 whole chicken breasts, boned, skinned, and split
Salt and pepper
½ cup olive oil
2–3 drops Tabasco

PUREE

3 tablespoons butter, plus ½ cup (1 stick) cold butter cut into pieces
1 fennel bulb, chopped
½ red bell pepper, diced
2 shallots, chopped
¼ cup dry white wine
¼ cup Chicken Stock (page 352)
2 teaspoons Pernod
Salt and pepper

Pound chicken breasts lightly so they are of uniform thickness (¼ inch thick) and sprinkle with salt and pepper. Mix oil and Tabasco and brush chicken with mixture on both sides. Set aside to marinate while making puree.

Heat 3 tablespoons butter in a small skillet or shallow saucepan. Sauté fennel, pepper, and shallots, covered, for about 15 minutes or until tender. Add wine and stock and cook over low heat, uncovered, for 10 minutes. Puree fennel mixture with Pernod and return to pan. Over low heat, add cold butter piece by piece, whisking constantly, until all the butter is incorporated. Taste for salt and pepper.

Preheat grill or broiler to very hot. Cook chicken 3 to 4 minutes on each side. Spread each chicken breast with fennel puree and serve.

Serves 6

Grilled Fennel with Sun-dried-Tomato Butter

3 large fennel bulbs, quartered lengthwise
1 teaspoon salt
3 tablespoons olive oil
½ cup (1 stick) butter
6 sun-dried tomatoes (packed in oil)
¼ teaspoon dried oregano
½ teaspoon freshly ground black pepper

In a large pot of boiling salted water, blanch (page 361) fennel for 2 minutes. Drain under cold water.

Preheat grill. Brush fennel with olive oil and place about 2 inches from heat. Cook about 5 minutes on each side. Remove and keep warm.

In a small skillet, melt butter. Add tomatoes, oregano, and pepper. Cook about 5 minutes over medium-high heat, then puree in a processor or blender and serve over fennel.

Serves 6

Fennel Fricassée

½ pound bacon, diced
1 large red onion, diced
2 cloves garlic, minced
2 fennel bulbs, halved and sliced
3 carrots, cut into 1-inch sticks
½ teaspoon fennel seed, crushed
½ cup dry white wine
½ cup Chicken Stock (page 352)
Salt and pepper
Freshly grated Parmesan cheese

In a medium skillet, brown bacon, remove, and reserve. Pour off all but ¼ cup bacon fat. Sauté onion, garlic, fennel, and carrots over medium-high heat about 5 minutes, until barely tender. Add fennel seed, wine, and stock and bring to a boil. Boil about 2 minutes, cover, and simmer about 15 minutes, or until vegetables are tender. Taste for salt and pepper. Sprinkle with Parmesan cheese and reserved bacon and serve.

Serves 4–6

Fennel and Honey Rye Muffins

1½ cups all-purpose flour
½ cup rye flour
1 teaspoon baking powder
1 teaspoon baking soda
1½ tablespoons fennel seed, toasted (page 360)
½ teaspoon salt
¼ cup vegetable oil
1 egg
3 tablespoons honey
1 cup dairy sour cream

Preheat oven to 375 degrees; grease 12 muffin tins.

In a large mixing bowl, combine dry ingredients until well blended. In a medium bowl, mix remaining ingredients until smooth and stir into dry ingredients. Mix until just blended. Fill muffin tins two-thirds full and bake about 20 minutes.

Yield: 1 dozen

Lemon Fennel Pound Cake

½ cup (1 stick) butter, room temperature
1½ cups sugar
Pinch of salt
5 large eggs
2 cups all-purpose flour
2 tablespoons fennel seed, toasted (page 360) and crushed
1 tablespoon grated lemon zest (page 363)
1 teaspoon vanilla extract
2 tablespoons fresh lemon juice

Preheat oven to 325 degrees. Grease and flour a 9-inch tube pan with a removable bottom.

In a large mixing bowl, cream butter, sugar, and salt. Add eggs one at a time, beating well after each addition, stirring in a bit of the flour after the third egg. Add remaining flour, fennel seed, and zest, mixing until well combined. Add vanilla and lemon juice and blend well. Pour batter into prepared pan and bake 1 hour.

Remove cake from oven, then cool in pan on a wire rack for about 15 minutes. Remove the cake from the pan. When cool, store covered with plastic wrap or foil. Serve with Fenneled Figs and Fresh Raspberries (page 96) or good vanilla ice cream.

Serves 8–10

Fenneled Figs and Fresh Raspberries

2 cups water
½ cup sugar
1 tablespoon fennel seed
1 2-inch strip lemon zest (page 363)
1 tablespoon Pernod
1 pound dried figs
2 cups fresh raspberries
Crème Fraîche (page 359), dairy sour cream, or plain yogurt

In a medium saucepan, bring water, sugar, fennel, and zest to a boil. Continue to boil for 10 to 15 minutes, or until syrupy. Strain sauce, return to saucepan, and add Pernod and figs. Bring to a boil again, remove from heat, and let cool. When ready to serve, stir in fresh raspberries. Serve with Crème Fraîche or over Lemon Fennel Pound Cake (page 95).

Serves 6

Mint

LORE AND LINEAGE

I have even knowed people to pick briar leaves, peppermint, and pepper grass and cook it together. Now, I never did try that because that didn't sound too good to me.

—LINDA PAGE GARLAND AND ELLIOTT WIGGONTON, EDS.
Foxfire Book of Appalachian Cookery, 1984

People who don't like mint have to stay on the alert. This persistent little herb can show up in any course of the meal, from salad to dessert. It may even crop up *after* dinner, in dinner mints; or in mint-flavored liqueurs. Mint, moreover, is a part of American regional eating, from vegetable dishes in Appalachia to Armenian shish kabobs in California's San Joaquin Valley. And to make matters even more unavoidable, the mint family consists of 3,200 species which include over twenty varieties of minty-tasting plants, although produce departments usually simplify the issue by labeling them all "mint."

The most common of these are Spearmint (*Mentha spicata*), with its sharp pointed leaves, and Peppermint (*M. piperita*), with darker, less crinkly leaves, a cool stimulating scent, and slightly heavier taste. Though often used interchangeably, Spearmint is considered the best all-purpose variety. Applemint (*M. rotundifolia*) has rounded woolly leaves with the flavorful taste and smell of apples. Some mint experts credit it with the finest flavor of all, especially fresh and raw in salads, cold soups, and sauces. Pennyroyal (*M. pulegium*) has tapering leaves, an exotic fragrance, and full minty flavor for sauces and stuffings. Eau-de-Cologne Mint, Bergamot Mint, Lemon Mint, and Orange Mint (*M. citrata*) are all the same variety. They have smooth, round shiny leaves and a citrus taste and aroma. They are good added to orange-flavored or sweet dishes, or, as one of their names suggests, to a nice, hot bath. There are also such varieties as Ginger Mint, Corsican Mint, Water Mint, and Pineapple Mint. All mints contain menthol, which raises the temperature at which the skin's cold receptors discharge. This is why minted drinks taste colder than they are and minted foods cool the mouth. Like some varieties of basil and coriander, mint is a cooling herb often combined with hot spices to provide relief and counterpoint in Indian, Southeast Asian, and Mexican dishes.

Some variety or other of mint has been used for culinary purposes in this country for as long as there are records. Wild American Mint (*M. arvensis*), the only indigenous variety, is common from Maine to California and was used widely by Native Americans. The early colonists found it similar to their accustomed Spearmint and Peppermint. American Pennyroyal, which still grows wild along the Eastern Seaboard, is called Squaw Mint and provided a Native American tea, a medicine, and even a contraceptive. Native Americans dried the leaves to flavor a delicious recipe for piñon nut soup; they made nut butters from ground acorns, nuts, or seeds and spiked them with mint and honey.

Mint was certainly one of the first herbs the Pilgrims brought to America. According to herbalist Helen Noyes Webster, "In Plymouth, by the Pilgrim Spring, grows today the descendent of a mint, planted, if not in the first year of the settlement, then very soon after." By 1672 "Spear Mint" was included in John Josselyn's list of New England's thriving plants and, a century later, in John Randolph's accounting of Virginia's herbs. By 1801 Peppermint and Spearmint were described as familiar herbs in James E. Landing's *American Essence.*

SIGNATURE DISH: LAMB AND MINT JELLY

Mint jelly may (temporarily) be out of favor with grown-up gourmets; but most will admit that, as children, this bright green, candy-sweet accompaniment was the main reason they looked forward to lamb dinners.

Early colonial mint recipes exist for teas and sauces and such English favorites as *yonge pessene ryalle*, a rabbit dish with saffron and mint. Mint vinegar was used as a flavoring in itself and also as a basis for mint sauce when fresh mint was not available. Mint was important in the Liberty Teas which substituted for real tea during the boycotts of the Revolutionary era. In the first American cookbook (1796), Amelia Simmons advises boiling peas "with a few leaves of mint." She includes among "Herbs, useful in cookery" the Pennyroyal, a "spontaneous herb in old ploughed fields." Around this same time, the Shaker communities were creating such delicacies as asparagus in minted lemon cream sauce and making mint-scented drinks called herbades. Country folk in the eastern colonies started a still-extant tradition of weed wines and herb wines made from mint and other aromatics.

Cookbooks such as Mary Randolph's *The Virginia Housewife*, first published in 1824, offered exotica like "To Make an Ollo—a Spanish dish," which called for "a handful of mint chopped." Other authors confined mint to confectionery, such as "To Prepare Peppermint Drops" (*A New System of Domestic Cookery*, 1807). By century's end, Fannie Farmer's cookbook included two mint sauces, one made with confectioner's sugar and vinegar and the other with currant jelly and orange rind.

Probably the most famous American culinary use of mint also had its medicinal purposes. The renowned mint julep was reputed to ward off malaria. Consequently, those who administered to themselves a dozen glasses before breakfast as the "usual allowance" could do so in the name of preventive medicine. Though generally made with bourbon, ice, and mint, the julep had many interpretations, including those made with rum, brandy, Madeira, or whisky. Henry Clay, as noted in his diary, required that his juleps be made only in a silver goblet in which choice fresh mint leaves had to be pressed with a silver spoon. Fannie Farmer must have been harking back to the possible health benefits when she included in her julep directions orange juice, strawberry juice, lots of lemon, and a bit of claret, the whole to be diluted with a quart of water.

To early American entrepreneurs, mint meant big business. The village of Cheshire, Massachusetts, had two productive commercial distilleries of peppermint in the 1790s. In 1816, a Mr. Barnett of Wayne County, New York, distilled peppermint leaves to produce "pimentol." Ashfield, Massachusetts, became, in 1819, the first commercial producer of spearmint oil, also known as green mint. By 1835 a full-fledged peppermint oil industry was established in St. Joseph's County, Michigan, taking its crop from the large peppermint plantations of northern Indiana and southern Michigan. These mint oils spurred other nineteenth-century enterprises, including John Hart's mint cordials, which were sold in gallon containers. Today the United States supplies 75 percent of the world's mint oil, with our most productive mint farms located in Washington State's Yakima Valley.

Not only do we grow it here, we use it here. The Portuguese of San Francisco still celebrate the Feast of the Holy Spirit on the last Sunday in

June with their traditional *sopa de espirito santo*, a thick, rich soup served over sprays of fresh mint. In the large Greek community of Tarpon Springs, Florida, people still bring their mint-and-rice–stuffed lamb to the town bakery to be roasted in the big ovens for Easter. In New Mexico and Arizona, mint figures in the mix of herbs used for stews, pork dishes, and braised steak.

Mint also is becoming the darling of trendy eaters and their current fascination with non-Western cuisines. At Vietnamese restaurants, rice-flour spring rolls are redolent of fresh mint; so also are Asian raw chutneys, curries, garnishes, dipping sauces, and sambals. The fragrance of mint fills the room at Thai places featuring such favorites as *yam nang mu* (pork-skin salad). Moroccan meals traditionally end with a ritual of sweet spearmint tea poured, with remarkable accuracy, from several feet above their little tea-cup targets. A North African minted tomato salad juxtaposes the herb with hot red chiles. Middle Eastern salads begin with mint-spiked yogurt or tabouleh or haloumi cheese. The Lebanese *hulus* eggplant dish and *fatouch*, a bread salad, depend on mint and parsley to temper a preponderance of onions.

Perhaps the ubiquitous popularity of mint is based on its ease of propagation. As any amateur mint grower knows, you may as well be lavish in your use of the herb because you can't get rid of it once you've got it. So in Pennsylvania, they pack bunches of mint with the grain because it is supposed to keep away rats. Farm workers there drink a special mint brew to prevent heat prostration. In Massachusetts, an old cure for mosquito bites includes a good dose of mint. Mint's reputation for strengthening the mind is based on its etymology: *mentha* from *mens*, "the mind." For some reason, it has the opposite effect when stufffed into a small pillow and slipped under the head: there it reportedly promotes sleep and sweet dreams. As one of the traditional strewing herbs, mint is the all-time favorite air-freshener. Scattered across the dining room table, mint leaves are said to stimulate the appetite. Postprandially, mint might again be called upon to quell an overindulged stomach or, on the morning after, to relieve a throbbing sensation in the head. People have used mint to prevent conception, cure dog bites, and whiten teeth, though not necessarily simultaneously.

According to research by Euell Gibbons, mint has the same amount of vitamin C as oranges and more vitamin A than carrots, if taken in equivalent weights. Such massive doses might easily be consumed by those who have kept up the old southern custom of multiple mint juleps. For the rest of us, we have the following, far more sober, alternatives.

VINTAGE RECIPE

This recipe is from *The Boston Cooking-School Cook Book* by Fannie Merritt Farmer (Boston: Little, Brown, 1909).

Mint Julep

1 quart water
2 cups sugar
1 pint claret wine
1 cup strawberry juice
1 cup orange juice
Juice 8 lemons
1½ cups boiling water
12 sprigs fresh mint

Make syrup by boiling quart of water and sugar twenty minutes. Separate mint in pieces, add to the boiling water, cover, and let stand in warm place five minutes, strain, and add to syrup; add fruit juices, and cool. Pour into punch bowl, add claret, and chill with a large piece of ice; dilute with water. Garnish with fresh mint leaves and whole strawberries.

Consumer Guide

Also known as: Arabic—na'nā; French—menthe; German—Minze; Greek—diosmo; Italian—menta; Mexican—yerba buena; Thai—by kaprow.

LATIN: *Mentha spicata (spearmint)*
M. piperita (peppermint)
(and other species of Mentha)

Common varieties: Spearmint, Peppermint, Pineapple Mint, Apple Mint, Orange Bergamot Mint.

Selection: Look for bright green, unblemished leaves and fresh minty fragrance.

Storage: Wrap in damp paper towels and seal in plastic bag. Will keep in refrigerator for about 10 days.

Fresh vs. dried: We do not recommend dried mint, as it imparts a musty taste and odor.

Compatible herbs and spices: Parsley, coriander, peppers, garlic.

RECIPE LIST

Grape Gazpacho
Fried Chicken Wings with Lemon–Mint Sauce
Chicken and Ruby Red Grapefruit Salad
Fettuccine with Mint Salsa
Lamb Kabobs with Mint and Mustard
Salmon in Saffron–Mint Cream
Minted Potatoes with Sherry Vinegar
Warm Minted Cherry Tomatoes
Winter Fruit Salad with Cranberry–Mint Dressing
Minted Berry Cream

Grape Gazpacho

2 thick slices French bread, crusts removed
3 tablespoons olive or vegetable oil
3 tablespoons white wine vinegar
2 cloves garlic
1 small sweet onion
1 English cucumber, peeled, seeded, and cut into chunks
1 sprig mint
2 sprigs parsley
2 cups Chicken Stock (page 352)
Salt and pepper
1½ cups seedless green grapes
Mint leaves for garnish

Tear bread into chunks and place in small bowl. Combine oil and vinegar and pour over bread and marinate until the bread has absorbed all the liquid. Place bread, garlic, onion, cucumber, mint, and parsley sprigs in a food processor or blender and puree. While machine is running, pour in

stock and process until fairly smooth. Taste for salt and pepper and remove to serving dish. Stir in grapes and garnish with mint leaves. Serve chilled.
Serves 6

Fried Chicken Wings with Lemon–Mint Sauce

3 pounds chicken wings
½ cup honey
3 tablespoons lemon juice
½ cup all-purpose flour
½ cup yellow cornmeal
1 teaspoon salt
¼ teaspoon ground red pepper
1 cup vegetable shortening for frying

LEMON–MINT SAUCE
½ cup dry white wine
½ cup Chicken Stock (page 352)
1½ cups heavy cream
3 tablespoons chopped mint
1 teaspoon lemon zest (page 363)
Salt and pepper

Place chicken in a large noncorrosive bowl. Combine honey and lemon juice and pour over chicken and marinate for at least 3 hours. Remove chicken from marinade; reserve about 2 tablespoons of the marinade. In a plastic bag, combine flour, cornmeal, salt, and red pepper. Shake several chicken wings in bag to coat well with flour mixture. Place on rack and chill in refrigerator for 30 minutes or in freezer for 10 minutes.

In a large skillet, heat shortening until the surface ripples (about 350 degrees). Fry chicken wings in one layer, turning until chicken is golden and tender on all sides; this should take about 15 minutes. Remove chicken to serving plate and keep warm.

To make sauce, pour fat from skillet, leaving brown bits in bottom of pan. Pour in wine and stock and bring to a boil while scraping bottom of pan. Over high heat, reduce liquid by one-half. Add cream, mint, zest, and reserved marinade. Cook over medium-high heat for about 5 minutes, or until sauce is thick enough to coat a spoon. Add salt and pepper to taste. Serve as a dipping sauce for chicken wings or pour over chicken.

Serves 6 as an appetizer

Chicken and Ruby Red Grapefruit Salad

1 large red or pink grapefruit, peeled and sectioned
1 large skinned and boned whole chicken breast, cooked and cut into julienne (page 362)
½ pound bacon, cooked until crisp and crumbled
1 bunch green onions, thinly sliced
⅓ cup toasted pecans (page 360)
3 tablespoons chopped mint
1 jalapeño pepper (page 361), cut into very fine julienne (page 362)
¼ cup orange juice
1 tablespoon lemon juice
⅓ cup olive oil
¼ teaspoon ground cumin
½ teaspoon sugar
Salt and pepper
Red leaf lettuce

Make sure all membrane is removed from grapefruit sections. Cut each section into 3 pieces. In a large bowl, combine grapefruit, chicken, bacon, green onions, pecans, mint, and jalapeño pepper. In a small bowl, mix orange and lemon juice, olive oil, cumin, and sugar until well blended. Pour over chicken mixture and toss well to combine. Add salt and pepper to taste. Serve on lettuce leaves.

Serves 6

Fettuccine with Mint Salsa

1 clove garlic
1–2 jalapeño or serrano peppers, seeded and deveined (page 361)
2 pounds ripe tomatoes, or 1 28-ounce can, seeded
3 tablespoons chopped mint
1 teaspoon sugar
1 teaspoon ground cumin
1 teaspoon salt
1 tablespoon lemon juice
3 tablespoons olive oil
1 pound fettuccine, cooked until al dente
1 cup Greek black olives, pitted

Place all ingredients except fettuccine and olives in a food processor and process until coarsely chopped. Toss with hot pasta and olives. (This dish is especially tasty when hot, but also refreshingly delicious when served at room temperature.)

Serves 6

Lamb Kabobs with Mint and Mustard

½ cup plain yogurt
1 tablespoon honey mustard
2 tablespoons finely chopped mint
1 large clove garlic, put through press
1 tablespoon lemon juice
½ teaspoon salt
½ teaspoon freshly ground black pepper
3 pounds boneless leg of lamb, cut into ¾-inch cubes

Mix all ingredients except lamb in a medium bowl until well blended. Stir in lamb pieces and marinate in refrigerator overnight.

Preheat grill or broiler until very hot. Thread lamb cubes onto 12 skewers, reserving marinade. Place on grill or in broiler, turning and basting with marinade from time to time. Cooking time should be 8 to 10 minutes. Serve 2 skewers per person.

Serves 6

Salmon in Saffron–Mint Cream

½ cup dry white wine
1 cup water
1 tablespoon lemon juice
¼ teaspoon saffron threads
½ teaspoon salt
4 salmon steaks, 6 ounces each, and ¾ inch thick
¾ cup heavy cream
2 tablespoons (¼ stick) butter, in pieces
2 tablespoons chopped mint

In a medium skillet or sauté pan, place wine, water, lemon juice, saffron, and salt and bring to a boil over high heat. Reduce to a simmer and add salmon. Cover and cook over low heat for 10 minutes. Remove salmon and keep warm. Boil poaching liquid until it reduces to ½ cup.

Add cream to pan and cook over medium-high heat for about 3 minutes, or until sauce is thick enough to coat a spoon. Swirl in butter 1 tablespoon at a time until sauce is satiny smooth. Stir in chopped mint and cook another minute. Place salmon on serving plates and top with sauce.

Serves 4

Minted Potatoes with Sherry Vinegar

1/4 cup olive oil
1 1/2 pounds red potatoes, cubed
3 tablespoons sherry wine vinegar
1 teaspoon salt
1/2 teaspoon freshly ground black pepper
1/4 cup coarsely chopped mint, loosely packed

In a large skillet, heat oil until hot. Add potatoes and sauté about 15 minutes, stirring every so often until lightly browned. Pour in vinegar and cook another 3 minutes. Sprinkle with salt, pepper, and mint. Serve hot or warm.

Serves 6

Warm Minted Cherry Tomatoes

1/4 cup (1/2 stick) butter
1 shallot, chopped
3 tablespoons chopped fresh mint
2 pounds ripe cherry tomatoes
Salt and pepper

In a large skillet, heat butter. Add shallot, mint, and tomatoes and cook, tossing, over medium heat for about 3 minutes, or until tomatoes are just heated through. Taste for salt and pepper and serve.

Serves 6

Winter Fruit Salad with Cranberry–Mint Dressing

2 navel oranges, peeled and sectioned
2 tangerines, peeled and sectioned
2 grapefruits, peeled, sectioned, and sections cut in half
2 small bananas, sliced
½ cup coarsely chopped dried apricots
½ cup toasted and coarsely chopped pecans (page 360)
½ cup cranberry sauce
2 tablespoons bourbon
2 tablespoons olive oil
1 tablespoon lemon juice
6 mint leaves, finely chopped

In a serving bowl, combine fruits with pecans. Whisk together cranberry sauce, bourbon, olive oil, and lemon juice. Toss with fruits and sprinkle with mint leaves.

Serves 6

Minted Berry Cream

16 ounces fresh berries (your favorite or a mixture)
⅓–½ cup sugar, depending on sweetness of fruit
1 tablespoon orange-flavored liqueur
½ cup plain yogurt
1 tablespoon chopped fresh mint plus whole leaves for garnish

Partially freeze berries by placing them in freezer in a single layer on a baking sheet for about 15 minutes. Remove from freezer and place berries in a food processor bowl with sugar and liqueur. Process mixture until slushy. With machine running, pour in yogurt and process until smooth. Stir in chopped mint by hand. Pour into wine glasses and serve immediately, or chill for up to 20 minutes. Garnish each serving with a mint leaf.

Serves 6

Oregano and Marjoram

LORE AND LINEAGE

They are not exceeded even by the Chinese in that loyalty to native food which I call the patriotism of the stomach.

—EDWARD A. STEINER, Writing of Greeks in America
On the Trail of the Immigrant, 1906

At least one herb in this country is linked to the peculiar development of the motion picture industry. When movie theaters first opened, there was no one in the lobby selling popcorn or candy. Instead, people stopped in neighborhood confectionery shops for little treats to bring into the theaters. Many of these local shops were owned or run by Greeks, who immigrated here in great numbers between 1900 and 1920. Once theaters opened their own candy counters, the sweet shops either went out of business altogether or were converted into coffeehouses, lunchrooms, and restaurants. That's where oregano comes in.

In these little eating places, Greek cooks prepared their native dishes, flavored lavishly with oregano, the "king of Greek herbs." The food included *kolokithya dolmades* (stuffed grape leaves); the crusty, vertically grilled lamb called *doner kabob,* or gyros; *arni psito* (roast lamb); moussaka; and anything "à la Grecque." Such menu items turned many of these restaurants into instant gathering centers for homesick Greeks, but the most successful places also served chops, steaks, and plain old American food, with perhaps a surreptitious spiking of oregano.

The term "greasy spoon"—a pejorative pun on the word *Greece*—gives some indication of the quality and style of the fare. With the proliferation of these Greek-American restaurants, oregano was starting to get around. By 1913, Chicago had 600 Greek-owned eating places, New York, 200; thousands more opened their doors wherever Greeks settled, from Lowell, Massachusetts, and Nashua, New Hampshire, to South Omaha, Nebraska. Fifteen years later there were at least 7,000 such eateries nationwide and several chains, including one called Lambropoulos, which thrived in the unexpected settings of Virginia and the Carolinas. (By then the expression, "When Greek meets Greek, they start a restaurant," was already a cliché.)

The South had not been a popular destination for incoming Greeks since the tragic failure of the Florida colony of New Smyrna in the 1700s. This ill-fated community did include some Minorcans, however, whose Spanish influence—oregano and all—lives on there to this day. In her recipe for Minorcan gopher stew, Marjorie Kinnan Rawlings begins with one decapitated "gopher," actually a nickname for a type of Florida turtle.

In the Southwest, the oregano traditions of Spanish America are intrinsic. New Mexico's *posole,* a lime-husked hominy and pork stew, is often flavored with oregano, as are many "classic" Southwestern salsas and chiles—such as Cochiti Pueblo's red chile stew. A Native American favorite of roasted kid sprinkled generously with oregano leaves remains a popular tradition in New Mexico. From Mexican and Aztec cooks, who developed the idea of "dry soups," we inherit such wonders as the oregano-lush *sopa seca de fideos* (made with vermicelli-style noodles), and *sopa seca de tortillas y chorizo* (with fried tortilla strips and sausage).

But it was probably Italian food in general that paved a permanent path for oregano in most areas of this country. In spaghetti houses, pizza parlors, and other "red ink joints"—named for the ubiquitous bottle of Chianti on the table—oregano began to win permanent converts. This happened as a result of *oligata,* a garlic-oil sauce from Calabria used on broiled fish; and as a result of the Neapolitan-Campanian *bistecca alla pizzaiola* with its oregano-flavored tomato sauce; but most conversions happened because oregano is the essential herb of the classic Neapolitan pizza. Italians call oregano *erba da funghi* because it goes so well with mushrooms; but the French call it *l'herbe à pizza.*

Oregano also became popular because of accomplishments outside the culinary. Early colonists chewed its seeds for toothaches, used its tops as a purple dye for woolens, and made a balm that eradicated bruises. It was also a preservative and flavoring for beer and ale before the widespread use of hops. A bundle of oregano placed in the dairy during thunderstorms was supposed to keep milk from turning sour.

Oregano can be confusing. For example, Mexican oregano, also called Mexican sage, is from a different botanical family and has a somewhat sharper taste. It is a basic ingredient in Mexican chile-powder mixtures. True oregano *(Origanum vulgare)* is sometimes called "shepherd's thyme"; it is chemically similar to thyme and often tastes like it. Oregano may also be confused with marjoram, and for good reasons. Both are from the mint family and resemble each other closely in appearance and taste.

SIGNATURE DISH: PIZZA "AMERICANA"

Since this country's first pizzeria opened in New York in 1895, at 53½ Spring Street, Americans have become increasingly possessive about this Neapolitan import. In fact, several restaurants along Wooster Street, in New Haven, Connecticut, display "documented" claims to having invented pizza or calzone or both.

Oregano is known as wild marjoram, and one of marjoram's names is *Origanum majoram.* Marjoram is generally considered sweeter than oregano, more delicate, though both have aromatic, bitter undertones. Marjoram was an early transplant to New England, where settlers grew it to make tea. Fresh or dried, it appeared in the earliest recipes, such as those for "Margerum" cakes and, mixed with parsley, nutmeg, and capers, for "Breast of muton." In the first American cookbook (1796), Amelia Simmons lists it as her second entry under "Herbs, useful in cookery." "Sweet Marjoram is used in Turkeys," she advises, and also "To Dress a Calve's Head, Turtle fashion."

The Pennsylvania Germans called marjoram the *Wurstkraut,* or "sausage herb," and used it accordingly. With garlic, paprika, and other flavorings, marjoram is essential in the pork and veal sausage *Bratwurst,* tongue sausage *Blutwurst,* and in *Braunschweiger, mortadella,* and *Knackwurst.* In early August, during Czech Festival days, Nebraska towns like Wilber, Biatriz, and Bruno perpetuate its use in the liver dumpling soups, blood sausages *(jelita),* mushroom barley casseroles *(kuba),* and homemade bologna *(klobasy)* they have been making since their arrival a century ago. Farther south, Tex-Czech spinach is a regional specialty, often served with Texas pecan butter, made with marjoram and chopped chives. At another point in the country's culinary spectrum, *Miss Parloa's New Cook Book* (1880) included marjoram in the little muslin bag (with "summer savory, four cloves and twelve allspice" to be exact) to be cooked with leg of lamb à la Française.

Marjoram is especially delicious in biscuits, with yams and turnips, and for apple-marjoram salads. While some claim the differences between oregano and marjoram are appreciable, we often use them interchangeably, which you may like to do in these recipes. Indeed, no less an herb authority than Irma Goodrich Mazza confesses "the difference in taste, while plainly discernible, is nothing to sit up nights about."

VINTAGE RECIPE

This recipe is from *Miss Parloa's New Cook Book and Marketing Guide,* by Maria Parloa (Boston: Estes and Lauriat, 1880).

Leg of Lamb à la Française

Put a leg of lamb, weighing about eight pounds, in as small a kettle as will hold it. Put in a muslin bag one onion, one small white turnip, a few green celery leaves, three sprigs each of sweet marjoram and summer savory, four cloves, and twelve allspice. Tie the bag and place it in the kettle with the lamb; then pour on two quarts of boiling water. Let this come to a boil, and then skim carefully. Now add four heaping tablespoonfuls of flour, which has been mixed with one cupful of cold water, two tablespoonfuls of salt and a speck of cayenne. Cover tight, and set back where it will just simmer for four hours.

Oregano: Consumer Guide

Also known as: Arabic—anrār; Dutch—wilde marjolein; French—origan; German—Oregano; Greek—rigani; Italian—origano.

LATIN: *Origanum vulgare*

Common varieties: Mexican Oregano is very pungent; European is more subtle.

Selection: Dried oregano should have a pungent odor and somewhat green color. (If it is gray, it has expired.) Fresh oregano has a milder aroma than dried. Fresh leaves should be unblemished and perky looking.

Storage: Dried oregano will keep well for up to 6 months in an airtight container kept away from light. Fresh oregano should be stored in plastic wrap in the refrigerator for no more than 5 days.

Fresh vs. dried: Dried oregano has more flavor and should be used with caution, as it can be overwhelming. When substituting dried for fresh, use half the amount called for in recipe.

Compatible herbs and spices: Garlic, parsley, thyme, cumin, cinnamon.

Marjoram: Consumer Guide

Also known as: Arabic—marzanjūsh; Dutch—marjolein; French—marjolaine; German—Marienkraut; Italian—maggiorana; Spanish—majorana.

LATIN: *Origanum majorana*

Common varieties: Sweet marjoram with its fuzzy gray-green leaves is the variety most often found in food markets.

Selection: Marjoram is most commonly found on the spice shelves of supermarkets. It should have a similar but more delicate aroma than oregano. Fresh marjoram should have green, unblemished leaves.

Storage: Wrap fresh marjoram in paper towels and seal in plastic bag in refrigerator for up to 5 days. It does not freeze well due to its delicate flavor. Dried marjoram should be kept in an airtight container in a cabinet.

Fresh vs. dried: May be used interchangeably, substituting half the amount dried marjoram for fresh.

Compatible herbs and spices: Parsley, dill, basil, thyme, nutmeg, cinnamon.

RECIPE LIST

Pinto and Pasta Soup
Endive and Goat Cheese Soup
Clam Oregano Pizza
Greek Salad Pita Sandwich
Eggplant and Sausage Pasta
Artichoke, Carrot, and Mushroom Ragout
Scallops Baked with Oregano Crumbs
Marinated Lamb Oregano
Garlic Oregano Biscuits
Sautéed Mushroom and Egg Salad Sandwiches
Sautéed Yams with Pine Nuts and Marjoram
Turkey Crepinettes

OREGANO

Pinto and Pasta Soup

1 pound dried pinto beans
3 sprigs fresh oregano, or 2 teaspoons dried, plus additional for garnish
1 onion, quartered
¼ cup olive oil
2 cloves garlic, minced
3 large tomatoes, coarsely chopped
3 cups water
3 cups tomato juice
1 cup dried pasta, broken into short pieces
Salt and pepper

Place beans, oregano, and onion in a large pot with enough water to cover by 2 inches. Bring to a boil and let simmer 3 minutes. Remove from heat and allow to stand, covered, for 1 hour.

In a stockpot, heat oil. Sauté garlic and tomatoes for about 2 minutes. Add water and tomato juice and bring to a boil. Drain beans and add to soup. Cook, partially covered, for about 1 hour. Add pasta and continue to cook another 5 minutes. Taste for salt and pepper and sprinkle with additional oregano before serving.

Serves 6–8

Endive and Goat Cheese Soup

¼ cup (½ stick) butter
1 bunch green onions, sliced
2 heads Belgian endive, cored and thinly sliced
4 teaspoons fresh oregano, or 2 teaspoons dried
¼ pound mild goat cheese
4 cups Chicken Stock (page 352)
1 cup half-and-half
Freshly ground black pepper

In a medium saucepan, heat butter. Cook green onions and endive about 4 minutes, or until wilted. Add oregano and goat cheese and cook over low heat until cheese melts. Add stock, bring to a boil, and simmer 5 minutes. Add half-and-half and cook over very low heat for another 5 minutes. Serve with a generous grinding of fresh pepper.

Serves 6

Clam Oregano Pizza

1 recipe Herbed Pizza Dough (page 355)
¼ cup olive oil
3 cloves garlic, minced
2 7-ounce cans chopped clams, drained and liquid reserved
¼ cup chopped parsley
2 tablespoons fresh oregano, or 1 tablespoon dried
Salt and pepper

Preheat oven to 450 degrees. Roll out pizza dough to fit a 15-inch pizza pan.

Spread dough with 2 tablespoons olive oil. Then sprinkle with garlic, clams, parsley, and oregano. Mix 2 tablespoons reserved clam liquid with remaining olive oil and sprinkle over clam mixture. Bake for 12 minutes. Add salt and pepper to taste.

Serves 6

Greek Salad Pita Sandwich

½ pound imported feta cheese, crumbled
1 English cucumber, peeled, seeded, and diced
2 tomatoes, seeded and coarsely chopped
4 green onions, chopped
1 cup black olives (preferably Greek-style), pitted and coarsely chopped
¼ cup chopped parsley
2 eggs, hard-boiled and coarsely chopped
2 tablespoons red wine vinegar
¼ cup olive oil
2 teaspoons fresh oregano, or ½ teaspoon dried
Salt and pepper
6 pita breads
Young spinach or lettuce leaves

In a medium bowl, combine first 7 ingredients. In a small bowl, whisk together vinegar, oil, and oregano. Toss with salad ingredients just until moistened. Taste for salt and pepper. Heat pita breads just until warm. Make slit at one end and fill with salad and spinach or lettuce.

Yield: 6 sandwiches

Eggplant and Sausage Pasta

1 pound mild Italian sausage
1 onion, chopped
1 small eggplant (about 1 pound), cubed
1 green or yellow bell pepper, seeded, deveined, and cut in strips
1 28-ounce can imported Italian tomatoes, drained and coarsely chopped
½ cup dry white wine
3 tablespoons tomato paste
2 teaspoons fresh oregano, or 1 teaspoon dried
Salt and pepper
¼ cup heavy cream
1 pound pasta, fresh or dried
¼ cup chopped parsley
Grated Parmesan cheese

In a large skillet, sauté sausage until most of the fat is rendered. Remove sausage and set aside. In same skillet, sauté onion, eggplant, pepper, and tomatoes, about 6 minutes over medium-high heat. Add wine, tomato paste, and oregano, bring to a boil, cover, and simmer 10 minutes, adding reserved sausage during the last 2 minutes. Taste for salt and pepper, stir in cream, and keep warm while making pasta. Cook pasta according to directions, drain well, and toss with sauce in pasta bowl. Sprinkle with parsley and serve. Pass the cheese.

Serves 4–6

Artichoke, Carrot, and Mushroom Ragout

¼ cup (½ stick) butter
1 onion, thinly sliced
8 small artichoke hearts (page 360), or frozen and defrosted, quartered
1 pound carrots, sliced 1½ inches thick
½ pound fresh mushrooms, quartered
2 tablespoons fresh oregano, or 1 tablespoon dried
2 tablespoons all-purpose flour
½ cup Chicken Stock (page 352)
½ cup dry white wine
2 tablespoons tomato paste
Salt and pepper

In a medium sauté pan, heat butter. Add onion, artichokes, carrots, mushrooms, and oregano. Cook until well coated with butter, cover, and continue cooking over low heat for 20 minutes. Sprinkle flour over mixture, stir well, and pour in stock, wine, and tomato paste. Bring to a boil and simmer 5 minutes. Add salt and pepper to taste and serve hot, warm, or at room temperature.

Serves 6

Scallops Baked with Oregano Crumbs

¼ cup fresh oregano, or 2 tablespoons dried
1 cup parsley leaves
2 cloves garlic
½ cup grated Parmesan cheese
½ cup (1 stick) butter, room temperature
1 cup dry bread crumbs
Salt and pepper to taste
2 pounds bay scallops
2 tablespoons lemon juice

Preheat oven to 425 degrees. Place oregano, parsley, garlic, cheese, butter, bread crumbs, salt, and pepper in a food processor and process until a coarse paste is formed. Place scallops in a buttered baking dish in one layer and sprinkle with lemon juice. Spoon oregano paste on top. Bake 10 minutes, or until bubbly. Serve with steamed rice or noodles.

Serves 6

Marinated Lamb Oregano

1 leg of lamb (about 6 pounds), boned and butterflied
Salt and pepper
4 cloves garlic, minced
2 tablespoons fresh oregano, or 1 tablespoon dried
2 tablespoons fresh thyme, or 1 teaspoon dried
½ cup lemon juice
½ cup olive oil

Blot lamb dry with paper towels and rub well with salt and pepper. Mix remaining ingredients and rub half the mixture all over the meat. Reserve the other half for basting. Allow to marinate at room temperature for 4 hours or overnight in the refrigerator.

Preheat grill or broiler until quite hot. Place lamb about 5 inches from heat and cook a total of 40 minutes, turning and basting with reserved juice every 10 minutes. Allow to rest off heat 20 minutes before slicing.

Serves 6–8

Garlic Oregano Biscuits

1½ cups all-purpose flour
½ cup semolina flour
1 tablespoon baking powder
1 teaspoon baking soda
¼ teaspoon salt
2 teaspoons fresh oregano, or 1 teaspoon dried
1 clove garlic, put through press
½ cup (1 stick) cold butter, in pieces
½ cup buttermilk
2 tablespoons cream or melted butter

Preheat oven to 450 degrees, grease a baking sheet.

In a large mixing bowl, combine dry ingredients, oregano, and garlic. Cut in cold butter pieces until mixture is crumbly. Add buttermilk and stir until mixture comes together to form a dough.

On a floured surface, knead dough 1 minute. Roll out dough to ½-inch thickness. Cut biscuits with 2-inch round cutter, then re-roll scraps gently and cut again. Place on baking sheet, brush tops with cream, and bake for 12 to 15 minutes, or until golden.

Yield: Approximately 1 dozen

MARJORAM

Sautéed Mushroom and Egg Salad Sandwiches

3 tablespoons butter
1 shallot, chopped
½ pound fresh mushrooms, chopped
1 teaspoon lemon juice
1 sprig fresh marjoram or ¼ teaspoon dried, plus ¼ teaspoon dried marjoram
4 eggs, hard-boiled and shelled
6 strips bacon, cooked and crumbled
¼ cup mayonnaise
Salt and pepper
Red onion rings
Young spinach leaves or butter lettuce leaves
8 slices egg bread

In a medium skillet, heat butter. Sauté shallot and mushrooms for about 5 minutes. Sprinkle with lemon juice and stir in fresh marjoram or ¼ teaspoon of dried. Allow to cool slightly. Chop eggs and place in bowl with mushroom mixture, bacon, remaining dried marjoram, and mayonnaise. Combine well. Taste for salt and pepper.

Make sandwiches by layering egg–mushroom mixture, red onion rings, and spinach leaves between 2 slices of bread.

Yield: 4 sandwiches

Sautéed Yams with Pine Nuts and Marjoram

2 pounds yams, cut into ¼-inch-thick slices
¼ cup (½ stick) butter
2 large tart apples, quartered and sliced ¼ inch thick

1 teaspoon fresh marjoram or ½ teaspoon dried
¼ cup toasted pine nuts (page 360)

Cook yams in boiling salted water for 10 minutes. Drain and set aside. In a large skillet, heat butter. Sauté apples for 5 minutes over medium heat. Add yams and marjoram and continue cooking another 10 minutes. Sprinkle with pine nuts and serve.

Serves 6

Turkey Crepinettes

1 pound ground turkey
½ cup cooked white long-grain rice
¼ cup currants, soaked in ¼ cup brandy for 30 minutes
1 small onion, chopped
1 clove garlic, minced
¼ cup chopped parsley
1 teaspoon fresh or dried marjoram
1 teaspoon salt
½ teaspoon freshly ground black pepper
¼ teaspoon grated nutmeg
1 egg beaten with 1 tablespoon heavy cream
8 strips bacon
2 tablespoons (¼ stick) butter

In a large mixing bowl, stir all ingredients except bacon and butter until well combined. Form eight 3- to 4-inch patties. Place bacon strip around each pattie. In a large skillet, heat butter. Cook patties over medium-high heat for about 8 minutes on each side. Drain on paper towels and serve.

Serves 4

Parsley

LORE AND LINEAGE

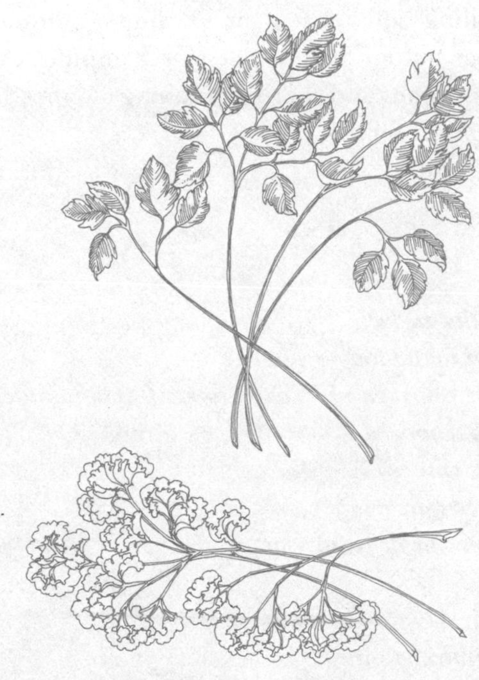

I wouldn't want to be Parsley
only to be sprinkled on things at the end
going around the edges of platters
garnish to the good stuff,
making the pallid look palatable.
What kind of reward is that for
keeping yourself green all the time
lying seductively on the carrots till
you're picked off?

Some people might say:

Parsley, you may not actually contribute

to the taste of anything,

but you won't detract from it either.

Still, I wouldn't want to be parsley,

I wouldn't want to be her.

—J.F.

Let's face it. We've all been guilty of treating parsley as just another pretty herb. Who among us could deny that at least once we have allowed our own parsley sprig to be "thrust aside with forks and returned to the kitchen, thence to slip into the refuse pail"? When cookbook author Irma Goodrich Mazza made this accusation nearly fifty years ago, she had hopes that parsley would soon be used for more than a mere green dust to cover a corner of the dinner plate. This chapter is intended to help us mend our ways; but in defense, we have traced this form of parsley abuse back to quite an honorable American source.

In the first cookbook written by an American (1796), Amelia Simmons advised that parsley is "much used in garnishing viands." That set the tone—parsley could be used for its good looks. In all fairness, Simmons also includes parsley in recipes for stuffing a leg of veal, a parsley sauce for fowl, and a dressing for turtle. She mentions three types of parsley, recommending that "the thickest and branchiest is the best." We're not so sure. True, the frilly leafed type does provide some rich foliage for the undercrowded dinner plate. But the more professional-looking flat-leafed type, called Italian or French Parsley, usually has a finer, more pronounced flavor.

There actually are all kinds of parsleys: Hamburg Parsley, a potherb used by Germans and Poles, among others, has its leaves ignored altogether and is cultivated for its delicious carrot-shaped root, which looks rather like an anemic parsnip. Japanese Parsley, also known as *mitsuba,* trefoil, or Chinese Parsley, is becoming more available with the ever-expanding interest in Asian cooking; this "exotic variety" is actually fresh coriander. "Fool's Parsley" or "Dog's Poison" looks like flat-leafed parsley though it has won its name for obvious reasons. American Indians in the West knew thirty true species of parsley and some mountain parsleys that are botanically unrelated. They used them all, mostly their roots, which they ate raw, baked, or dried and ground up as flour.

Parsley is one of the oldest and most universally used herbs in history. Its name in Greek *(Petroselium sativum)* means "rock celery"; its origin, judging from its appearance in virtually all Roman sauces and salads, is probably Mediterranean. As the subject of a poem, parsley was an enchanting entry in a fifteenth-century English gardening book; it was soon a popular part of most recipes in manuscripts of English cooking. Consequently, our first colonists knew parsley well and planted it here almost immediately, listing it among those New England rarities "as do thrive there." Settlers in New Netherlands grew it also, according to a description of early plants by Adriaen van der Donck. A report from the Virginia settlements by Alexander Whitaker has it firmly established, along with "time, hysop, marjorum," by 1610. And the Swedes and Hollanders who settled Delaware in the mid-1700s planted it, along with red pepper and peppergrass.

A century later, fried parsley became a popular garnish, recommended by eminent cookbook writers like Mrs. Sarah Tyson Rorer as an accompaniment to fried frogs. In Virginia, slices of veal, flattened and sprinkled with parsley and spices, were rolled up and cooked on skewers; they emerged looking like their name: veal olives. According to another Virginia recipe, sweet herbs and parsley were used "To Dress Ducks with Juice of Oranges." In Michigan, the Cornish who came to work in the iron mines in the late 1800s flavored their meat-filled pasties *(PASS-tees)* with parsley, thyme, and marjoram. These hearty, crescent-shaped pastries, designed to be carried in the pocket into the mines, were adopted by the newly arriving Finns, Italians, Germans, French, Swedes, and

Poles, all of whom soon vied for the honor of making the best "Cornish" pasty.

About the same time, Basque sheepherders immigrated to Idaho, Nevada, and California, bringing with them such highly seasoned dishes as *ezkualdun itarrak,* unpronounceable by all but Basques. This bean dish consists of *chorizo,* bacon, pinto beans, and big handfuls of fresh parsley. The French chefs who became society's darlings in New York's *haute* nineteenth-century eating establishments used the herb by bushels for the standard *beurre maître d'hôtel* (parsley butter), *persillades,* bouquets garnis, and fines herbes. In Greek neighborhoods, parsley was abundant in the spinach and feta pie called *spanakopita* as well as in richly flavored meatballs called *keftedes.*

SIGNATURE DISH: BOUQUET GARNI

Parsley is the one constant in many of the herb and spice combinations, from traditional fines herbes and bouquets garnis to the more American-sounding soup spirits, herb bundles, and sweet bags.

The Pennsylvania Dutch still make parsley dumplings and cook them in stews or with shortribs. An interest in tabouleh salad, made with abundant amounts of parsley and bulgur; and in hummus, a sesame-seed spread bursting with garlic and parsley, has migrated from Middle Eastern communities in New York and California to natural foods stores across the country. *Lahmajoun,* an Armenian "pizza" in which parsley is the sole herb, is even beginning to appear in the frozen food departments right next to its Neapolitan neighbors. In the hill country around the Pedernales River in Texas, some German families permit parsley to invade a few of their recipes—oven-roasted doves, for one example. But those who try to duplicate that region's German potato salad should think twice before introducing anything as unorthodox as a sprig of parsley. ("Parsley?"

reacted one horrified, old-time cook. "You mean like they put in the Friday Fish Plate at the Ranch Room? Why honey . . . don't you know God meant for potato salad to be plain?")

She may not have minded so much if she thought about the nutritional value of parsley, one tablespoon of which supplies the recommended daily allowance of vitamins A and C and iron! In fact parsley, which contains more vitamin C than almost any other food and more vitamin A than cod liver oil, is often more nutritious than the food it adorns. Aside from these health-giving attributes, parsley has been used to lighten freckles, cure hangovers, prevent baldness, and alleviate rheumatism. An old southern superstition warns that it is bad luck to transplant parsley from an old home to a new one. And some venerable Pennsylvania wisdom assures that planting parsley in the house means that someone will surely die. Parsley oil is used in condiments and commercial ice cream. According to one old American "receipt," the herb can be made into a perfume which will reveal the future (assuming you throw in some fleawort seeds and violet root).

There is one ominous parsley legend which does concern us here. It is supposedly bad luck to give parsley away to anyone, to receive it from anyone, or even to snip some sprigs in the garden—especially if you are in love. Fortunately, there are other ways to get hold of the herb, as we overheard in the grocery store recently.

"Do you know any way to preserve parsley?" one shopper asked another. "I only need a few tablespoons and I never know what to do with the rest."

"No, but I do have a solution," her friend said brightly. "When I need just a little, I always steal it. They'll never miss a few sprigs of parsley in this store."

This solution should help one escape the legend, if not the store manager. But in the interests of honesty, we hereby present enough parsley recipes to use up an entire bunch.

VINTAGE RECIPE

This recipe, devised by the U.S. Army to feed the citizenry following the 1906 earthquake, was probably more appreciated than many of the more famous San Francisco dishes. Adapted from "The Refugees Cook Book" (quoted in *San Francisco Chronicle,* April 5, 1986, p. 13).

Earthquake Stew

1/4 cup (1/2 stick) butter
2 onions, chopped
3 pounds boneless beef, cut in bite-size pieces
Flour for dredging
3 carrots, diced
3 turnips, diced
3 potatoes, cut in chunks
2 parsnips, sliced
1/2 cup chopped parsley
1 bay leaf
Salt and pepper

In a large frying pan, melt butter and sauté onions until brown. Dredge meat in flour and, in same pan, brown well on all sides. Put meat and onions in large stew pot, cover with boiling water, and cook over low heat for 2 hours, adding more water if necessary. Add remaining ingredients and cook 1 hour longer. According to the original recipe, you can now "thicken it with one-half cup of flour and teaspoon of caromel [*sic*]."

Consumer Guide

Also known as: French—persil; German—Petersilie; Greek—maitano; Italian—prezzemolo; Spanish—perejíl.

LATIN: *Petroselinum crispum (curly)*
P. sativum (flat-leaf)

Common varieties: Curly Parsley (delicate in flavor), Italian Flat Leaf (more robust).

Selection: Bright green, unblemished leaves.

Storage: Shake off excess moisture, wrap in 2 layers of paper towels, and seal in plastic bag. Refrigerate and use as needed. Will keep well for about 1 week.

Fresh vs. dried: Only fresh parsley should be used, as it is available all year. Dried parsley has almost no flavor.

Compatible herbs and spices: Dill, oregano, thyme, garlic, peppers.

RECIPE LIST

Salmon Tartare in Cucumber Cups
Two-Lettuce Cream Soup with Parsley and Chives
Parsley and Potato Chowder
Parslied Chicken Dumplings in Chicken Broth
Carrot and Olive Tart
Winter Wheat Salad with Parsley and Mint
Fresh Vegetable Salad with Parsley Vinaigrette
Veal in Parsley and Caper Sauce
Roast Cornish Game Hen with Parsley Pancetta Stuffing
Fried Parsley
Parsley Pasta with Clam Sauce

Salmon Tartare in Cucumber Cups

1 pound boneless, skinless salmon, fat removed
4 green onions, trimmed
2 cloves garlic
1 cup parsley leaves, loosely packed, plus chopped parsley for garnish
⅓ cup fresh dill, or 1 teaspoon dried
2 tablespoons lemon juice
2 tablespoons hot mustard
3 tablespoons olive oil
1 teaspoon salt
1 teaspoon freshly ground black pepper
2 large cucumbers, preferably English, sliced 1 inch thick

In a food processor, coarsely chop salmon. Remove to bowl. Place remaining ingredients except cucumber in processor bowl and process until blended. Add to salmon and mix well. Hollow out the center of each cucumber slice with a melon baller, leaving just a thin membrane, and fill with 2 tablespoons of salmon mixture. Sprinkle with additional chopped parsley and serve.

Serves 8–10 as an appetizer (about 30 pieces)

Two-Lettuce Cream Soup with Parsley and Chives

3 tablespoons butter
1 head butter lettuce, shredded
1 small head romaine lettuce, shredded
1 leek (white part only), sliced
½ cup parsley leaves, plus ½ cup chopped parsley, loosely packed
4 cups Chicken Stock (page 352)
1 cup heavy cream or half-and-half
Salt and pepper
¼ cup chopped chives

In a 4-quart saucepan, melt butter. Add lettuces, leek, and parsley and cook over low heat until wilted. Add stock, bring to a boil, and simmer, partially covered, for 10 minutes. Puree soup in food processor, blender, or food mill and return to saucepan. Add cream, salt and pepper to taste, and chopped parsley. Heat through and serve garnished with chives.

Serves 6

Parsley and Potato Chowder

¼ cup (½ stick) butter
1 onion, chopped
2 cloves garlic, minced
5 cups Chicken Stock (page 352)
2 red potatoes, cubed
1 sweet potato, cubed
1½ cups half-and-half or light cream

1 cup chopped parsley, loosely packed
Salt and pepper

In a medium saucepan, heat butter. Sauté onion and garlic about three minutes, or until tender. Add stock and bring to a boil. Add potatoes and simmer, covered, about 12 minutes until tender. Add half-and-half and parsley. Heat but do not boil. Taste for salt and pepper and serve.

Serves 6

Parslied Chicken Dumplings in Chicken Broth

1/4 pound skinned and boned chicken breast, chilled
1 egg white
1/2 teaspoon salt
1/2 teaspoon freshly ground black pepper
1/2 teaspoon grated nutmeg
1/2 cup heavy cream, chilled
1/2 cup chopped parsley, loosely packed
2 quarts Chicken Stock (page 352)

Remove all fat and gristle from chicken and cut into small pieces. In a food processor, puree chicken with egg white, salt, pepper, and nutmeg. While machine is running, add cream slowly until thick. Mix in parsley by hand and chill mixture about 1 hour.

In a large pot, bring stock to a simmer. Using 2 teaspoons, form dumpling mixture into ovals and place ovals in simmering soup.

Simmer very gently, covered, for 10 minutes. Serve immediately.

Serves 6–8

Note: Dip spoons in cold water before forming each dumpling; this makes it easier to push dumplings off spoon.

Carrot and Olive Tart

1 recipe Pâte Brisée (page 354), fitted into a 9-inch tart shell, and partially baked
3 tablespoons butter
3 carrots, shredded
¾ cup chopped parsley, loosely packed
2 eggs
½ cup heavy cream
½ teaspoon salt
½ teaspoon freshly ground black pepper
½ cup olive spread (may be purchased in gourmet shops)

Preheat oven to 375 degrees. Have tart shell ready to be filled.

In a large skillet, heat butter. Sauté carrots over medium-high heat for about 5 minutes. Allow to cool about 5 minutes.s Mix with ½ cup parsley, plus eggs, cream, salt, and pepper. Spread olive mixture on bottom of tart shell. Pour carrot mixture over olive spread and bake 25 minutes, or until top is golden and puffy. Sprinkle with remaining parsley. Allow to rest at least 15 minutes before serving.

Serves 6

Winter Wheat Salad with Parsley and Mint

18 ounces bulgur (cracked wheat)
½ cup raisins
½ cup coarsely chopped dried apricots
1 orange
1 tangerine
1 tablespoon grated orange rind
1 tablespoon grated tangerine rind
6 tablespoons lemon juice
2 tablespoons orange juice
1 tablespoon Dijon mustard
1 cup olive oil
1 teaspoon ground cinnamon
1 teaspoon ground cumin
Salt and pepper
1 small red onion, chopped
½ cup chopped mint, loosely packed
½ cup chopped parsley, loosely packed
1 cup coarsely chopped toasted almonds (page 360)

In a large bowl, soak bulgur in cold water to cover for 1 hour. Drain well and return to bowl.

In a small bowl, soak raisins and apricots in warm water to cover for about 20 minutes. Drain and reserve.

Peel and section the fresh fruits. Add to bulgur along with grated rinds, raisins, and apricots. Whisk together lemon and orange juices, mustard, oil, cinnamon, cumin, and salt and pepper to taste. Pour over bulgur, add onion, mint, and parsley and toss well. Sprinkle with toasted almonds.

Serves 6–8

Fresh Vegetable Salad with Parsley Vinaigrette

1 bunch red radishes, sliced
¼ pound fresh mushrooms, thinly sliced
1 bunch green onions, sliced
2 large carrots, shredded
10 cherry tomatoes, halved
½ head romaine lettuce, shredded

VINAIGRETTE
1 bunch parsley
1 large clove garlic
1 teaspoon Dijon mustard
2 tablespoons lemon juice
2 tablespoons red wine vinegar
½ cup olive oil
Salt and pepper

In a large bowl, mix vegetables. Place vinaigrette ingredients in food processor or blender and mix until smooth. Add salt and pepper to taste. Pour over vegetables and toss well.

Serves 6–8

Veal in Parsley and Caper Sauce

12 veal scallops (about 3 ounces each)
½ cup all-purpose flour
½ teaspoon salt
½ teaspoon ground red pepper
3 tablespoons butter
½ cup dry white wine
½ cup Chicken Stock (page 352)

½ cup chopped parsley, plus additional for garnish, loosely packed
2 tablespoons capers, rinsed and drained
¼ cup heavy cream

Blot veal dry with paper towels. Dredge in flour mixed with salt and red pepper. In a large skillet, heat butter. Sauté veal until golden, about 3 minutes on each side. Remove and keep warm. Add the wine and stock to the skillet. Bring to a boil while scraping the bottom of the pan. Cook over medium-high heat about 3 minutes, or until slightly thickened. Add parsley, capers, and cream and cook about 4 minutes, until somewhat reduced. Pour half the sauce on the serving plate, top with veal, and pour remaining sauce over veal. Sprinkle with additional chopped parsley.

Serves 6

Roast Cornish Game Hen with Parsley Pancetta Stuffing

4 rock cornish game hens
2 teaspoons salt
2 tablespoons lemon juice
¼ cup melted butter
1 tablespoon paprika

STUFFING
¼ cup (½ stick) butter
¼ pound pancetta (Italian non-smoked bacon), diced
1 small onion, chopped
1 cup fresh white bread crumbs
½ cup fresh whole wheat bread crumbs
½ cup pine nuts
1 cup Chicken Stock (page 352)
1 cup chopped parsley, loosely packed
Salt and pepper

Preheat oven to 400 degrees. In a large skillet, melt butter. Sauté pancetta and onion for about 5 minutes. Add bread crumbs and pine nuts and cook another 2 minutes. Remove from heat and stir in stock and parsley. Taste for salt and pepper.

Salt each hen cavity with ½ teaspoon salt and sprinkle with lemon juice. Stuff the cavities loosely with the stuffing. Mix melted butter with paprika and brush each bird with mixture. Place hens on their sides on a rack in roasting pan. Roast 15 minutes, baste with drippings, turn breast side up, and roast another 15 to 20 minutes, or until birds are golden brown all over. Remove from roasting pan to serving platter, pour pan juices over, and serve.

Serves 4

Fried Parsley

3 bunches parsley
6 chives
Oil for deep-frying

Divide the 3 bunches of parsley into 6 equal bunches. Tie each bunch at the stem end with a chive. In a large pot of salted boiling water, blanch (page 361) parsley for 30 seconds. Remove with slotted spoon and blot dry. In a large, deep skillet, heat 1 inch of oil to about 375 degrees. Fry parsley a few minutes, turning occasionally. Drain on paper towels and serve immediately.

Serves 6

Parsley Pasta with Clam Sauce

¼ cup olive oil
3 cloves garlic, minced
1 shallot, minced
2 15-ounce cans whole baby clams
1 small tomato, seeded and coarsely chopped
¼ cup chopped parsley, loosely packed
¼ cup dry white wine
Salt and pepper
1 recipe Herbed Pasta Dough (page 355), substituting ¼ cup chopped parsley for mixed herbs

In a medium skillet, heat oil. Add garlic and shallot and cook about 4 minutes, until wilted. Drain clam juice from canned clams into skillet. Add tomato, parsley, and wine and bring to a boil. Simmer about 4 minutes until slightly syrupy. Add clams, taste for salt and pepper, and heat through. Cook pasta in boiling salted water until tender, about 3 minutes. Then toss with sauce and serve.

Serves 4–6

Rosemary

LORE AND LINEAGE

Now hoppin-john was F. Jasmine's favorite food. She had always warned them to wave a plate of [it] . . . before her nose when she was in her coffin, to make certain there was no mistake; for if a breath of life was life in her, she would sit up and eat, but if she smelled the hopping-john, and did not stir, then they could just nail down the coffin and be certain she was truly dead.

—CARSON MCCULLERS
The Member of the Wedding, 1946

Imagine the worst. It's raining, you're hungry, you're supposed to be on vacation, and you've been driving around for hours on the back roads of South Carolina looking for a place that's open on New Year's Day. You finally end up in a little storefront café—to be told they're serving only one thing today, something you've never heard of. Hoppin' John, the waiter called it. And when you tell him you never heard of it, the whole roomful of people look over and laugh out loud. It may not sound like the makin's for a happy New Year, but if there's any truth in legends, it very well could be.

Turns out, Hoppin' John is a traditional southern dish eaten for good luck on New Year's Day. This soul-food dish comes from Africa by way of the West Indies, and is associated with the Gulla country near Charleston. The word may be a corruption of *pois à pigeon,* for the pigeon peas of which it was originally made; but there are as many other explanations of the name as there are versions of the recipe. Whatever the formula, however, the dish itself is symbolic as is every ingredient in it.

Pigeon peas are part of the formula, of course, or a reasonable substitute like black-eyed peas which, along with the hog jowl, signify luck; rice is for purity, mustard for steadfastness, and, finally, rosemary for friendship.

SIGNATURE DISH: HOPPIN' JOHN

This old, southern New Year's dish, which is supposed to bring luck in the new year, has as many symbolic associations as it has versions. It is basically a highly seasoned rice and bean combination, cooked long and seriously with hog jowl or beef bone, salt pork, or cracked ham bones.

If the rosemary is the most memorable taste in the meal, that fits right in with the mythology of this herb that resembles pine needles. Because it signifies remembrance, rosemary is an important flower in the dainty nosegays called "tussie-mussies" that southern debutantes carry at their coming-out parties. According to another custom, students are advised to put rosemary in their hair when studying for exams to stimulate the memory, while some of their professors may utilize rosemary for its reputed ability to prevent baldness. In fact, this ancient herb is generally good for the head. Many of today's shampoos contain rosemary oil because it preserves both color and curl and keeps hair shiny. American colonists usually took their rosemary in the form of teas, fruit punches, candied flowers, herb vinegars, and a curious dessert called French curds.

Meanwhile, rosemary's culinary potential was being developed in such seemingly unrelated locations as Lebanon, New York; North Union (now Shaker Heights), Ohio; and Pleasant Hill, Kentucky. These are all sites of communal farms run by the Shakers. The Shakers were great herbalists; they grew over 350 herbs and seeds—chives, rosemary, basil, and savory, among others—which they sold in packets with relevant recipes printed on them, most of them their own. Of the most famous are rosemaried potatoes, Shaker spinach with rosemary, and rosemary biscuits.

The colonists had not been too successful with the herb, according to John Josselyn's 1672 report, which said "Southernwood is no plant for this Country, Nor Rosemary, Nor Bayes." But the plant's beautiful, pale blue blossoms, so attractive to bees, made it important in the bee gardens which many kept for honey before sugar was widely available. Rosemary figures in the British-based cookery of New England for dishes like jugged hare with rosemary and juniper or steak and kidney pie. Its presence in colonial Virginia is confirmed by Governor Lord Culpeper, who recommended the smoking of rosemary cigars to cure consumption. Another early reference, supposedly by the unknown American author of *A Lytel Herball,* advised "Take the flowers of Rosemary and put them in a lynen clothe, and so boyle them in fayre cleane water . . . and drynke it for it is much worth against all the evyls in the body." In her 1824 edition of *The American*

Frugal Housewife, Mrs. Lydia Maria Child gives a recipe for Hungary water, which is made by stuffing rosemary flowers tightly into a glass retort and then filling it with "as much spirits of wine as the flowers can imbibe." This was supposed to cure paralysis, but even if it didn't, all that wine might have made it more bearable.

Rosemary, a Mediterranean herb meaning "dew of the sea," is often referred to as *the* Tuscan herb. Like several other spices and condiments, it became even more familiar to the American palate with the influx of Italians early in this century. From Boston's North End to Rhode Island's Federal Hill, from the Bronx's Arthur Avenue to Barre, Vermont, where many northern Italian stone quarriers made their homes, Italian cooking radiated rosemary. This included *capretto brodettato* (suckling kid); *ceci* soup and *pasta e fagioli* (macaroni and bean soup); *abbacchio,* the traditional Easter lamb dish; *panini de rosmarino,* a traditional Easter bread; and even a Tuscan chestnut cake, scattered with rosemary leaves. In Seattle, the Greeks spit-roast the Paschal Lamb with rosemary and garlic stuck into the flesh. In Nevada, the Basques cook pinto beans with sausage and rosemary, while in the Midwest an Austrian and Hungarian bean dish, *ungarishes Bohengulyás,* combines dried beans in a goulash of ham and potatoes.

In his book, *The Food Lover's Garden,* Angelo Pellegrini calls rosemary one of the Indispensable Dozen herbs and uses it even metaphorically: "Many, many Americans have made the happy discovery that there is neither sin nor wickedness in a sprig of rosemary and a glass of wine. . . ." Yet not everybody loves rosemary. In spite of her passion for Mediterranean cuisines, Elizabeth David thinks it good "as a decoration only. . . ."

A small bit of this aromatic, slightly camphorous member of the mint family goes a long way; it can make a masterpiece of boiled meats and game. It perks up such robust vegetables as cabbage and beets and complements green beans, zucchini, and artichokes. Its new popularity may be due to its effectiveness when thrown over the mesquite coals for grilling fish and meats. Recent findings have shown that rosemary and sage exert a bacterial reaction that helps preserve meats.

In combination with parsley, sage, and thyme, rosemary makes a nice little folksong. Children encounter it for the first time in various fairy tales; it is the herb that almost—but not quite—awakens Sleeping Beauty. Speaking of beauty, infusions of rosemary are supposed to maintain skin tone and prevent crow's feet.

Finally, people who don't want the neighbors to know their domestic business should be careful about planting rosemary in the front yard. According to legend, "Rosemary will not grow well unless . . . the mistress is master."

VINTAGE RECIPE

This recipe is adapted from various printed recipes and descriptions.

Shaker Spinach with Rosemary

2 pounds spinach leaves, washed and chopped
2 bunches green onions, chopped
2 tablespoons (1/4 stick) butter
1 teaspoon chopped fresh rosemary
1/4 cup chopped parsley
Salt and pepper to taste

In a heavy pot, place all ingredients. Cook, covered, for 6 minutes, or until tender.

Serves 4

Consumer Guide

Also known as: Arabic—iklil al-jabal; French—romarin; Italian—rosmarino; Spanish—romero.

LATIN: *Rosmarinus officinalis*

Selection: Fresh rosemary should have dark green, pine-needlelike leaves. Dried rosemary should be used in leaf form rather than ground.

Storage: Fresh rosemary may be wrapped in plastic and stored in refrigerator for up to 10 days. Dried rosemary will lose some of its potency after 6 months.

Fresh vs. dried: Dried rosemary may be substituted successfully for fresh, reducing quantity of dried by half. Best commercial dried variety is Select Origins.

Compatible herbs and spices: Parsley, thyme, sage, garlic, oregano.

RECIPE LIST

Swordfish and Leek Chowder
Red Chard and White Bean Soup
Chicken and Carrot Thread Salad
Pasta with Red Onion and Rosemary
Prawn and Scallop Stew in Rosemary–Garlic Sauce
Chicken Cutlets with Oranges and Rosemary
Braised Lamb Shanks in Rosemary Mustard
Parsnip, Mushroom, and Green Onion Gratin
Braised Turnips with Rosemary and Pine Nuts
Rosemary–Raisin Whole Wheat Corn Muffins
Rosemary Garlic Bread
Oranges and Black Grapes in Rosemary-scented Syrup

Swordfish and Leek Chowder

6 ounces bacon, cut into thin strips
3 large leeks (white part only), sliced
3 cloves garlic, minced
4 cups water
2 cups Fish Stock (page 353)
1 pound potatoes, peeled and cubed
2 carrots, diced
1 tablespoon fresh rosemary leaves, or 1 teaspoon dried
2 teaspoons salt
1 teaspoon freshly ground black pepper
1 pound boneless, skinless swordfish, cut into 1-inch pieces
1 cup half-and-half or milk

In a large saucepan, sauté bacon, leeks, and garlic until bacon is browned and leeks are tender. Pour off excess fat. Add water and stock to pot and bring to a boil. Add potatoes, carrots, rosemary, salt, and pepper and simmer gently about 15 minutes, or until potatoes are tender. Add swordfish and cook gently another 5 minutes. Stir in half-and-half, heat, and serve.

Serves 6

Red Chard and White Bean Soup

¼ cup olive oil
3 cloves garlic, minced
1 onion, chopped
1 bunch red chard, stems cut in 1-inch pieces and leaves cut in chiffonade (page 362)
2 yellow summer squash, quartered lengthwise and sliced ½ inch thick
2½ quarts Chicken or Beef Stock (pages 352, 353)
2 cups small white beans, soaked in cold water to cover overnight, or quick-soak (page 363)
1 large sprig rosemary
Salt and pepper
2 tablespoons sherry wine vinegar
Grated Parmesan cheese

In a 6-quart stockpot, heat oil. Add garlic, onion, chard stems and leaves, and squash and sauté about 3 minutes. Add stock, bring to a boil, and add beans and rosemary. Simmer, partially covered, for about 1½ hours. Taste for salt and pepper. Just before serving, remove rosemary and stir in vinegar. Sprinkle each serving with Parmesan cheese.

Serves 8–10

Chicken and Carrot Thread Salad

1 sprig rosemary
2 cloves garlic
1 teaspoon salt
½ teaspoon freshly ground black pepper
1 whole chicken breast, skinned
3 large carrots, peeled and cut into julienne (page 362)

DRESSING
1 tablespoon minced fresh rosemary, or 1 teaspoon dried
½ cup olive oil
3 tablespoons lemon juice
1 tablespoon Dijon mustard
Salt and pepper to taste

Bring 4 quarts water to a boil with rosemary, garlic, salt, and pepper. Add chicken breast and simmer very gently, covered, for 15 minutes. Remove chicken and garlic and reserve. Add carrots to the boiling water, cook 2 minutes, then drain. Place in a bowl of ice water. When chicken has cooled, remove from bones and cut into thin strips. Drain carrots thoroughly from ice water and place in bowl with chicken.

To make dressing, mash reserved garlic and mix with dressing ingredients. Add to chicken and carrots and toss well.

Serves 6

Pasta with Red Onion and Rosemary

3 tablespoons butter
3 tablespoons olive oil
1 large sprig rosemary plus 1 tablespoon finely minced fresh rosemary, or 1 teaspoon dried
4 red onions, thinly sliced

Salt
Freshly ground black pepper
½ cup dry white wine
1 tablespoon chopped parsley
1 pound pasta, such as penne or ziti
Grated Parmesan cheese (optional)

In a large skillet, heat butter and oil. Add rosemary sprig and onions and cook over low heat, stirring occasionally to prevent onions from burning. Cook about 20 minutes until onions are soft. Add salt and pepper to taste. Add wine and cook about 5 to 7 minutes until all liquid has evaporated. Stir in parsley and minced rosemary. Cook pasta according to package directions and drain. Remove rosemary sprig from sauce, toss pasta with sauce, and sprinkle with Parmesan cheese.

Serves 6

Prawn and Scallop Stew in Rosemary–Garlic Sauce

⅓ cup olive oil
¾ pound prawns, shelled and deveined
¾ pound scallops (cut in half if large)
4 cloves garlic, crushed
1 cup dry white wine
2 ripe tomatoes, seeded and coarsely chopped
2 tablespoons finely minced fresh rosemary, or 1 tablespoon dried
1½ cups heavy cream
Salt and pepper
2 tablespoons (¼ stick) butter, in pieces
¼ cup chopped parsley

In a large skillet, heat oil. Sauté prawns, scallops, and garlic, stirring constantly, for about 1 minute, or until prawns turn pink. Remove and reserve. Add wine, tomatoes, and rosemary. Cook about 3 minutes, or until bubbly. Add cream and cook over medium heat another 3 minutes, or until slightly thickened. Add salt and pepper to taste. Whisk in butter, stirring until sauce is smooth. Return prawns and scallops to sauce and just heat through. Serve over freshly cooked pasta or rice, and sprinkle with fresh parsley.

Serves 6

Chicken Cutlets with Oranges and Rosemary

2 tablespoons fresh rosemary leaves, or 1 tablespoon dried, very finely minced, plus additional rosemary sprigs for garnish
½ cup all-purpose flour
1 teaspoon salt
½ teaspoon freshly ground black pepper
3 boned and skinned whole chicken breasts, split and lightly pounded
¼ cup (½ stick) butter
2 tablespoons olive oil
¼ cup orange marmalade
2 small oranges, peeled and sliced ¼ inch thick
1 cup dry white wine
½ cup Chicken Stock (page 352)
Pinch of ground red pepper

Mix rosemary leaves, flour, salt, and pepper. Dredge chicken breasts in this mixture, coating well on both sides. In a large skillet, heat half the butter and the olive oil. Sauté chicken breasts about 6 minutes on each side, until golden. Remove and keep warm. Add remaining butter to skillet along with marmalade and cook about 3 minutes. Add orange slices and cook over medium-high heat for about 2 minutes.

Remove the orange slices and set aside. Add wine, stock, and red pepper to skillet and cook over medium-high heat, scraping bottom of pan, for 5 minutes, until sauce becomes syrupy. Return chicken and oranges to sauce just to heat through. Serve each chicken breast topped with sauce and orange slices and garnish with a small sprig of rosemary.

Serves 6

Braised Lamb Shanks in Rosemary Mustard

6 tablespoons olive oil
6 artichoke hearts, fresh or frozen, cooked and quartered (page 360)
1 carrot, finely chopped
1 celery stalk, finely chopped
1 onion, finely chopped
1 tablespoon minced fresh rosemary, or 1 teaspoon dried
6 lamb shanks (about 3 pounds)
½ cup all-purpose flour
1 cup dry vermouth
1 tablespoon Dijon mustard
1 tablespoon tomato paste
Salt and pepper

In a large sauté pan, heat oil. Sauté artichoke hearts, stirring about 5 minutes, then remove and set aside. In the same pan, sauté carrot, celery, onion, and rosemary over medium-high heat for about 5 minutes. Dredge lamb shanks in flour and brown with vegetables in same pan.

In a separate bowl, mix vermouth with mustard and tomato paste. Pour over lamb and bring to a boil. Simmer, covered, about 1½ hours, or until lamb is very tender. Remove lamb to serving platter. Skim fat from sauce and puree vegetables with liquid in a food mill or food processor. Return to pan, add artichoke hearts, and salt and pepper to taste, and heat through. Pour over lamb shanks and serve.

Serves 6

Parsnip, Mushroom, and Green Onion Gratin

¼ cup (½ stick) butter
3 parsnips, blanched (page 361) and sliced
½ pound fresh mushrooms, quartered
1 bunch green onions, chopped
2 tablespoons minced fresh rosemary, or 1 tablespoon dried
1 teaspoon salt
1 teaspoon freshly ground black pepper
½ cup heavy cream
1 egg
1 cup fresh bread crumbs
¼ cup grated dry Monterey Jack cheese
3 tablespoons olive oil

Preheat oven to 375 degrees. In a large skillet, heat butter. Sauté parsnips, mushrooms, green onions, and rosemary over medium-high heat for about 7 minutes. Place vegetables in a 9-inch ovenproof dish (a ceramic quiche dish is fine). Mix salt, pepper, cream, and egg and pour over vegetables. Sprinkle with bread crumbs and cheese and drizzle with oil. Bake about 25 minutes, or until top is golden.

Serves 6

Braised Turnips with Rosemary and Pine Nuts

2 pounds small turnips, peeled, or medium turnips cut into 1-inch cubes
6 tablespoons (¾ stick) butter
1 clove garlic, minced
1 tablespoon fresh rosemary leaves, or 1 teaspoon dried
¼ cup lemon juice
1 teaspoon sugar
Salt and pepper
¼ cup toasted pine nuts (page 360)

Preheat oven to 375 degrees. In a medium ovenproof dish with a cover, place turnips in 1 layer. Cut butter into small pieces and place over turnips, along with garlic and rosemary. Combine lemon juice and sugar and pour over all. Cover and bake about 25 minutes, or until turnips are tender. Stir occasionally to prevent turnips from sticking to bottom of pan. Taste for salt and pepper. Just before serving, toss with pine nuts.

Serves 6

Rosemary–Raisin Whole Wheat Corn Muffins

½ cup yellow cornmeal
½ cup whole wheat flour
1 cup all-purpose flour
1 teaspoon baking powder
1 teaspoon baking soda
½ teaspoon salt
¼ cup sugar
1 tablespoon chopped fresh rosemary, or 1 teaspoon dried
2 eggs, lightly beaten
1 cup plain yogurt or dairy sour cream
½ cup (1 stick) butter, melted
1 cup golden raisins

Preheat oven to 400 degrees. Butter 12 muffin cups.

In a large bowl, combine dry ingredients. In a medium bowl, mix rosemary, eggs, yogurt, and melted butter until well blended. Pour yogurt mixture into dry ingredients and beat just until combined. (It's okay if mixture has a few small lumps.) Stir in raisins. Fill muffin tins two-thirds full. Bake 20 minutes, or until tester inserted comes out clean. Allow to cool a few minutes before removing muffins from pan.

Yield: 1 dozen

Rosemary Garlic Bread

7 cups all-purpose flour
3 teaspoons salt

---

2 packages dry yeast proofed (page 362) in 3¼ cups warm water with 2 tablespoons sugar
2 cloves garlic, minced
2 tablespoons fresh rosemary leaves or 1 tablespoon dried, finely minced
2 tablespoons cornmeal

In a large bowl combine flour and salt. Pour in yeast mixture and mix well until you have a soft dough. Turn out on a floured surface, knead until smooth and elastic, about 5 minutes. Add additional flour as needed. Place dough in greased bowl and cover with plastic wrap. Let rise in warm spot until doubled—about 1 hour.

Punch dough down and turn out onto a floured surface. Knead for about 1 minute. Divide dough in half. Roll out half at a time to a 15- x 10-inch rectangle. Sprinkle with half the garlic and rosemary and roll up tightly on long side, like a jelly roll. Repeat with other half. Place dough seam side down on a cookie sheet that has been sprinkled with cornmeal. Place in a warm spot and allow to rise 30 minutes. Meanwhile, preheat oven to 400 degrees. With a sharp knife or razor make diagonal cuts on top of loaves. Brush with water and bake about 35 minutes. Breads should give a hollow sound when tapped. Allow to cool on racks before slicing.

Makes 2 loaves

Oranges and Black Grapes in Rosemary-scented Syrup

2 cups water
1 cup sugar
Zests of 1 orange and 1 lemon (page 363)
2 long rosemary sprigs, plus rosemary sprigs for garnish
3 cups black grapes
3 oranges, peeled and sectioned

Bring water to a boil with sugar, zests, and 2 rosemary sprigs. Boil 10 minutes, until syrupy. Strain and chill. Arrange orange sections in petal fashion around grapes. Pour syrup over fruit and serve.

Serves 6

Sage

LORE AND LINEAGE

The classic baloney sandwich may not be a culinary masterpiece, but it is a genuine American artifact. It has the kind of innocence that appeals to our down-to-earth, frontier heritage. When Archie Bunker adds baloney to his daughter's shopping list of things to get at the natural foods store, we understand his reasoning. As he puts it, "What could be more natural than baloney?" Best of all, for our interests here, baloney even harbors an herb.

SIGNATURE DISH: THANKSGIVING STUFFING

With cornbread, wild rice, or just plain torn-up bread, sage is the taste remembered from the steamy hot stuffings that often are—in terms of pure nostalgia—more important than their surrounding big birds.

It is this same herb, sage, that almost always spikes the stuffing of wild rice or cornbread for the Thanksgiving Day turkey or the Christmas goose. Sage resounds in many Pennsylvania German dishes: Amish preaching soup, Mennonite pork pie, Pennsylvania Dutch French goose (really pig's stomach stuffed with vegetables and sausage), and *mummix und hexel,* a hash or omelet of leftovers. Sage-wrapped eel (*Aalsuppe)* and eel soup flavored with sage were traditional German dishes that inspired the eel puree which eventually became the pride of Salisbury, Pennsylvania.

Sage is the essential flavoring of scrapple, a creation dating from the first arrival of Germans in Philadelphia in the 1680s. This dish, basically a mixture of pork, cornmeal, sage, and other seasonings, was a true expression of the American melting pot, a union of the Pennsylvania German sausage expertise and the native American know-how with corn.

As many Germans moved south and westward, they brought their sage —and their scrapple—with them, making both common fare wherever they settled. (In *American Food: The Gastronomic Story* [1975], Evan Jones tells of the somewhat confused traveler in the South who recorded his meeting with a family named Scrapple, who served him a wonderful dish called biddle.) In Texas, German settlers in the Pedernales River region responded to their culinary surroundings by combining hot pepper with the traditional sage to produce the spicy Hill Country scrapple. The hot pepper and sage combination also flavored one of the earliest Kentucky dishes we know of: a stew made of boiled buffalo, deer, elk, bear, or whatever wandered in. In Appalachia, sage is the only stuffing herb, and it is used for everything from wild turkey and hog's head to "Will Singleton's Raccoon."

Aside from scrapple, German cooks know sage is really in its element in sausages. Hence, Lebanon (Pennsylvania) sausage and Lebanon bologna are fragrant with sage. So is the white Usinger bratwurst from Milwaukee, a blend of pork or veal with nutmeg, mace, lemon juice, caraway, and generous pinches of sage. German delis feature sage-spiced head cheese with touches of savory, juniper berries, and sometimes pistachios. The same deli case may also feature the German sausage called *Schmerkäse*; but look carefully, because the same word, in Pennsylvania Dutch country, means cottage cheese. Wisconsin Germans make a stuffed crown roast of frankfurters, sewing the links together and filling the center with a sage-chestnut stuffing. A German communal group which settled Aurora, Oregon, made that town famous for its sage-fragrant sausages.

One of America's earliest sage-spiced favorites were Oxford sausages. The Anglo heritage inspired New World versions of sage and onion stuffings, pork stews, and herb-flavored cheeses. In Derbyshire cheese, for example, sage leaves are blended into the curds and then pressed. Derbyshire is now a Vermont specialty served at Christmas. Sage tisane, sweetened with maple syrup or rum, has also become a Vermont tradition.

Euell Gibbons laments that sage is woefully underused by Americans; nonetheless, we do import more than 2 million pounds a year. It is excellent in toasted cheese sandwiches, cheese omelets, and soufflés; it adds sparkle to legumes, pâtés, terrines, garbanzos, and all kinds of nuts. Italian Americans spread sage onto buttered bread, and cook it with white beans and *saltimbocca.* The flavors of Mormon split-pea soup, Shaker sage cakes, and Shaker pork-and-sage "hand pies" spring from sage, which was one of the major herbs of the Shaker religious communities.

Nutritionally, sage is so rich in vitamins A and C that some people chew or smoke sage leaves, while the less adventuresome make sage tea, lacing it with sage honey. Chemically speaking, according to Harold McGee, sage acts like phenolic substances in inhibiting the oxidation of fats, which means that it actually helps preserve the flavor of the food. Sage's ability to aid digestion explains its use with sausages, goose, and other fat- and oil-rich foods.

Etymologically, sage (*Salvia*) is from the same root as *salve*. Its traditional uses bear out this association. It has been gargled for throat ailments, rubbed on the skin for snakebites, breathed vigorously as snuff, and brushed on teeth and gums to whiten and clean. It has an age-old reputation for turning gray hair black and, if that doesn't work, it's also supposed to mitigate grief. People who grow sage are supposed to live forever. Even more intriguing, sage, like rosemary, is said to thrive only where the woman rules the household. This has led some to point out that the French meaning of *sage* is "wise," and others to respond that they don't care what the French meaning of *sage* is.

Aside from the most common sage (*Salvia officinalis*), there are hundreds of species varying enormously in aroma, flavor, and color. Most are decorative, especially in name: Lavender Sage, Cyprus Sage, Moroccan Ash-leaved Sage. Some, like Wormwood and Ragweed, smell nice but have marginal value in the kitchen. And others—Sagebrush, South African Wild Sage, Russian Sage, and Jerusalem Sage, among them—are not sage at all. Pineapple Sage (*S. rutilans*) contributes a fruity aroma and taste to punch and fruit desserts. Wild Dalmatian Sage, from the hills of Yugoslavia or Serbia, is reputed to have the finest flavor of all. Clary Sage (*S. sclarea*), which supposedly has psychedelic properties, is the most versatile of the lot: its large leaves can be dipped in batter and fried as an unusual appetizer; its flowers can be steeped for tea; its oil is used in perfumes; its aromatic properties give wine a flavor similar to Muscatel. Clary wine once had a particularly devoted following, in the days when it was considered an aphrodisiac. Pioneers on the Oregon Trail were rejuvenated by the stimulating smell of wild sage after a rainstorm. From White Sage leaves, American Indians made a delicious tea—sissop—with which they also washed their hair. Those living in the Southwest and along the Pacific Coast roasted seeds, nuts, and acorns with Chia—a rough-leaved member of the sage family. From this they made a gruel which they offered to the first European sailors to reach California's shores. One tablespoon of Chia seeds was supposed to sustain life for a full day. By the 1890s, its value was well recognized and it became an expensive herb, costing over $6 a pound. Chia is now being touted again as a high-energy food and can be found in many natural foods stores. Whatever variety of sage you find, here are some delicious ways to enjoy the complexity and range of its flavor.

VINTAGE RECIPE

This recipe is adapted from the Prudence Penny binding of *The United States Regional Cook Book,* edited by Ruth Berolzheimer (Chicago: Culinary Arts Institute, 1939).

Stuffed Crown Roast of Frankfurters

20 frankfurters
2 cups sauerkraut
½ teaspoon sage

Arrange frankfurters side by side, with curved side up. Using a large needle and string, sew through all the frankfurters ½ inch from the bottom—and then the same way ½ inch from the top. Tie the ends of the top string, bringing the first and last frankfurter of the row together. Repeat with the bottom string. Stand the frankfurters on end, and you have a most attractive crown of frankfurters. (Concave side should be out.) Fill the center of the crown with sauerkraut mixed with sage and bake at 375 degrees for about 20 minutes. As a variation, fill center with sage stuffing.

Serves 10

Consumer Guide

Also known as: Arabic—mariyamiya; Dutch—salie; French—suage; German—Salbei; Italian—salvia; Spanish—salvia.

LATIN: *Salvia officinalis (and other species of Salvia)*

Common varieties: Garden Sage is the most common and best for all-purpose cooking. Other culinary varieties include Pineapple Sage, Golden Sage, and Dwarf Sage.

Selection: Fresh Garden Sage is available in some markets. Leaves should have a silvery green color and unblemished appearance. Dried sage is found on spice shelves in 2 forms: whole leaf and ground. The whole leaf is superior. Best commerical dried variety is Select Origins.

Storage: Fresh sage may be wrapped in paper towels, sealed in plastic bags, and stored in refrigerator for up to 4 days. Dried sage should be stored in airtight containers on spice shelf.

Fresh vs. dried: Dried sage in leaf form may be substituted for fresh, reducing the quantity of dried by half. Best commercial dried variety is Select Origins.

Compatible herbs and spices: Rosemary, thyme, parsley, garlic.

RECIPE LIST

Eggplant Spread with Garlic and Sage
Grilled Cheese Sandwiches with Sage
Cream of Banana Squash Soup
Sage and Salt Cornmeal Flats
Cheese Timbales in Sage Cream
Sage-scented Swordfish
Sage-and-Apple-Stuffed Veal Chops
Chick-Peas, Sausage, and Sage
Roast Ducklings with Mushroom–Sage Stuffing
Creamed Yellow Squash with Sherry Vinegar and Sage

Eggplant Spread with Garlic and Sage

2 eggplants (about 1½ pounds)
1 small onion, quartered
2 cloves garlic
½ cup parsley leaves
5 fresh sage leaves, or 1 teaspoon crumbled dried
2 tablespoons tomato paste
3 tablespoons lemon juice
⅓ cup olive oil
¼ teaspoon ground red pepper
Salt and pepper
Toasted baguette slices or crackers

Preheat oven to 400 degrees. Prick skin of eggplants and place in baking dish. Bake for about 45 minutes, or until eggplants are soft and almost collapsed. Let cool completely.

Discard stems from eggplants and cut into chunks. Place eggplant in food processor with remaining ingredients except bread. Process until smooth. Taste for salt and pepper. Serve as an appetizer with bread or crackers.

Yield: 2 cups

Grilled Cheese Sandwiches with Sage

8 slices firm white bread, crusts removed
2 tablespoons (1/4 stick) butter, room temperature
2 tablespoons mustard of your choice
4 slices sharp cheddar cheese, to fit bread
4 thin red onion slices
8 sage leaves
2 eggs, beaten with 2 tablespoons milk
1/4 cup vegetable oil

Spread 4 slices of bread with butter and remaining 4 with mustard. On the mustard-topped bread slices, arrange in order: a slice of cheese, onion slice, and 2 sage leaves. Top with remaining bread slices, butter-side down. Pour egg mixture into a shallow bowl and dip sandwiches on all sides. In a large skillet, heat oil. Brown sandwiches on each side—about 3 minutes. Serve immediately or keep warm in 250-degree oven.

Yield: 4 sandwiches

Cream of Banana Squash Soup

3 tablespoons butter
1 leek (white part only), chopped
1 celery stalk, chopped
2 pounds banana (winter) squash or pumpkin, peeled and diced
3 cups Chicken Stock (page 352) or water
1 cup milk
2 teaspoons chopped fresh sage, or 1 teaspoon crumbled dried
1/4 cup heavy cream
2 teaspoons fresh lemon juice
Salt and pepper

In a medium saucepan, heat butter. Sauté leek and celery until tender. Add squash, stock, and milk and bring to a boil. Reduce heat to a simmer, cover, and cook about 25 minutes, or until squash is tender. Puree mixture in blender or food processor and return to pot. Add sage, cream, and lemon juice and heat through. Taste for salt and pepper and serve.

Serves 6

Sage and Salt Cornmeal Flats

1 package active dry yeast
¾ cup warm water (105°–115°)
Pinch of sugar
2 cups all-purpose flour
1 cup yellow cornmeal
½ teaspoon salt
6 tablespoons olive oil
2 teaspoons kosher (coarse) salt
3 large fresh sage leaves, or 1 teaspoon crumbled dried

In a small bowl, mix yeast, water, and sugar and let stand about 5 minutes, until foamy. In a large bowl, mix flour, cornmeal, and salt. Make a well in center and pour in yeast mixture along with 3 tablespoons oil. Combine until dough forms. On a floured surface, knead gently about 4 minutes, until smooth. Place dough in a greased bowl, cover with plastic wrap, and let rise about 1 hour, until doubled in bulk. Punch dough down, knead to get air bubbles out, and let rest, covered, with a towel for about 15 minutes.

Preheat oven to 425 degrees. Divide dough into 8 pieces. On a floured surface, roll out each piece to a 4-inch circle. Brush with oil and sprinkle with salt and sage. Place flats on a baking sheet dusted with cornmeal. Bake 15 minutes, or until golden brown and crisp. Serve warm or at room temperature. Great with soups, salads, and appetizers.

Yield: 8 breads

Cheese Timbales in Sage Cream

½ cup grated Vermont cheddar cheese
6 ounces cream cheese
2 eggs
½ cup heavy cream
2 fresh sage leaves, chopped, or ½ teaspoon crumbled dried
Salt and pepper

SAGE CREAM
3 tablespoons butter
1 tablespoon all-purpose flour
1½ cups heavy cream
4 fresh sage leaves, or 2 dried, left whole
Salt and pepper

Preheat oven to 350 degrees; butter six 3-inch ramekins.

Blend cheese, cream cheese, eggs, cream, sage, and salt and pepper until very smooth. Pour into ramekins. Place ramekins in a baking pan and pour hot water into the pan until it reaches halfway up the sides of the ramekins. Cover entire pan with a sheet of parchment paper or buttered foil. Bake for 20 minutes, or until a knife comes out clean when inserted in center. Keep warm in water bath.

To make sauce, melt butter in a medium saucepan. Add flour and cook about 1 minute, until blended. Add cream, stirring continuously, then add sage and cook until slightly thickened. Taste for salt and pepper. Remove sage and unmold timbales. Serve surrounded with sage cream.

Serves 6 as a first course

Sage-scented Swordfish

4 swordfish steaks or any firm, white-fleshed fish (6 to 8 ounces each), 1 inch thick
1 teaspoon salt
1 teaspoon freshly ground black pepper
12 fresh sage leaves, or 1 tablespoon crumbled dried
1/4 cup lemon juice
1/4 cup orange juice
1/2 cup olive oil
1/2 cup (1 stick) butter, cut into pieces

Blot fish dry with paper towels and score on both sides. Rub salt and pepper into flesh and place fish in 1 layer in a noncorrosive dish. Combine remaining ingredients except butter and pour over fish. Cover with plastic wrap and refrigerate about 5 hours, turning fish once.

In a large skillet, heat half the butter. Sauté fish over medium-high heat for about 5 minutes on each side. Remove and keep warm. Pour remaining marinade into skillet, and reduce over high heat until slightly syrupy. Swirl in remaining butter, piece by piece, until sauce is smooth. Serve fish with 2 tablespoons sauce over each steak.

Serves 4

Sage-and-Apple-Stuffed Veal Chops

6 loin veal chops, about 6 ounces each, cut 1 inch thick
Salt and pepper
3 tablespoons oil
½ cup apple cider
½ cup Chicken or Veal Stock (pages 352, 353)
Sage leaves for garnish

STUFFING
2 tablespoons oil
½ pound ground veal or beef
1 shallot, chopped
½ apple, cored and coarsely chopped
1 teaspoon salt
½ teaspoon freshly ground black pepper
2 teaspoons chopped fresh sage, or 1 teaspoon crushed dried

Make stuffing first. In a medium skillet, heat oil. Brown meat over medium-high heat, then add shallot and apple and cook until tender. Add seasonings and cook another minute. Set aside.

Make a pocket in the side of each chop with a sharp knife. Fill each pocket with 2 to 3 tablespoons of stuffing. Close pocket with a skewer or toothpick. Salt and pepper the chops. In a large skillet, heat oil. Brown chops on both sides, then remove from pan. Deglaze skillet (page 361) with apple cider and stock, cooking over medium heat. Return chops to same skillet, reduce heat, and cover. Cook over low heat for about 20 to 25 minutes, or until veal is tender. Serve veal with pan juices.

Serves 6

Chick-Peas, Sausage, and Sage

2 cups dried chick-peas (garbanzo beans)
1 pound medium-hot sausage, sliced
1 onion, chopped
2 tablespoons tomato paste
2 teaspoons chopped fresh sage, or 1 teaspoon crushed dried
Salt and pepper
2 tablespoons olive oil
1 clove garlic, chopped
2 pounds spinach, coarsely chopped

Place chick-peas in a large pot and cover with about 6 cups water. Leave to soak overnight.

Drain the chick-peas. In a medium skillet, sauté sausage and onion for about 5 minutes. Add to chick-peas, along with tomato paste and sage. Add enough water to cover beans and bring to a boil. Cover and simmer about 1½ hours, or until peas are tender. Taste for salt and pepper.

In a large skillet, heat oil and garlic. Sauté spinach just until wilted. Place a bed of spinach on a serving plate and top with chick-pea mixture. Or serve as a cold salad with fresh, raw spinach leaves as a base. Great both ways.

Serves 8

Note: The quick-soak method for beans can be used here. Cover the chick-peas with water, bring to a boil, and cook one minute. Take the pot off the heat and let stand for one hour. Drain the chick-peas and continue.

Roast Ducklings with Mushroom–Sage Stuffing

2 ducklings, 3½ pounds each
1 lemon, cut in half
½ cup fresh orange juice
1 tablespoon lemon juice
½ cup Chicken Stock (page 352)
1 clove garlic, crushed
½ cup Port wine
½ cup heavy cream
Salt and pepper

STUFFING
¼ cup (½ stick) butter
2 bunches green onions, chopped
1 pound fresh mushrooms, chopped
6 chopped fresh sage leaves, or 2 teaspoons crumbled dried
2 cups fresh bread crumbs
1 egg
1 teaspoon salt
½ teaspoon freshly ground black pepper
1 tablespoon orange-flavored liqueur

Make stuffing first. In a medium skillet, heat butter. Sauté green onions, mushrooms, and sage for about 5 minutes. In a large bowl, mix sauté mixture with remaining stuffing ingredients.

Preheat oven to 375 degrees. Blot duckling cavities dry and rub cavities and skin with cut lemon. With a skewer or other pointed instrument, prick skin all over. Place breast side down on a roasting pan rack. Combine orange and lemon juices, stock, and garlic. Brushing some marinade on ducks every 20 minutes, roast ducklings about 1½ hours, turning them breast side up for the last 30 minutes of cooking. Leg should move easily when done, and juices should run clear when skin is pricked. Remove ducks to serving platter and keep warm.

Skim fat from pan juices and deglaze (page 361) with wine. Cook until syrupy, then add cream. Cook over medium-high heat until sauce is thick enough to coat a spoon (about 5 minutes). Taste for salt and pepper. Cut ducks into quarters and serve with stuffing and some sauce over each portion.

Serves 4

Creamed Yellow Squash with Sherry Vinegar and Sage

3 tablespoons olive oil
1 pound yellow summer squash, coarsely shredded
2 tablespoons sherry wine vinegar
2 teaspoons finely chopped fresh sage, or 1 teaspoon crumbled dried
1/3 cup heavy cream
1/3 cup dairy sour cream
Salt and pepper

In a medium skillet, heat oil. Sauté squash about 4 minutes, just until lightly browned. Remove and set aside. Deglaze pan (page 361) with vinegar, and reduce liquid to a few drops. Add sage and both creams, and mix well. Taste for salt and pepper. Return squash to skillet and heat through.

Serves 6

Sorrel

LORE AND LINEAGE

Soup is something you can make when there's nothing much left in the larder. Sorrel soup is a possibility when there's nothing left in the garden, either. Except weeds, that is. Sorrel fans might argue that not all types of sorrel are weeds, but once planted, it does persist in the manner of the hardiest, most unwanted weed. Sorrel is more commonly found on the edges of private gardens than in the vegetable department of supermarkets. But wherever you find a big bunch of it, you might think about putting the kettle on. As anyone knows who has ever cooked sorrel, it quickly liquifies, like some sort of natural-style, instant soup.

Although sorrel is only now becoming more known in the contemporary kitchen, sorrel soup recipes have a significant American past. *Shav* is the Jewish "version," but it, in turn, has endless variations. Some are made only with water, others with chicken stock, and in still others vegetables are added. In the Jewish congregation of Charleston, South Carolina, which was originally established in 1749 by Sephardic Jews from the West Indies, collard greens flavored the stock used for their Passover matzo ball soup. We know of an old Kansas recipe that uses sheep sorrel, and a Shaker recipe called Sister Amelia's herb soup in which chervil, tarragon, and chives are added to the melted sorrel and chicken broth.

Even the earliest American cookbooks often called for a bit of sorrel, along with marjoram and mint and other herbs, to flavor all kinds of soup. Sorrel was among the "faggot of herbs" in such intriguingly named recipes as Cheap Soup or Soup for the Poor, one of which begins: "Wash an oxhead very clean; break the bones." Some colonists made the enigmatically named English herb soup Pottage Without the Sight of Herbs. Actually this meant that the herbs were pounded to a paste with oatmeal and seemed to disappear as they were stirred into the boiling broth. French settlers brought over their *potage à l'oseille* and a richer sorrel soup, sometimes served cold, *potage Germiny.* It was also a French custom to add a chiffonade of sorrel to *potage Santé,* a kind of health soup.

Nineteenth-century cookbooks, like Catherine Beecher's *Domestic Receipt Book* of 1857, contained directions for "Soup Powder" or "Soup Herb Spirit." These were mixtures of sorrel and other herbs, dried, pounded, and sifted. They were stirred into stock or water to make soup during the winters, when no fresh herbs could be had. "Portable Soup" was similar, though it often took a form not unlike today's bouillon cube. We know of at least one such formula from a 1763 collection of Mrs. Sylvester Gardiner of Gardiner, Maine. The process began with "about fifty pounds weight" of beef plus flavorings, which were boiled, strained, gelled, and cut into small, hard squares. One could take a cube along and dissolve it in hot water whenever the urge for soup arose—a presage to the current cup-a-soup generation. Perhaps the most fascinating approach to sorrel soup—or any soup, for that matter—comes from Vermont. The cook would make a giant kettle of thick, concentrated soup and set it in a cold place with a piece of wood protruding from its center. Once frozen, the solid soup was unmolded from the kettle and hung outside from the roof beams by its wooden handle. During the cold months, big chunks of soup were chipped off and reconstituted as needed.

Nutritionally speaking, sorrel soup is a good idea. One cup of cooked sorrel provides 22,000 IU of vitamin A, compared with 7,900 for one carrot and 11,000 for a whole pound of broccoli. The same quantity of sorrel contains twice as much vitamin C as a small orange: 110 mg compared to 54. Like spinach, sorrel has a high oxalic acid content, which hinders the absorption of calcium. Because it reacts with iron, which makes it turn black and metallic-tasting, sorrel should be cut with and cooked in stainless steel.

There are many sorrels, all from the dock family of weeds. Though they all share the same chemistry, French Sorrel (*Rumex scutatus)* is often praised as the most succulent type because of its muted acidity and fleshier leaves. Two other varieties, Garden Sorrel or Old English Sorrel (*R. acetosa*) and Sour Grass or Sheep Sorrel (*R. acetosella*), can be used successfully in cooking. Beware of one imposter, however, called Good King Henry, a look-alike with no culinary virtues.

Sorrel is good for lots of things besides soup. The earliest transplanted recipes were English, and they include sorrel purees, gravies for roast goose, and condiments like gooseberry sauce with sorrel juice, coddled gooseberries, butter, and ginger. "To make Sirrup of Wood Sorrel," a seventeenth-century recipe advised that the cook put pulverized sorrel in a "canviss bagg & press it in a booksellers press." But it was the French who brought diversity into the American sorrel legacy. They use it in stuffings for many-boned fish, such as shad, and the acid content of the herb virtually dissolves the bones. French chefs also dip large sorrel leaves in batter and deep-fry them as fritters or *beignets.* Sorrel is also cooked down and potted or preserved like jam; it is served, like applesauce, with pork, duck, and fish. Today, preserved sorrel can be purchased in Jewish delis or European-style specialty shops. For Polish Americans, the sour-cream–sorrel sauce *sos szezawiowy* is traditional with veal, beef, and egg dishes.

SIGNATURE DISH: SORREL SAUCE

Especially good with fish because of its tart, almost lemony flavor, this classic fish herb was well known among Native Americans of the eastern woodland tribes, who baked shad with spicebush berries, nannyberries, and an abundance of chopped sorrel leaves.

Sorrel is a great substitute for salt, vinegar, spinach, and lemon. It also acts as an effective meat tenderizer when its large leaves are wrapped around beef roasts for stewing or braising. But perhaps its most unexpected culinary application is in desserts. The Dutch ate cooked sorrel leaves with butter and raisins. Sorrel fool was a colonial sweet. Like other unlikely candidates on the frontier, Sheep Sorrel became a wagon-train treat sweetened with molasses and baked into a pie. Sorrel was brewed with rum into a drink called "sorrel bounce" and Native Americans made a drink with its juicy leaves that tasted like lemonade. They also knew its importance as a scurvy preventative, owing to its vitamin C content, and so instructed the settlers.

From Virginia, we get the first mention of sorrel in the New World. In his *True Declaration* (1610), John Smith says, "Many herbes in the Spring time are commonly dispersed throughout the woods—food for broths and sallets, as Violets, Purslins, Sorrel &c." Sorrel is included among the wild plants in early New England lists, such as William Woods' 1634 catalog of "all manner of Hearbes for meate." It was recorded in Adriaen van der Donck's 1653 description of New Netherlands' early plants. Writing of the middle colonies a century later, the traveler Peter Kalm observed, "They prepare greens of a kind of sorrel that grows at the edge of cultivated fields. Green leaves are gathered in April by everyone everywhere [and] used in the same way Swedes prepare Spinach. . . . But they generally boil the leaves in the water in which they had cooked meat. . . . It is served on a platter and eaten with a knife."

Medically, "salts of sorrel" (oxalic acid) was considered excellent for purifying the blood and dissolving kidney stones. Its attributes read like the labels on elixirs from the proverbial medicine man: a bleach for stains on linen and on the hands, an effective antiseptic, a soap base. Sorrel is supposed to improve both the complexion and the appetite as well as fasten the teeth.

But some people are fond of sorrel not for what it can do but for what it once was. According to some sources, sorrel may well be descended from the ancient shamrock of Ireland.

VINTAGE RECIPE

This recipe and the accompanying note are excerpted from *Mrs. Rorer's Philadelphia Cook Book: A Manual of Home Economies* by Sarah Tyson Rorer (Philadelphia: Arnold and Company, 1886).

Sorrel Soup

2 tablespoons of butter
1 pint of sorrel
1 quart of stock
Yolks of two eggs
Salt and pepper to taste

Put the butter in a sauce-pan, set it on the fire, and as soon as melted, put the sorrel in, and stir one minute; then add the stock, salt and pepper; boil three minutes. Beat the yolks lightly, put them into the tureen, pour the boiling soup over gradually, stirring all the while till thoroughly mixed. Serve with croutons.

(Note: Another *very* important point is to have a porcelain-lined or better still a granite iron soup kettle with a close cover. Why? Because the juices of the meat are always acid and will act upon a metallic kettle thereby giving the soup an inky, bitter taste. A close cover [is needed] to keep in the steam and prevent evaporation and also to keep the dust and smoke out.)

Consumer Guide

Also known as: Dutch—zurin; French—oseille; German—Sauerampfer; Italian—sauro; Polish—szczaw; Spanish—acedera.

LATIN: *Rumex scutatus (French sorrel)*
R. acetosa (Garden sorrel)

Selection: Sorrel may be found in the fresh herb section of your market. Look for unblemished leaves of good green color, small to medium in size.

Storage: Wrap in a layer of paper towels, seal in a plastic bag, and store in refrigerator. Will keep well for about 5 days.

Fresh vs. dried: No contest, as no commercially dried sorrel exists.

Compatible herbs and spices: Parsley, chives, thyme, oregano, nutmeg.

RECIPE LIST

Sorrel and Ricotta Mousse

3 tablespoons butter
12 sorrel leaves, cut into chiffonade (page 362)
1 shallot, minced
8 ounces whole milk ricotta cheese
3 ounces cream cheese
½ cup heavy cream
3 eggs
1 teaspoon salt
½ teaspoon freshly ground black pepper

In a medium skillet, heat butter. Cook sorrel and shallot until wilted. Set aside.

Preheat oven to 350 degrees. In a food processor, combine remaining ingredients until smooth. Stir in sorrel and shallot. Butter 6 small ramekins and fill two-thirds full. Cover tops with a sheet of buttered parchment paper or foil. Place in pan of hot water and bake for about 20 minutes, or until a knife comes out clean when inserted in center. Allow to cool slightly before serving. May be served directly from ramekin or unmolded onto individual plates. Serve with toasted baguette slices.

Serves 6

Carrot and Sorrel Bisque

3 tablespoons butter
3 carrots, grated
2 cups shredded sorrel leaves
3 cups Chicken Stock (page 352)
1 cup heavy cream
Salt and pepper

In a medium saucepan, heat butter. Add all but ½ cup each of carrots and sorrel and cook about 5 minutes, until wilted. Add stock, bring to a boil, and simmer 10 minutes. Puree with cream in a food processor or blender and add salt and pepper to taste. Garnish with remaining carrots and sorrel. Delicious served hot or cold.

Serves 4–6

Salmon and Sorrel Tart

1 recipe Pâte Brisée (page 354), fitted into a 10-inch tart shell and partially baked
2 tablespoons (¼ cup) butter
¾ pound sorrel leaves
½ pound spinach leaves
½ cup parsley leaves
4 eggs
1 cup heavy cream
Salt and pepper
4 ounces Emmanthaler cheese, grated
½ pound boned, skinned, and cooked salmon
2 tablespoons fresh dill

Preheat oven to 375 degrees. Have tart shell ready to be filled.

In a medium skillet, heat butter. Cook sorrel and spinach until just slightly wilted. Drain off liquid and remove vegetables to mixing bowl. Combine with parsley, 2 eggs, ½ cup cream and salt and pepper to taste. Pour mixture into tart shell. Sprinkle with cheese. Puree remaining eggs and cream with the salmon and dill and pour on top of cheese mixture. Bake about 30 to 35 minutes, or until top is golden. Allow to cool about 10 minutes before serving.

Serves 8 as a main course or 12 as a first course

Sorrel Soufflé

½ cup grated asiago cheese
5 tablespoons butter
2 cups chopped sorrel
3 tablespoons all-purpose flour
1 cup milk, room temperature
3 egg yolks
Pinch of salt
¼ teaspoon grated nutmeg
5 egg whites

Preheat oven to 400 degrees. Butter a 1½-quart soufflé dish and sprinkle with 1½ tablespoons cheese.

In a small skillet, heat 2 tablespoons butter and cook sorrel until wilted. Set aside.

In a medium saucepan, heat remaining butter until foamy. Add flour and cook, stirring, for about 2 minutes. Add milk, stirring constantly, and cook over low heat about 3 to 4 minutes, until mixture thickens. Remove from heat and whisk in egg yolks, remaining cheese, salt, nutmeg, and sorrel. Beat egg whites just until soft peaks form. Fold whites into yolk mixture and pour into prepared dish. Bake for 5 minutes and turn heat down to 375 degrees. Bake another 20 to 25 minutes, or until puffy and golden brown. Serve immediately.

Serves 4–6

Poached Halibut with Sorrel Mayonnaise

2 cups packed sorrel leaves
½ cup parsley leaves
2 egg yolks
1 tablespoon lemon juice
2 teaspoons mild mustard
½ teaspoon salt
1 cup olive or vegetable oil
Salt and pepper
1 small red onion, diced
1 cucumber, peeled, seeded, and diced
6 small halibut steaks or filets (about 6–8 ounces each), poached and cooled

In a medium saucepan, blanch sorrel and parsley for 1 minute (page 361). Drain and squeeze excess liquid from leaves. Set aside to cool completely.

In a food processor or a blender, combine yolks, lemon juice, mustard, and salt. With machine running, add oil in slow, steady stream until mixture becomes thick. Add parsley and sorrel and process until smooth. Taste for salt and pepper. Stir in red onion and cucumber and serve over or alongside halibut.

Serves 6

Corn Custards with Sorrel Sauce

2 cups corn kernels, fresh or thawed
4 eggs
¼ cup grated Monterey Jack cheese
1 cup heavy cream
2 tablespoons chopped chives
Salt and pepper

SAUCE
1 tablespoon butter
1 cup shredded sorrel
1 cup heavy cream
Salt and pepper

Preheat oven to 375 degrees. In a food processor, puree corn, eggs, cheese, cream, chives, and salt and pepper until fairly smooth. Pour into 6 buttered 8-ounce custard cups or ramekins. Place in a pan of hot water and cover the whole with parchment paper or buttered foil. Bake about 25 minutes, or until custard is set.

Meanwhile, heat butter in a small saucepan. Add sorrel and cook until completely wilted. Add cream and simmer until reduced to ¾ cup. Taste for salt and pepper.

Turn out custards on serving plates and spoon some sauce over each.

Serves 6

Sorrel and Sole Timbales

5 tablespoons butter
1 shallot, chopped
2 cups chopped sorrel
Salt and pepper to taste
Pinch of grated nutmeg
¼ cup heavy cream
4 sole fillets (about 4 ounces each)

Preheat oven to 400 degrees. In a small skillet, heat 3 tablespoons butter. Sauté shallot and sorrel until wilted. Add salt, pepper, nutmeg, and cream and cook about 4 minutes, or until thick. Score filets on darker side in 2 or 3 places. Butter 4 custard cups or ramekins, 6- to 8-ounce size. Line each ramekin with 1 filet, with the lighter side out, pressing gently to cover as much of the inside surface as possible with the fish. Fill the centers with sorrel mixture and dot with pieces of remaining butter. Place ramekins in baking pan and pour hot water around molds to reach halfway up sides. Cover all with parchment paper and bake about 15 minutes.

Drain timbales by holding a small plate over each mold and tipping out juices. Unmold on a serving plate and serve with Tomato Cream Sauce (page 358).

Serves 4

Tarragon

LORE AND LINEAGE

. . . the alliance of the United States with France in 1778 . . . began an infiltration of French customs, including culinary ones, that has never ceased. . . . To the extent that French cookery would affect American eating habits, the process would be one of gradual . . . percolation, beginning among wealthy sophisticates and moving slowly and imperfectly into lower levels of society.

—RICHARD J. HOOKER
A History of Food and Drink in America, 1981

Tarragon is traditionally an herb not for the cook but for the chef; and specifically, the French chef. In this country, the French chef, embodying the aristocratic and cultural traditions of his native land, suddenly became, in the wake of the American Revolution, the object of many kinds of desire. Americans who wanted some of that aristocracy and culture hired themselves a French chef. This was a fortunate situation for tarragon lovers, for it was these professional practitioners who introduced this elegant *haute* herb to the American repertoire.

This was also a fortunate situation for the chefs and pastry cooks fleeing Paris during the French Revolution, for they found ready and appreciative employment right from the beginning—and the beginners—of the nation. George Washington hired a French steward, John Adams turned into a Francophile in spite of himself (a mission to France converted him), and Jefferson made a Frenchman, Julien Lemaire, the first chef at the White House. Jefferson kept him well supplied with choice ingredients by personally writing to France for such items as olive oil and tarragon vinegar.

Other chefs worked for or opened their own inns, cafés, boardinghouses, and restaurants. Jean Baptiste Jullien, chef to the archbishop of Bordeaux, went to Boston in 1794 to open Jullien's Restarator. It was to Jullien, who became famous as the Prince of Soups, that Brillat-Savarin, author of *The Physiology of Taste* and another aristocrat seeking refuge, came when in town. At another Boston French establishment, Sign of the Alliance, the palates were as sensitive as the politics. Nearby, the Tremont House was to set the highest standards for French cuisine and service.

Around this same time, French-trained chefs fled to this country to escape the Haitian revolution, finding refuge in many port cities. Soon they were running restaurant kitchens in New York, Philadelphia, and Baltimore, the latter city called by Oliver Wendell Holmes "the gastronomic metropolis of the Union." In New York, French chefs eventually presided over fare in famous hotels like the Brunswick and Astor House, or in the private kitchens of their patrons, the Vanderbilts, Goulds, Astors, Schuylers, Lorillards, Havemeyers. At Taylor's Restaurant, woodcocks were stewed with French truffles and crawfish; Chef J. Pinteux attracted the wealthy to his ostentatiously appointed Café de Mille Colonnes; Maison Dorée on Union Square was equally glamorous. But for truly prestigious French eating, Delmonico's was *de rigueur.* Under the direction of chef

Charles Ranhofer, whose seven-page *carte du restaurant Français* offered all the classics, Delmonico's was even regal enough for the likes of the visiting Charles Louis-Napoleon, who became Emperor Louis Napoleon III.

Philadelphia had its French-style Petry's to serve the wealthy. In a more democratic spirit, the U.S. Centennial Exposition, held in Philadelphia, sponsored several French restaurants which offered authentic French fare to fair-goers.

In New Orleans, almost every eating place was synonymous with fine French food. Antoine Alciatore came to the Crescent City from Marseilles to found the famous Antoine's, birthplace of oysters Rockefeller. Although the official recipe has never been divulged, the licorice taste of tarragon is its one constant distinguishing flavor. Chicken Rochambeau is another famous tarragon-scented New Orleans specialty, created and named for the commander of the French forces supporting Washington's army. This and other Creole dishes were perfected at the city's rapidly proliferating new French restaurants: Madame Eugene's; Moreau's, near the French Market; Madame Venn's; Fleches; Victor's; the St. Charles Hotel; Arnaud's. There were also the slightly less expensive cafés on Chartres Street, like Les Quartre Saisons and Le Pelerin, which served full dinners for half a dollar.

SIGNATURE DISH: OYSTERS ROCKEFELLER

Supposedly a never-revealed secret, this creation of chef Jules Alciatore at New Orlean's Antoine's usually consists of a grand mashing up of green onions, celery, tarragon, bread crumbs, Tabasco, and butter, splashed with anisette or a reasonable facsimile; a plump spoonful of all this should be placed on each oyster, put in a broiler, and browned.

The Midwest had its Kinsley's, often called the Delmonico's of Chicago, and, further west, Georgetown, Colorado, had its Hotel de Paris which became world renowned for Chef Louis Dupuy's cassoulet Toulousain and mushroom omelets.

The first French chefs to visit California were brought as part of the usual entourage assembled by wealthy businessmen who came to check on their western investments. When the business was over, the chefs often stayed behind, impressed with the possibilities for starting their own businesses as innkeepers and restaurateurs. At least one was a French woman, known as Ma Tanta, whose French peasant-style restaurant was a center of activity on Washington Street in San Francisco. Other French chefs in that city were soon plying their trade—which meant introducing dishes distinguished by tarragon—at Jacques, Marchand's, Maison Tortoni, and Maison Riche. A western version of Delmonico's was established when Jules Harder came to San Francisco from his exalted position at the New York restaurant to become the first chef at the opulent Palace Hotel. Under his direction, the grill room became the model of stylish and authoritative cuisine. It was there, in fact, that tarragon reached center stage during the run of the wildly popular play *Green Goddess,* starring George Arliss. The Palace chef created green goddess dressing in Arliss's honor (see page 45). The dressing included tarragon vinegar and generous snippets of the fresh herb.

San Francisco can boast more than its share of Franco-Americana, apocryphal or otherwise. One story concerns an early restaurant, Poulet d'Or, named for a brightly gilded chicken at its entrance. Because of the way people pronounced—or mispronounced—it, the name eventually became slurred into the "Poodle Dog." In fact, when one of its waiters left and started his own version, he called it The Pup.

The French language was a difficulty that menu writers never quite mastered; but probably nobody noticed and certainly nobody cared. Nineteenth-century menus are full of such "Frenglish" offerings as *"Currie of Veal en Bordured de Riz," "Tenderloin of Mutton à la Maire d'Hote," "Hors d'noeurves,"* and *"Poummie de terre Dauphin."* Other words slipped from the French into the American vernacular almost unmolested: *bouillon, consommé, fricassée, ragout, croutons, croquette,* and, of course, the word *restaurant* itself.

Tarragon also sailed with French cuisine along the Mississippi and Ohio on the luxury steamboats. Their chefs, masters of *la grande cuisine,* were often black cooks from Louisville and Natchez, from the French trading posts and plantations along the Mississippi. By 1868 tarragon was riding the rails with the chef of yet another "Delmonico's," the first railroad dining car built by the Pullman company. This was an era of some famous tarragon recipes: Northern Pacific French dressing, Pennsylvania Railroad's famous salad dressing, and the stuffed tomatoes Bretonne served on the Chicago, Rock Island, and Pacific dining cars. Everything came full circle a few years later when "smart eateries" were being designed to look like railroad dining cars.

The earliest references to tarragon in this country call it Dragon Wort; it is listed among the herbs recorded in New Netherlands by Adriaen van der Donck in 1653. Martha Washington's cookbook records that although the herb was "so dear to the French" it was used very little elsewhere. Nonetheless, she allows a smidge of it in the recipe "To Boyle Pigeons Wth Puddings."

In the early nineteenth century, the high excitement over everything French led to the publication of some French-style cookbooks. In Philadelphia a translation of Louis Eustache Ude's classic *The French Cook* was published in 1828. A few years later, Eliza Leslie, also of Philadelphia, collected (some would say pirated) several recipes published under the title *Domestic French Cookery, Chiefly Translated from Suplice Barne* (1832). In her tarragon vinegar recipe, from a later book, she instructs: "Tarragon should be gathered on a dry day, just before the plant flowers. Pick the green leaves from the stalks, and dry them a little before the fire. Then put them into a wide-mouthed stone jar, and cover them with the best vinegar" to steep for a few weeks. (Still, many in the nineteenth century remained suspicious of French frippery, among them Harriet Beecher

Stowe. In her *House and Home Papers* (1865), she wrote "O we can't give time here in America to go into niceties and French whim-whams.") Tarragon had come a long way toward reaching the common people, or at least some of the people, by Fannie Farmer's day. She includes in her 1909 cookbook a recipe for saddle of lamb *à l'estragon,* with a sauce made from stock "infused with one tablespoon tarragon one hour."

Although tarragon came to our shores almost entirely through the cuisines of the French, we have inherited a few Italian ways with it as well. Italians from Siena make an artichoke dish with tarragon-speckled stuffing (*carciofi al dragoncello)* and Tuscans have contributed a tarragon sauce for fish *(salsa di dragoncello).* Tarragon also flavors the more Anglo-Saxon tartar sauce, beet dishes, grilled meats, and roast chicken with sour cream. Because of its high oil content, tarragon can be preserved successfully in vinegar. It makes a delicious mustard and a wonderful flavored butter, which is also a convenient way to preserve it. And, it is an excellent salt substitute.

The word *tarragon* probably comes from the Arabic, *tarkuhn.* Its similarity to the Greek word *drakonteion,* for dragon, has given it a reputation as the dragon herb, though some say its dragon identity comes from the fact that its roots are coiled like a serpent. Whatever its past, tarragon may well be the herb of the future, since recent experiments suggest that the plant actually thrives on exhaust fumes.

There are two types of tarragon: French and Russian. The former has been described as licoricelike, a cross between anise and vanilla. Russian Tarragon is more easily described, since it has virtually no taste at all. In San Francisco's Russian community, one important tarragon recipe will probably have the same effect with either tarragon—or even none at all. It's called Tarragon vodka, made from a lot of vodka mixed with a whisper of the herb. Bottom's Up, *Salud, Skol,* or, as they say in San Francisco, *Na Zdorovie!*

VINTAGE RECIPE

Recipe from *Recipes from the Russians of San Francisco* by Margaret H. Koehler (Riverside, Connecticut: The Chatham Press, 1974), page 109.

Tarragon Vodka

1 quart vodka
1 branch fresh tarragon
5 black peppercorns
2 cubes sugar

Mix vodka with the other ingredients, rebottle, and let stand for at least a week before using it.

Consumer Guide

Also known as: Arabic—tarkuhn, French—estragon; German—Estragon; Greek—drakonteion; Italian—dragoncelle; Russian—estragon; Spanish—estragón.

LATIN: *Artemesia dracunculus (French tarragon)*

Common varieties: Although both French and Russian tarragon are found in nurseries, only the French variety has the full flavor desired for culinary purposes.

Selection: Fresh tarragon leaves should be a silvery green color and unblemished. Both fresh and dried tarragon should have a licoricelike scent when leaves are rubbed between fingers. Select Origins, an herb and spice company, packages the best dried tarragon that we know of.

Storage: Wrap fresh tarragon in paper towels and seal in plastic bag. It will keep refrigerated for up to 1 week. May also be preserved in vinegar, but must be carefully rinsed before using.

Fresh vs. dried: Fresh tarragon is highly superior to dried. Use one-third the amount of dried as you would fresh.

Compatible herbs and spices: Parsley, oregano, thyme, garlic.

RECIPE LIST

Twice-baked Tarragon–Tomato Toasts
Shrimp Pâté with Tarragon and Mustard
Spinach Salad Supreme
Tomato–Tarragon Soup with Vodka
Baby Trout with Yellow Tomatoes and Tarragon
Sea Bass Baked in Leeks and Cream
Pan-fried Game Hens with Mustard and Tarragon
Veal in Tarragon, Olives, and Toasted Walnuts
Grilled Skirt Steak with Tomato–Tarragon Relish

Twice-baked Tarragon–Tomato Toasts

12 slices French bread
5 tablespoons olive oil
1 clove garlic, cut in half
¾ pound fresh mushrooms, finely chopped
2 green onions, finely chopped
4 sun-dried tomatoes (packed in oil), finely chopped
2 tablespoons fresh tarragon leaves or 1½ teaspoons dried
1 tablespoon lemon juice
¼ cup dairy sour cream
Salt and pepper
¼ cup shredded fontina cheese

Preheat oven to 450 degrees. Brush each bread slice with a little olive oil, about 1 tablespoon altogether, and place on an oiled baking sheet. Bake about 5 minutes, until light golden brown. Rub cut garlic clove on surface of each slice of bread and set aside.

In a medium skillet, heat remaining 4 tablespoons oil. Sauté mushrooms, green onions, 3 sun-dried tomatoes, tarragon, and lemon juice for about 5 minutes, until mushrooms are tender and most of the liquid has evaporated. Add sour cream and cook another 2 minutes over medium heat. Taste for salt and pepper. Spread each bread slice with mushroom mixture, sprinkle with cheese, and top with some of the reserved sun-dried tomato. Return to oven and bake about 3 minutes, or until cheese is melted.

Serves 6 as a first course

Shrimp Pâté with Tarragon and Mustard

1 pound shrimp, cooked, shelled, and deveined
1 tablespoon fresh lemon juice
2 tablespoons brandy
1 tablespoon fresh tarragon leaves, or 1 teaspoon dried
Pinch of ground red pepper
1 tablespoon mild mustard
½ cup (1 stick) butter, room temperature
Salt and pepper
Crackers or baguette slices

Place first 6 ingredients in a food processor and process until finely chopped. Add butter in 4 portions and process until smooth after each. Taste for salt and pepper. Place mixture in a 2½-cup crock or mold and chill about 4 hours. Serve with crackers or lightly toasted slices of baguette.

Yield: 2½ cups

Spinach Salad Supreme

2 pounds spinach, washed, dried, and stemmed
1 cup shredded Jarlsberg cheese
1 whole chicken breast, cooked, boned, skinned, and cut into julienne (page 362)
½ pound bacon, cooked and crumbled
2 red apples, cored and coarsely shredded

DRESSING
2 tablespoons white wine vinegar
1 tablespoon lemon juice
1 egg
1 tablespoon strong mustard
1 tablespoon fresh tarragon leaves, or 1 teaspoon dried
½ teaspoon salt
¼ teaspoon freshly ground black pepper
½ cup vegetable or olive oil, or a mixture of both

To make dressing, combine first 7 ingredients until smooth. Add oil slowly until dressing is thick. This can be done very successfully in a food processor. Set aside.

If spinach leaves are large, tear into small pieces. Place in a salad bowl and toss with about half the dressing. Arrange remaining ingredients in concentric circles over spinach leaves and pass remaining dressing separately.

Serves 6–8

Tomato–Tarragon Soup with Vodka

¼ cup (½ stick) butter
2 large shallots, finely chopped
2 tablespoons fresh tarragon leaves, or 1 teaspoon dried
1 28-ounce can imported tomatoes, chopped

½ cup vodka
2 cups tomato juice
Pinch of sugar
Dash of Tabasco
Salt and pepper
Lemon slices

In a medium saucepan, heat butter. Sauté shallots about 5 minutes, until soft. Add tarragon, tomatoes, and vodka and cook about 8 minutes, or until some of the liquid has evaporated. Add tomato juice, sugar, and Tabasco. Simmer 15 minutes, partially covered. Pass soup through a food mill and taste for salt and pepper. Garnish with lemon slices. Delicious served hot or cold.

Serves 4–6

Baby Trout with Yellow Tomatoes and Tarragon

4 boneless baby trout, heads and tails removed and butterflied
½ cup all-purpose flour
¼ cup yellow or white cornmeal
¼ teaspoon salt
Pinch of ground red pepper
6 tablespoons (¾ stick) butter
2 cups yellow cherry tomatoes, seeded and chopped
1 tablespoon minced shallot
1 teaspoon honey
1 tablespoon fresh tarragon leaves, or 1 teaspoon dried
¼ cup Fish or Chicken Stock (pages 353, 352)
Salt and pepper

Blot trout dry with paper towels. On a flat plate, combine flour, cornmeal, salt, and red pepper. Dredge both sides of trout in mixture. In a large skillet, heat 4 tablespoons of butter. Sauté trout about 2 minutes on each side, or until light golden brown. Remove and keep warm by covering with foil and placing in warm oven.

Add remaining 2 tablespoons butter to skillet and heat. Add cherry tomatoes, shallot, honey, and tarragon and cook over medium-high heat for about 3 minutes. Add stock, bring to a boil, and cook about 2 minutes, or until slightly thickened. Place trout on serving plates and spread with sauce.

Serves 4

Sea Bass Baked in Leeks and Cream

6 large sea bass filets (about 6–8 ounces each)
Salt and pepper
1 tablespoon fresh tarragon leaves, or 1 teaspoon dried
1 cup dry white wine
3 tablespoons butter
3 leeks (white part only), thinly sliced
½ cup heavy cream

Preheat oven to 350 degrees. Blot fish dry and sprinkle with salt and pepper. Place in buttered baking dish, sprinkle with tarragon, and add wine. Cover with foil and bake 10 minutes.

Meanwhile in a large skillet, heat butter. Sauté leeks about 5 minutes, or until almost tender. Carefully pour the liquid surrounding the fish into the skillet containing the leeks. Add cream and cook at medium until reduced by half. Spread leek mixture over fish, return to oven, and bake another 10 minutes, or until top is bubbly.

Serves 6

Pan-fried Game Hens with Mustard and Tarragon

3 game hens, split
Salt and pepper
2 tablespoons minced fresh tarragon, or 2 teaspoons dried
2 tablespoons strong mustard
2 tablespoons hot-sweet mustard
1 egg
¼ cup heavy cream
2 cups dry bread crumbs
Oil for frying

Make small slits in the skin of the hens with point of small knife and blot dry; season with salt and pepper. Mix half the tarragon with mustards, egg, and cream. Spread this mixture on both sides of hen halves. Mix remaining tarragon with bread crumbs. Coat both sides of the hens with the bread crumb mixture. Place on a large plate in 1 layer and refrigerate 3 to 6 hours.

Heat 1½ inches of oil in a pan large enough to hold all hen pieces. Fry about 20 minutes, turning every so often until hens are golden brown and crisp. Drain on paper toweling and serve immediately.

Serves 6

Veal in Tarragon, Olives, and Toasted Walnuts

¼ cup olive oil
2 cloves garlic, cut in half
2½ pounds veal stew meat, cut into 1½-inch cubes
Salt and pepper
Flour for dusting
1 cup dry white wine
¼ cup sherry wine vinegar
½ cup Chicken Stock (page 352)
2 large tomatoes, seeded and coarsely chopped
1½ cups Niçoise olives, pitted
1 tablespoon fresh tarragon leaves, or 1 teaspoon dried, plus chopped tarragon for garnish
1½ cups coarsely chopped toasted walnuts (page 360)

In a large pan, heat oil. Sauté garlic until golden and then discard. Blot veal dry and sprinkle with salt, pepper, and flour. Brown veal in same skillet, then add wine, vinegar, and stock. Cook until liquid has reduced by half. Add tomatoes, olives, and tarragon and simmer, covered, for about 1½ hours, or until veal is tender. Just before serving stir in 1 cup of walnuts. Sprinkle each serving with some additional walnuts and garnish with chopped tarragon leaves, if desired.

Serves 6

Grilled Skirt Steak with Tomato–Tarragon Relish

2 pounds skirt steak, trimmed of fat and cut into 6 pieces
1/3 cup olive oil
1/4 cup red wine vinegar
1/4 cup lime juice
1/4 cup orange juice
1 clove garlic, minced
1/2 teaspoon ground cumin
1/4 teaspoon ground red pepper
1/2 teaspoon salt

RELISH
3 tomatoes, peeled, seeded, and chopped
1/2 papaya, diced
3 green onions, chopped
1 tablespoon fresh tarragon leaves, or 1 teaspoon dried
2 tablespoons oil
1 tablespoon lemon juice
Pinch of ground red pepper
Salt and pepper

Place steak in a noncorrosive dish. Mix oil, vinegar, lime and orange juices, garlic, cumin, red pepper, and salt. Pour over steak, cover, and refrigerate at least 6 hours, turning meat in marinade every so often.

To make relish, combine ingredients until well blended. Refrigerate for 1 to 5 hours before using.

Preheat broiler or grill until very hot. Remove meat from marinade and cook about 5 minutes on each side. Serve with the relish.

Serves 6

Thyme

LORE AND LINEAGE

Anyone who has seen too many cowboy pictures as a child knows what people ate in the Pacific Northwest. All those pioneers and adventurers on the Oregon Trail have left a legacy of hearty appetites and stick-to-your-ribs cuisine, better known as grub. Today they may no longer roast their buffalo and reindeer over open pits, as they did during those Saturday morning movies so long ago. And yet, the regional specialties do include oxtail stews, venison with spaetzle, reindeer ragouts, elk meatballs in sour cream, and buffalo roasted with hard cider. And mingling in many of these muscle-flexing meals is the flinty, half-wild taste of thyme.

An herb whose name means to "burn sacrifice," thyme seems at home in the woodsy setting of Washington, Idaho, and Oregon. But in this country it is equally popular way down yonder in Mardi Gras country where, according to the *New Orleans City Guide* of the Federal Writers' Project, ". . . no Creole kitchen is complete without its iron pots, bay leaf, thyme, garlic, and cayenne pepper." Cajun and Creole dishes make copious use of thyme, the one taste, aside from chile peppers, that presides in so many dishes. This includes mudhens, bobolink, and black bear; turtle soups; crawfish bisque, balls and étouffée; and the famous Cajun dish, made with whatever shows up, called *le make-do*. Thyme is used in shrimp-stuffed mirliton, a Louisiana squash also known as vegetable pear, chayote, christophine, or brionne, which is now gaining popularity in other areas as well. Thyme is the compelling freshness in Acadian roast wild goose with oyster stuffing, baskets of frogs legs, redfish courtbouillon, crab chops, and braised pintail duck. Most gumbos have thyme plus just about anything else: catfish, duck, sausages, shrimp, even muskrat. As one cookbook describes it, "a muddle in Carolina Low Country is a fish stew, but when it has okra it's called gumbo . . . ." One vegetarian recipe, *gumbo z'herbes*, traditionally made with seven greens, is supposed to be eaten for good luck on Holy Thursday. Any greens may be used but, according to good authority (Sheila Hibben's *American Regional Cookery*, 1946), "onions, red pepper, and thyme must figure in it." Another authentic old version, called cow gumbo, is a fresh thyme-laced beef stew, the ceremonial dish at the traditional Acadian-style hoedowns called *fais dodo*.

SIGNATURE DISH: GUMBO

Made from everything from catfish to muskrat, gumbos are almost always flavored with thyme and thickened with filé, which also has a thymelike flavor.

Gumbo is one of those dishes, like chili, that everyone has the only authentic version for; consequently it is subject to drastic transformations as it travels from cook to cook and from cookbook to cookbook. One nineteenth-century recipe, for example, which directs that the cooked ingredients be sieved through a colander, concludes with the unappetizing suggestion: "Dish the jelly to eat with toast." From this same era, we inherit General Winfield Scott's gumbo, a military-size version that includes twenty-three spoonfuls of sassafras powder (filé) and some cut-up chicken, along with his instructions to "boil them to rags." Another famous-name gumbo is that of Lillian Hellman, who, in her book *Eating Together*, admitted modestly that there were probably better recipes than hers; "but," she added enticingly, "mine is easier."

Red beans and rice, the traditional New Orleans Monday noon meal, is now a favorite in many parts of the South. Thyme is one of the dish's herbs.

The cookery of Louisiana and environs includes many influences—Spanish, African, Native American, West Indian, Mexican, Cuban, Haitian—but it is probably its French connections that have made thyme so pervasive a flavor. Thyme sparkles through many Cajun dishes, a legacy from the fishermen, farmers, and trappers who settled near the bayous around New Orleans. Expelled from Nova Scotia (Acadia) in 1755 because of their refusal to swear allegiance to Britain, these Acadians (hence Cajuns) were French-Canadians. Their language, or *patois*, sounds more like that of eighteenth-century Quebec than of modern Paris, and their food is likewise connected to centuries-old, French culinary traditions.

Creole cooking, by contrast, is usually considered city food, sophisticated and with subtle blendings of flavors. It speaks of the intermarriage of French, Spanish, and other European settlers with each other and with the native population. Its dishes reflect the cooking of slaves who worked for the wealthy in private homes and in the restaurants of New Orleans. The French heritage of thyme was passed along through classic bouquets garnis (along with sage, parsley, and marjoram) and in many fines herbes mixes (with burnet and parsley). Many cooks agree that the best thyme in the world still comes from the Vendée region of France.

The French influence brought thyme to many other areas of the country. For example, two-wheeled carts called *caleches* delivered thyme along with other produce to cooks in Vincennes, Indiana, settled by the French in the early 1700s. A century later thyme found its way into Jefferson's executive mansion in such "French" dishes as Dolley Madison's famous *pot au feu*, a recipe which may have been inspired by the Creole style which she strongly admired. She made the dish on several occasions, despite the reviews. (One guest commented that her version was a bit too much like a "harvest home supper" to be served at official state functions.) At Monticello, Jefferson's gardens teemed with a boundless variety of herbs. Many of them came directly from the Paris Botanical Gardens, the superintendent of which Jefferson came to know well during his term as U.S. Minister to France.

Thyme had been planted by the colonists in Virginia in 1610, in New Netherlands in 1653, and in the gardens of New England by 1672. Some of the crop was reserved for the bees, since common thyme was always regarded as excellent raw material for honey. But the kitchen also got its share. Amelia Simmons pronounced thyme "most useful and best approved in cookery." She has it in several recipes in America's first cookbook (1796), including one "To Dress a Turtle." Many early cookbooks also use thyme to flavor vinegars. In *The Virginia Housewife*, first published in 1824, author Mary Randolph, a cousin of Thomas Jefferson, provides a recipe for chicken pudding made with ten eggs, four chickens, and "a bundle of thyme."

In the Shaker communities, the Sisters kept giant vats of thyme-scented lard next to barrels of meat scraps. They transformed these unpromising treasures into loaves of head cheese, scrapple, and pressed or jellied meat dishes. They also used thyme in their herb dumplings and herbed breads.

A Mediterranean plant, thyme is a member of the mint family. It grows throughout the mountains of Crete on Parnassus, and along the hilly slopes of Smyrna. Greek Americans indulge their fondness for thyme on grilled lamb, in kabob dishes such as *souvlakia*, and with dishes combining two other favorite herbs, oregano and dill.

Thyme has a high concentration of thymol, an antiseptic twelve times stronger than carbolic acid; its medical uses as a disinfectant against salmonella and staphylococcus bacteria are scientifically well founded. It also has religious connections, being one of the manger herbs mixed with the bedding straw for Christmas crèches. Steeped in boiling water, thyme leaves produce a tea that soothes colds, sore throats, and other ailments. It is associated with motherhood and headaches, though not necessarily in that order.

There are many varieties of thyme, most detectable by even the most uneducated nose. Common Thyme (*Thymus vulgaris*) has dark leaves, strong flavor; in *The Food Lover's Garden*, 1970, Angelo Pellegrini calls it "the recognized culinary leader of the family." There are three forms of common thyme: Garden Thyme or English Broadleaf; German Winter Thyme or English Narrowleaf; and French Narrowleaf Thyme, with a sweet smell and silvery leaves. Lemon Thyme (*T. citriodorus*) complements veal and fish and adds a lemony tang to desserts like rhubarb compote, custards, ice creams, and sherbets. According to some cooks, Oregano Thyme (*T. nummularius*) tastes more like oregano than oregano. Caraway Thyme (*T. herba barona*), which is from Corsica, is named for its central role in baron of beef; when crushed, it provides a caraway perfume and an exotic flavor spicier than other thymes but less pungent than caraway. Other choices include a sweet-tasting Orange Balsam Thyme (*T. fragrantissimus*) and many delicious wild thymes.

Because of these many variations, thyme has been described as smelling like everything from peppermint, garlic, nutmeg, and coconut to lavender, pine, pepper, tangerine, varnish, and even soap. It is one of the important herbs in the liqueur Benedictine. Thyme is wonderful in stuffings and slow-cooking soups, pickled vegetables, and broiled rabbit and also rubbed on creamy goat cheese. In fact, we found a handy old cook's rule that testifies to the general appeal of this herb: "When in doubt, use thyme."

VINTAGE RECIPE

At the International Alligator Festival, one of the over ninety Cajun fairs in southern and southwestern Louisiana, new recipes are always being introduced. Still, it's nice to have an old, reliable alligator recipe around the house, such as this one. It is adapted from Andy Edmonds, *Let the Good Times Roll!: The Complete Cajun Handbook* (New York: Avon 1984), page 52.

Golden Meadow Alligator Steak

2 pounds alligator meat, cut into 6 serving-size pieces
½ cup Tabasco sauce
2 onions, chopped
Salt and pepper
1 tablespoon thyme
Juice of 1 lemon
¼ cup (½ stick) butter, cut into pieces

Place alligator pieces on foil, pour Tabasco sauce over meat, and put in deep dish. Sprinkle with onion, salt, and pepper and put in refrigerator for at least 1 hour. Add thyme and lemon juice. Put one pat of butter on each piece of alligator, cover loosely with foil, and bake at 325 for 20 minutes or until tender. Serve with lots of beer or strong Cajun coffee.

Serves 6

Consumer Guide

Also known as: Arabic—sa'tar; Dutch—tijm; French—thym; German—Thymian; Italian—timo; Spanish—tomillo.

LATIN: *Thymus vulgaris (and other species of Thymus)*

Common varieties: French Thyme has small pointy leaves and lavender flowers. Lemon Thyme, a bit less common, has glossy round leaves and lemon scent and taste. Other varieties include English Thyme, Caraway Thyme, and Oregano Thyme.

Selection: Fresh thyme is becoming more available in better supermarkets. Leaves should be unblemished and grayish green in color. Dried thyme should be aromatic.

Storage: Wrap fresh thyme in paper towels and store in plastic bag in refrigerator for up to 1 week. Dried thyme should be stored in an airtight container in a cool, dark place.

Fresh vs. dried: May be used interchangeably. Use twice the amount of fresh as dried.

Compatible herbs and spices: Oregano, sage, parsley, pepper, dill, mint.

RECIPE LIST

Mozzarella Cakes with Thyme–Tomato Pesto
Three-Pepper Thyme Soup
Thymed Cheese and Fresh Tomato Sandwiches
Green Gumbo
Sole and Scallop Stew with Noodles
Baked Zucchini Cream
Thymed Parsnip Crisps
Lemon Thyme and Rhubarb Compote

Mozzarella Cakes with Thyme–Tomato Pesto

1 pound whole milk mozzarella, shredded
2 eggs, lightly beaten
½ teaspoon salt
¼ teaspoon dried thyme
1 cup dry bread crumbs
¼ cup olive oil

PESTO
¼ cup sun-dried tomatoes (packed in oil)
¼ cup toasted pine nuts (page 360)
2 cloves garlic
½ teaspoon dried thyme
1 tablespoon tomato paste
¼ cup grated asiago cheese
¼ cup olive oil

In a large bowl, combine mozzarella, eggs, salt, and thyme. Form 8 patties and coat each with bread crumbs. Refrigerate for about 1 hour. Meanwhile, combine pesto ingredients in a food processor or blender until fairly smooth. Set aside.

In a large skillet, heat oil. Cook mozzarella cakes about 4 minutes on each side, or until lightly browned. Drain on paper towels and keep warm by covering with foil and placing in a warm oven. Serve topped with tomato pesto.

Serves 4

Three-Pepper Thyme Soup

¼ cup olive oil
1 yellow bell pepper, seeded and cut into strips
1 onion, chopped
2 cloves garlic, minced
1 teaspoon dried thyme
2 jalapeño peppers, seeded, deveined, and chopped (page 361)
4 red bell peppers, seeded, deveined, and diced
2 tablespoons tomato paste
5 cups Chicken Stock (page 352)
½ cup heavy cream
Salt and pepper

In a medium saucepan, heat oil. Sauté yellow pepper about 3 minutes, until just slightly softened. Remove and reserve. In same pan, cook onion, garlic, thyme, and jalapeño and red peppers about 12 minutes, until soft and wilted. Stir in tomato paste and stock, bring to a boil, and simmer, partially covered, for about 30 minutes. Puree soup in a blender or food processor, stir in cream, and taste for salt and pepper. Serve garnished with reserved yellow pepper.

Serves 6

Thymed Cheese and Fresh Tomato Sandwiches

½ pound cream cheese, preferably natural type made without preservatives
2 tablespoons plain yogurt
2 green onions, chopped
2 tablespoons fresh thyme leaves, or 1 tablespoon dried
½ teaspoon salt
1 teaspoon freshly ground black pepper
8 slices rosemary garlic bread (page 156), lightly toasted
2 ripe tomatoes, sliced

In a medium bowl, combine cream cheese with yogurt, green onions, thyme, salt, and pepper until creamy. Cover and refrigerate 24 to 48 hours to allow flavors to develop.

Bring cheese mixture to room temperature, then spread on 4 slices of bread. Add tomato slices and top with remaining slices of bread.

Yield: 4 sandwiches

Green Gumbo

⅓ cup vegetable or olive oil
⅓ cup all-purpose flour
2 bunches green onions, sliced
2 jalapeño peppers, seeded, deveined, and chopped (page 361)
1 green bell pepper, seeded and chopped
3 cloves garlic, minced
½ teaspoon dried oregano
1 teaspoon dried thyme
1 pound spicy sausage, sliced
2 quarts Chicken Stock (page 352)
2 tablespoons filé powder (optional)
¼ pound green beans, cut into 2-inch pieces
2 zucchini, sliced
¼ pound asparagus, cut into 2-inch pieces
Salt and pepper
½ cup chopped parsley
¼ cup chopped fresh basil
3 cups hot cooked white, long-grain rice

In a stockpot, heat oil until almost smoking. Stir in flour slowly, and, whisking continuously, cook until golden in color. This should take about 10 minutes; if the flour burns, start over. Add green onions, jalapeño and green peppers, garlic, oregano, thyme, and sausage. Cook, stirring constantly, for about 5 minutes.

Slowly add chicken stock in 3 batches, stirring after each addition until flour mixture is completely dissolved. Stir in filé. Bring to a boil and simmer, covered, 30 minutes. Add green beans, zucchini, and asparagus and cook about 5 minutes, or just until vegetables are tender. Remove from heat, taste for salt and pepper, and stir in parsley and basil. Serve over rice.

Serves 8–10

Sole and Scallop Stew with Noodles

¼ cup (½ stick) butter
1 leek (white part only), thinly sliced
1 celery stalk, thinly sliced
2 carrots, diced
3 tomatoes, seeded and coarsely chopped
½ teaspoon dried thyme
½ pound fresh mushrooms, quartered
½ cup dry white wine
2 cups Fish or Chicken Stock (pages 353, 352)
½ pound asparagus tips
1 pound sole filets, cut into strips
1 pound scallops, cut into quarters if large
½ cup heavy cream
1 egg yolk
Salt and pepper
1 pound angel's hair pasta or fine noodles, cooked
Chopped parsley

In a large pan, heat butter. Sauté leek, celery, carrots, tomatoes, thyme, and mushrooms over medium-high heat for 5 minutes. Add wine and stock, bring to a boil, and cook 5 minutes. Liquid should be somewhat syrupy.

Add asparagus and cook 4 minutes. Add sole and scallops, and simmer 1 minute. Combine cream and warmed yolk with ¼ cup stew liquid and stir into stew over very low heat. Cook about 2 minutes, or until sauce has thickened slightly. Taste for salt and pepper. Serve over hot noodles and sprinkle with parsley.

Serves 6

Baked Zucchini Cream

2 pounds zucchini, grated, blanched (page 361), and well drained
1½ cups heavy cream
4 eggs
½ teaspoon dried thyme
½ teaspoon salt
½ teaspoon freshly ground black pepper
½ cup grated Jarlsberg cheese

Preheat oven to 400 degrees. Puree all but ½ cup zucchini with the cream, eggs, thyme, salt, and pepper until smooth. Stir in reserved zucchini and cheese. Butter a 10-inch ovenproof quiche or pie pan. Pour in mixture and bake about 35 minutes, or until top is golden brown.

Serves 8

Thymed Parsnip Crisps

1 pound parsnips, grated
¼ cup all-purpose flour
½ teaspoon salt
¼ teaspoon freshly ground black pepper
1 teaspoon fresh thyme, or ½ teaspoon dried
1 egg
2 tablespoons milk or cream
1 tablespoon vegetable oil
Oil for frying

In a medium bowl, combine all ingredients except frying oil until well blended. In a large skillet heat ½ inch of oil until very hot (350° to 375°) but not smoking. Drop tablespoons of batter in the pan and fry until golden brown and crisp on both sides (about 1 minute per side). Do this in several batches for best results. Drain on paper towels and serve as a side dish or appetizer.

Yield: about 16 crisps

Lemon Thyme and Rhubarb Compote

¼ cup water
¼ cup dry red wine
½ cup sugar
1 pound rhubarb, cut into 1-inch slices
1 pint strawberries, halved
2 sprigs Lemon thyme or French thyme with the addition of a squeeze of lemon (do not use dried)

Place water, wine, sugar, and rhubarb in a medium saucepan. Bring to a boil and simmer, partially covered, about 10 minutes, or until rhubarb is tender. Remove from heat and stir in strawberries and thyme. Allow to cool and discard thyme. Serve at room temperature or chilled as an accompaniment to a savory roast or as an after-dinner sweet, garnished with a dollop of Crème Fraîche (page 359).

Serves 6

Watercress

LORE AND LINEAGE

Let's stop letting the abundance of wild watercress in this country go to waste. I think it is a poor reflection on Americans that it is mainly our foreign-born population which . . . appreciates the wealth of wild watercress in this land, and that it is largely ignored by the native born.

—EUELL GIBBONS
Stalking the Wild Asparagus, 1962

Judging from today's restaurant menus, people are finally rediscovering watercress the herb, as well as watercress the leafy, green vegetable. Discriminating cooks are composing salads of watercress, walnuts, gorgonzola cheese, sliced pears, wild rice, and perhaps roasted peppers. In such elegant company, one would never suspect that watercress has had a rather rough-and-tumble past in this country, right from the beginning.

Early colonists learned from the Indians to eat raw watercress, dandelions, and peppergrass as well as to boil them with wild game. There is actually more evidence that the Pilgrims ate watercress at the first Thanksgiving than they did turkey. But somehow, roast watercress with cranberry sauce and all the trimmings never garnered wide appeal.

Though it grows wild along waterways, watercress was also one of the first plants cultivated in New England, where it was used as garnish, herb, and salad. In Virginia, it was included in early gardens because of its "agreeable warm taste." The famous Virginia epicure, Thomas Jefferson, agreed. His favorite salad consisted of watercress, peppergrass, and other greens picked in the morning and "laid in cold water, which will be improved by adding ice." His recipe was immortalized in *The Virginia Housewife,* a cookbook by his cousin Mary Randolph, first published in 1824. By this time, watercress was acquiring a dual personality, simultaneously homey and elegant. Some cookbooks featured watercress in simple, honest soups, sauces, or herb butters; fancier cookbooks of the same era presented almost the same dishes dressed up with names like *velouté cressonnière, sauce verte,* and *beurre Montpellier.* Out West, in gold country, *berro* salad was favorite, named after the Spanish word for cress. Some found watercress useful for didactic purposes, or at least scare tactics, as demonstrated by the following New York street cry from the 1820s:

The Water Cress Girl

Oh! look at that poor little girl,
  So ragged, 'tis shocking to see,
All shivering and dripping with wet,
  How thankful then ought I to be.
That I am not like that poor child,
  Obliged to earn all that I eat;

> And if I could not sell my cress,
> Be scolded, be starved, and be beat.

By this century, Fannie Farmer was offering such recipes as watercress salad with cucumbers and French dressing, and cream of watercress soup. An old Yankee dish—Vermont spring soup—adds peas, asparagus, and nutmeg to the soup pot, while in nearby New Britain, Connecticut, the Ukrainian community decks their traditional Easter suckling pig with garlands of watercress. Greek Americans served lamb kabobs, or *souvlakia,* on lush beds of watercress. In California, watercress has achieved stardom as a central ingredient in Cobb salad, invented by Robert Cobb in 1936 at Hollywood's Brown Derby Restaurant at Hollywood and Vine (this is not the original hat-shaped restaurant on Wilshire Boulevard).

At teatime, watercress was mixed with nuts and mayonnaise or cheese, spread on thin bread, and cut into heart- and diamond-shape sandwiches to delight the bridge party. The mustardy crunch of watercress is good on real sandwiches, too, with spicy pastrami or salami. Watercress pasta, with the leaves chopped into the dough, is a delightful change in the noodle realm. Stir-fried with ginger and garlic, watercress can be splashed with soy sauce or sesame oil and served on rice. It can also be chopped with parsley and chives as a novel fines herbes combination for omelets and stuffings.

SIGNATURE DISH: COBB SALAD

Created at Hollywood's Brown Derby Restaurant by Robert Cobb in 1936, this famous American salad is a lyrical layering of watercress, chopped hard-boiled eggs, bacon, cooked chicken, blue cheese, tomatoes, and various greens.

A French watercress soup, called *potage santé,* was invented—as its name suggests—as a health food. By 1904, this particular soup had become a sign of the sophisticated diner, as is proved by its place on the Waldorf-Astoria menu of that year for the Eighth Annual Dinner of the New York Society of the Order of the Founders and Patriots of America.

Watercress has been used to cure everything from scurvy and liver problems to kidney stones. Its juices have been extracted to treat skin irritations. Besides making people wittier, watercress was supposed to help children grow faster. Considering how rich watercress is in vitamins and minerals, some of these medicinal applications were probably effective. In addition to iron, phosphorus, calcium, sulphur, and nitrogen, watercress has substantial amounts of vitamin A and twice as much vitamin C as spinach.

Although all "cresses" offer these benefits, some are more generally available than others. Garden Cress or Peppergrass *(Lepidium sativum)* has a pleasantly pungent, faintly mustardlike taste. Wintercress or Yellow Rocket *(Barbarea vulgaris)* is also called St. Barbara's Herb and the American Land Cress. Similar in flavor to watercress, it adds a piquant note to spring salads and makes a nice bunch of boiled greens. Authentic streamside Watercress *(Nasturtium officinale),* a native of Europe and western Asia, grows in every state and for most of the year. According to Euell Gibbons in *Stalking the Wild Asparagus, "officinale"* means it was once included among the official medicinal herbs rich in minerals and vitamins. The pretty garden flower nasturtium has such a similar peppery flavor that it was awarded watercress's Latin genus name. This causes some confusion, especially since the popular name for the flower nasturtium (whose scientific name is *Tropaeolum majus*) is Indian Cress. One legend has it that the orange nasturtium flowers, once abundant in the Inca territories of Peru, were brought back to England and there dubbed "Indian Cress." This sounds logical enough, as does another equally credible story of romantic proportions. According to Kimball and Anderson's *Art of American Indian Cooking* (1965), the pioneers in covered wagons traveling west over the Plains "found a kind of nasturtium growing wild. They named it Indian Cress because tribes of the area used both the blossoms and leaves to give their green salads a special pungency."

At any rate, if you wonder why watercress's Latin name means nose-twister *(Nasus tortus),* just take a big, generous sniff while you're chopping it up for one of the following recipes.

VINTAGE RECIPE

This recipe is excerpted from *The Dinner Year-Book* by Marion Harland (New York: Charles Scribner's Sons, 1878).

Lettuce and Cress Salad

Cut up lettuce and cresses, having washed both well, and pile in a salad bowl; then pour over them a dressing made by beating together four teaspoonfuls of vinegar, one teaspoonful each of salt and sugar, half as much mustard, and when these are well mixed, adding, gradually, two tablespoonfuls of best salad oil. Toss with a silver fork, and serve.

Consumer Guide

WATERCRESS

Also known as: French—cresson de ruisseau; German—Brunnekresse; Italian—crescione di fonte; Spanish—berro.

LATIN: *Nasturtium officinale (Streamside Watercress)*
Lepidium sativum (Garden cress)
Barbarea vulgaris (Wintercress)

GARDEN CRESS

Also known as: French—cresson cultive; German—Gatrenkresse; Italian—crescione de giardino; Spanish—masteurzo de jardín.

Selection: Look for bright green and perky leaves in the vegetable or herb section of your supermarket; avoid any with yellowing leaves.

Storage: Wrapped in a layer of paper toweling and sealed in plastic, watercress will keep fairly well in the refrigerator for up to 5 days.

Fresh vs. dried: No commercially dried watercress exists.

Compatible herbs and spices: Parsley, oregano, thyme, mustard.

RECIPE LIST

Watercress and Walnut Tartlets

1 recipe Pâte Briseé (page 354)
3 ounces cream cheese
1/4 cup milk
2 egg yolks
1/2 teaspoon salt
1/4 teaspoon freshly ground black pepper
1/2 cup finely chopped watercress
1/2 cup medium-chopped walnuts
24 walnut halves

Preheat oven to 375 degrees. Grease 24 2-inch tarlet tins or miniature muffin tins. Divide dough into 24 pieces and press each piece into a tartlet tin. Refrigerate while preparing filling.

Combine cream cheese, milk, and yolks until smooth. Stir in salt, pepper, watercress, and chopped walnuts. Fill tins two-thirds full with mixture, then bake for 12 minutes. Place a walnut half on each tartlet and continue to bake another 3 minutes. Allow to cool for about 10 minutes before removing from tins. Serve warm or at room temperature.

Yield: 2 dozen

Bay Shrimp and Watercress Sandwich

½ pound cooked bay shrimp or smallest available
1 tablespoon lemon juice
1 tablespoon capers, rinsed and drained
1 small carrot, grated
¼ cup chopped chives
¼ cup Herbed Mayonnaise (page 358) or plain
Salt and pepper
4 slices good egg bread or brioche
½ cup watercress leaves

In a medium bowl, combine shrimp, lemon juice, capers, carrot, chives, and mayonnaise. Taste for salt and pepper. Spread mixture on 2 slices of bread, top with watercress, and add remaining bread slices.

Yield: 2 sandwiches

Roasted Red Pepper and Watercress Soup

3 large red bell peppers
2 tablespoons olive oil
2 cloves garlic, minced
1 shallot, chopped
3 cups Chicken Stock (page 352)
1 cup heavy cream
1 bunch watercress leaves, coarsely chopped
Salt and pepper

Char red peppers over a gas flame or in broiler until skins are black and blistered. Place in plastic bag until cool enough to handle. Peel, seed, devein, and cut into eighths.

In a medium saucepan, heat oil. Sauté garlic, shallot, and peppers about 5 minutes, or until soft. Add chicken stock, bring to a boil, and simmer, partially covered, about 15 minutes. Puree mixture with cream in a blender or food processor. Return to saucepan, add watercress, and just heat through. Taste for salt and pepper. Serve hot or cold.

Serves 6

Sweet Potato Vichyssoise

1/4 cup (1/2 stick) butter
2 leeks (white part only), chopped
1 quart Chicken Stock (page 352)
3 sweet potatoes, peeled and sliced
2 cups half-and-half
Juice and grated zest (page 363) of 1 orange
1 bunch watercress, stemmed, plus additional for garnish
Salt and pepper

In a medium saucepan, heat butter. Sauté leeks until soft. Add stock and bring to a boil. Add sweet potatoes and simmer, partially covered, for about 18 minutes, or until potatoes are tender. Stir in half-and-half, orange juice, and zest and cook another 2 minutes. Place in a food processor or blender with watercress and puree. Taste for salt and pepper. Serve hot, cold, or at room temperature, garnished with additional watercress, if desired.

Serves 6

Salmon Fritters with Watercress Sauce

1¼ pounds fresh salmon, cooked, boned, and skinned
½ small onion
1 clove garlic
½ cup cooked long-grain white rice
½ cup heavy cream
1 egg
½–1 cup dry bread crumbs
½ teaspoon salt
Pinch of ground red pepper
Oil for frying

SAUCE
1 bunch watercress, stemmed
½ cup dairy sour cream
1 tablespoon lemon juice
½ cup mayonnaise
1 teaspoon Dijon-type mustard
Dash of Tabasco
Salt and pepper

In a food processor bowl, place salmon, onion, garlic, rice, cream, and egg. Process until pureed. Add remaining ingredients except oil and process just until blended. Chill mixture about 30 minutes.

In a large skillet, pour in 1 inch of oil and heat to about 350 degrees. Form salmon mixture into tablespoon-size ovals or rounds and fry, turning until brown and crisp (about 2 minutes per side) on both sides. Remove to a paper towel-lined tray and keep warm.

Puree all the sauce ingredients in a food processor or blender. Serve fritters as an appetizer in a basket with a small bowl of the sauce in center for dipping. (This sauce is especially good with fresh seafood, crudités, crab cakes, or fried chicken wings.)

Serves 6

Chicken Breasts Stuffed with Watercress and Prosciutto

3 boned and skinned whole chicken breasts, halved
2 cups watercress leaves, chopped, plus ½ cup, chopped
¼ pound prosciutto, diced
¼ pound Monterey Jack cheese, shredded
Salt and pepper
¼ cup (½ stick) butter
½ cup dry white wine
2 large tomatoes, peeled, seeded, and chopped
1 cup heavy cream
½ cup chopped watercress leaves

Preheat oven to 400 degrees. Pound chicken breasts to flatten slightly. Combine 2 cups watercress, prosciutto, and cheese. Spread one-sixth of filling on each chicken breast. Roll up and tie with kitchen string. Sprinkle with salt and pepper. In a large skillet, heat butter. Brown stuffed chicken breasts on all sides and remove to baking dish. Bake chicken, covered, for about 20 minutes. Remove from oven and cut strings. Cut each breast into 4 slices and keep warm.

Deglaze (page 361) baking pan with wine and pour into a small saucepan. Add tomatoes and cook about 10 minutes, until soft. Add cream and cook over medium-high heat until thickened. Stir in the remaining ½ cup watercress and taste for salt and pepper. Spoon sauce on plates and arrange chicken slices over sauce.

Serves 6

Poached Chicken Breasts with Watercress, Thyme, and Vegetables

1 quart Chicken Stock (page 352)
1 teaspoon salt
½ teaspoon freshly ground black pepper
3 sprigs fresh thyme, or ½ teaspoon dried
¼ cup dry vermouth or dry white wine
4 skinned and boned whole chicken breasts, split
1 cup snow peas
1 cup baby carrots, peeled
1 cup very small whole new potatoes
1 cup sliced zucchini
1 cup fresh mushroom caps

SAUCE
1 cup watercress leaves
½ teaspoon dried thyme
¼ teaspoon salt
1 teaspoon lemon juice
¼ cup (½ stick) butter, room temperature
¼ cup heavy cream

In a large saucepan, bring stock, salt, pepper, thyme, and vermouth to a boil. Add chicken breasts and simmer gently, covered, for 10 minutes. Remove chicken and keep warm in a covered dish. In the same pot, cook each vegetable separately until crisp-tender. Remove the vegetables to a plate and cover them with foil; place in a warm oven. Reserve ¾ cup of the stock.

To make sauce, puree watercress, thyme, salt, lemon juice, and butter. Set aside. In a small saucepan, reduce stock to ½ cup, add the cream, and boil for 1 minute. Whisk in the watercress puree 1 tablespoon at a time until smooth.

To serve, place a chicken breast half on each plate and surround with vegetables in a colorful pattern. Drizzle some sauce over chicken and vegetables and pass remaining sauce.

Serves 8

Watercress, Apple, and Pecan Salad

2 bunches watercress, tough stems removed
2 Red Delicious apples, cored and cut into ½-inch cubes
1 cup toasted and coarsely chopped pecans (page 360)
2 cloves garlic, chopped
1 teaspoon salt
¼ cup heavy cream
½ cup vegetable oil
¼ cup olive oil
2 tablespoons lemon juice
Freshly ground black pepper

In a salad bowl, combine watercress, apples, and pecans. In a small bowl, make a paste of the garlic and salt. Whisk in cream and then oils. Add lemon juice and stir until combined. Taste for pepper. Dress salad and serve.

Serves 8

Corn, Cress, and Potato Salad

24 very small red potatoes
1/4 cup olive oil
1/4 cup dry white wine
1/4 cup balsamic vinegar
1/2 cup plain yogurt
1/2 cup mayonnaise
2 cups cooked corn kernels, fresh or frozen
1 bunch watercress, leaves coarsely chopped
1/4 cup chopped chives
Salt and pepper

In a large pot, cook potatoes in salted, boiling water to cover about 10 minutes, or just until tender. Drain and cut into quarters while still warm. Place in a large bowl. Combine oil, wine, and vinegar and pour over still-warm potatoes. Toss to coat evenly. Allow to cool to room temperature.

Mix yogurt and mayonnaise, and add corn, watercress, and chives. Mix gently and taste for salt and pepper.

Serves 6–8

Garlic-poached Scallops and Watercress Salad

3 cloves garlic, halved
1 quart water
1 bay leaf
1 teaspoon salt
1 pound bay scallops
2 bunches watercress, stemmed
4 green onions, chopped
6 tablespoons heavy cream
1 tablespoon mild mustard

6 tablespoons olive or vegetable oil
1/4 cup fresh lemon juice
Salt and pepper to taste

In a medium saucepan, simmer garlic, water, bay leaf, and salt for 10 minutes. Add scallops and poach about 3 minutes. Place scallops and cooking liquid in refrigerator and chill at least 1 hour, or until you are ready to proceed with the rest of the salad.

In a medium salad bowl, place drained scallops, watercress, and green onions. Combine remaining ingredients until well blended and pour over scallops. Toss gently to combine. Serve immediately.

Serves 6

Lemon Rice with Walnuts and Watercress

1/4 cup (1/2 stick) butter
2 tablespoons walnut oil
1 cup long-grain white rice
2 1/2 cups Chicken Stock (page 352)
1 tablespoon grated lemon zest (page 363)
1 cup coarsely chopped toasted walnuts (page 360)
1/2 cup chopped watercress
Salt and pepper

In a medium saucepan, heat 2 tablespoons butter and oil. Add rice and cook, stirring, until translucent. Pour in stock and bring to a boil. Reduce heat to a simmer and cook, covered, for about 18 minutes. Stir in remaining ingredients and let rest, covered, off the heat for about 5 minutes. Stir in remaining butter and salt and pepper to taste and serve.

Serves 6

THE SPICES

Cinnamon

LORE AND LINEAGE

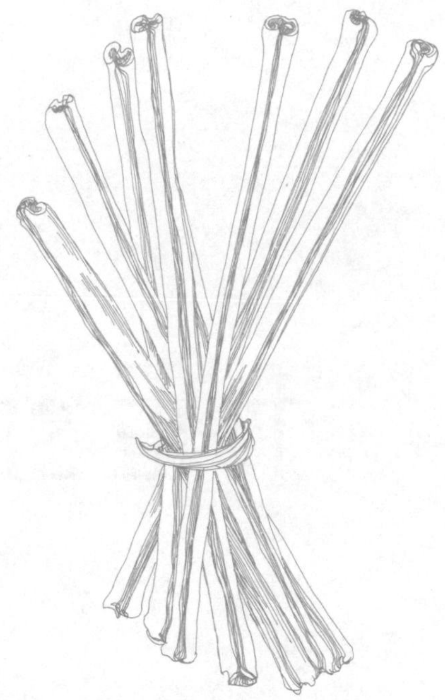

Even out on the old Chisholm Trail, bronc-busting, dust-breathing cowboys had a soft place in their hearts for apple pie. Of course, they had to be flexible about what an apple pie really needed to have and still be apple pie. It was all right if it didn't have a proper crust—they called them "boggy tops." It was even acceptable if there weren't any apples, in which case the pie might contain a chuckwagon interpretation made with soda crackers. But the one ingredient it had to have was cinnamon. Without cinnamon, it just didn't taste like apple pie.

And yet cinnamon itself was a scarce commodity. Of the early settlers, only the Dutch in New Netherlands had access to it because of Holland's control of the spice trade. New Englanders only dreamt of cinnamon toast at teatime and rum-laced, cinnamon-sweet "winter warmers." By the eighteenth century, however, the British East India Company had wrested the Ceylonese and Indian cinnamon trade from the Dutch and began shipping cinnamon into Boston. (One of the company's young employees, Elihu Yale, made his fortune in the spice trade and eventually used it to endow the university which bears his name.) Cinnamon began showing up in recipes in private manuscripts and, by 1796, Amelia Simmons's *American Cookery* included it in every kind of pie, from minced and apple to tongue, and in every kind of pudding, cake, and custard. Lydia Maria Child's *American Frugal Housewife* [1836] is lavish with the stuff, calling for "a great spoonful of . . . sifted cinnamon" in baked Indian pudding.

SIGNATURE DISH: CINNAMON TOAST

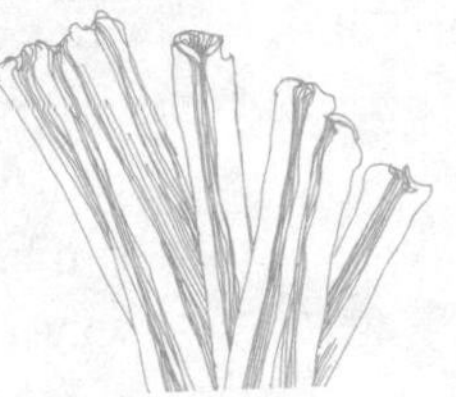

Bread, sugar, cinnamon: even a child can do it—and usually does. Other cinnamon-rich Americana are Indian pudding, shoo-fly pie, and bananas Foster.

By then, the various Shaker religious communities were stewing up quarts of Mount Lebanon Village "Oude (old) Sauce," with tomatoes, onions, peppers, horseradish, cloves, and cinnamon. In fact, as soon as it became readily available, cinnamon could be found in spice cupboards all over the country.

In Pennsylvania, for example, Lancaster Mennonites used it in shoo-fly pies; and most Pennsylvania Germans put it in *Zimsternes* (cinnamon stars), spiced beef, Moravian sugar cake, and even mead. The women of Germantown were soon bringing their freshly baked cinnamon buns to sell in Philadelphia's markets.

Throughout southern Appalachia, the mix of influences—Scotch-Irish, English, German, African—resulted in cinnamon's appearance in sauerkraut, chow-chow, gingerbreads, preserves, cushaw (a kind of squash) pie, and fig pudding.

All over the Midwest and, more specifically, along Chicago's 69th Street, Lithuanian bakers made cinnamon and spice mushroom-shaped cookies called *grybai,* while in the Jewish neighborhood bakeries there were coffee cakes and sweet noodle *kugel,* both speckled with cinnamon. Greeks showed the country how the sweet spice worked in savory dishes like *pastitsio* (a meat and macaroni custard), *avgolemono* (egg-lemon soup), moussaka, and stuffed anything. In Nebraska and Minnesota, cinnamon inspired Swedes to bake *pepparkakor* (pepper cookies), Danes to make rice fritters, and all Scandinavians to make *glögg.* Religious persecutions in the mid-1800s brought the Dutch back, this time to the upper Midwest; there they introduced *wijnsoep* (wine soup), *roode krentenbrij* (red currant soup), and other fruit soups made with raisins, blackberries, and generous quantities of nutmeg, cloves, and cinnamon.

Around Puget Sound, Washington, the culinary heritage of venison pies and game salamis was expanded considerably in the late 1800s with Slavonian contributions like *mostaccioli,* or "little mustaches," a tubular pasta served in a sauce made with cinnamon, herbs, beef, and pork; and *torta od orihe,* a flourless cinnamon-nut cake. In northern California, Portuguese farming families sprinkled cinnamon on *arroz doce* (rice pudding) and made a cinnamon-spiked wine and orange marinade for the grilled pork and sausage dish *carne de vinho e alhos.*

In New Orleans, of course, cinnamon always was essential in Creole fruitcakes and *café brûlot,* and is integral to bananas Foster, a creation of Brennan's restaurant, which named it to honor a favorite customer.

Today in Texas, San Antonio Christmases are distinguished by cinnamon-spiked *champurrado,* an Indian drink of chocolate, vanilla, and cornmeal. A week later, on New Year's Day, the traditional good luck ritual includes black-eyed peas with lots of garlic, nutmeg, and cinnamon. Texas stollen, an iced coffee ring based on the traditional Dresden fruitcake, was adapted in the German community of Fredericksburg as a breakfast treat.

Our cinnamon heritage is still being broadened, with influences as diverse as Italian and Vietnamese, Chinese and Moroccan. Cinnamon is even a basic element in the formulas for America's cola drinks, classic, light, caffeine-free, or otherwise. But in spite of its common use, cinnamon is the cause for some confusion, much of it deliberate. True cinnamon (*Cinnamomum zeylanicum*) comes from the inner bark of a small laurel-like tree. The bark is sun-dried and cut into strips that are then rolled together to form tan-colored sticks or quills. But people who think they are getting true cinnamon if they buy the quills are in for a surprise. False cinnamon (*Cinnamomum cassia*), also from the laurel family, is much less expensive; its quills are reddish-brown, but its flavor is not as delicate as true cinnamon. In England, the law requires that a clear distinction be made between the two spices; but in this country, the word *cinnamon* may be used legally for both. People may think they are buying true cinnamon, but they are actually getting the less-expensive cassia. This probably explains why six times as much cassia as cinnamon is consumed each year in this country.

At any rate, ground cinnamon, which deteriorates quickly, should be kept away from the sun and as airtight as possible. Cinnamon quills should be wrapped tightly, then kept in a dry, cool, dark place; they will keep indefinitely. If using whole quills, don't be alarmed when you check the cooking pot after awhile and find some debris floating around; the quills often uncurl during cooking.

VINTAGE RECIPE

This recipe is from *The Boston Cooking-School Cook Book* by Fannie Merritt Farmer (Boston: Little, Brown, and Company, 1909).

Horseshoes

Use Cinnamon Bar mixture [see below]. Cover with frosting colored with fruit red. Cut in strips six inches long by one-half inch wide. As soon as cut, shape quickly, at the same time carefully, in the form of horseshoes. Bake same as Cinnamon Bars. When cool, make eight dots with chocolate frosting to represent nails.

Cinnamon Bars

10 ozs. almond paste
5 ozs. confectioners' sugar
white 1 egg
½ teaspoon cinnamon

Mix same as macaroons. Dredge a board with sugar, knead mixture slightly, and shape in a long roll. Pat, and roll one-fourth inch thick, using a rolling-pin. After rolling the piece should be four inches wide. Spread with frosting made of white of one egg and two-thirds cup confectioners' sugar beaten together until stiff enough to spread. Cut in strips four inches long by three-fourths inch wide. This must be quickly done, as a crust soon forms over frosting. To accomplish this, use two knives, one placed through mixture where dividing line is to be made, and the other used to make a clean sharp cut on both sides of first knife. Knives should be kept clean by wiping on a damp cloth. Remove strips as soon as cut, to a tin sheet, greased with lard and then floured. Bake twenty minutes on centre grate in a slow oven.

Consumer Guide

Also known as: Arabic—qurfa; French—cannelle; German—Zimt; Italian—cannella; Spanish—canela.

LATIN: *Cinnamomum zelanicum (true cinnamon)*
C. cassia (false cinnamon or cassia)

Selection: Stick and ground cinnamon are widely available in every supermarket spice section. Cinnamon stick does not give off as much color in cooking as does ground, but the flavor is pretty much the same. Ground cinnamon is used almost exclusively in baking.

Storage: Keeps indefinitely in an airtight container on a cool, dry shelf.

Compatible herbs and spices: nutmeg, cloves, ginger.

RECIPE LIST

Braised Chicken and Leeks with Cinnamon Stick

1 large chicken (about 3½ pounds) cut into serving pieces
¼ cup (½ stick) butter
2 cloves garlic, minced
3 large leeks (white part only), cut into eighths lengthwise
3 tomatoes, seeded and coarsely chopped
½ cup dry red wine
1 bay leaf
1 2-inch piece cinnamon stick
1 teaspoon sugar
Salt and pepper
¼ cup chopped parsley

Blot chicken dry with paper towels. In a large sauté pan, heat butter. Brown chicken on all sides, then remove and reserve. In the same pan, sauté garlic and leeks until leeks are tender. Add tomatoes, wine, bay leaf, cinnamon stick, and sugar. Bring to a boil and simmer, covered, for 10 minutes. Return chicken to pan, cover, and simmer about 45 minutes, or until chicken is tender. Remove bay leaf and cinnamon stick and taste for salt and pepper. Sprinkle with chopped parsley before serving.

Serves 6

Hazelnut–Cinnamon Slices

2 cups all-purpose flour
1 teaspoon baking powder
1 teaspoon baking soda
¾ cup sugar
1 teaspoon ground cinnamon
1 cup coarsely chopped hazelnuts
2 eggs
¼ cup orange juice
¼ cup orange-flavored liqueur

Preheat oven to 375 degrees. Line a baking sheet with foil or parchment paper.

In a medium bowl, combine dry ingredients. In a separate bowl, beat eggs with orange juice and liqueur, and stir into dry mixture. Mix well until a slightly sticky dough forms, then shape into 2 long, slightly rounded cylinders and place on prepared baking sheet. Bake for 35 minutes.

Remove cylinders from oven and let rest about 5 minutes. Lower oven heat to 350 degrees. Cut cylinders into ¾-inch-thick slices and place cut side down on baking sheet. Return to oven and bake 12 minutes. Turn slices over and bake another 10 minutes. Allow to cool completely before storing.

Yield: about 1½ dozen

Cinnamon–Apple Noodle Soufflé

1 tablespoon butter
3 tablespoons ground walnuts
4 eggs, separated
¼ cup plus 2 tablespoons sugar
2 tablespoons ground cinnamon
8 ounces cottage cheese
1 large apple, peeled, cored, and grated
1 teaspoon grated lemon zest *(page 363)*
½ pound medium egg noodles, cooked and cooled

Preheat oven to 400 degrees. Butter 2-quart soufflé dish and dust with walnuts.

In a large bowl, beat yolks with ¼ cup sugar and 1 tablespoon cinnamon about 4 minutes, until thick. Stir in cottage cheese, apple, lemon zest, and noodles until well combined. In a separate bowl, beat whites until stiff. Fold into noodle mixture, then pour into soufflé dish. Sprinkle with remaining 2 tablespoons sugar and 1 tablespoon cinnamon. Bake for 10 minutes, then lower heat to 375 degrees and bake another 20 to 25 minutes, or until puffed and golden. Best if served immediately as dessert or a side dish.

Serves 6–8

Café Brûlot Pound-Cake Pudding

1 8-ounce pound cake, homemade or good-quality store-bought
1/4 cup strong brewed coffee
1/4 cup brandy
3 eggs, separated
3/4 cup confectioner's sugar
1 pound whole-milk ricotta cheese
3 ounces cream cheese
1/2 teaspoon each lemon and orange zest (page 363)
1 teaspoon ground cinnamon
5 ounces bittersweet chocolate, grated

Cut pound cake horizontally into slices 1/4 inch thick and then into 2-inch squares. Line the bottom of a 9- x 4-inch loaf pan with cake squares. Mix coffee and brandy and moisten cake in pan with half the mixture. In the medium bowl of an electric mixer, beat yolks with confectioner's sugar until thickened. Beat in both cheeses and zests until smooth. In a separate bowl, beat whites until stiff. Fold into cheese mixture.

Set aside 1 cup of egg-cheese mixture. Spread half of the remaining cheese mixture over cake in pan and sprinkle with half the cinnamon and chocolate. Add remaining cheese mixture, sprinkle with remaining chocolate and cinnamon, and top with remaining cake squares. Sprinkle with remaining coffee-brandy mixture. Spread reserved cheese mixture over cake. Cover with plastic wrap and refrigerate 2 hours or overnight.

To serve, cut through layers with a sharp knife to make 8 portions. Scoop out each portion with a spoon and serve in small bowls.

Serves 8

Cappuccino Sorbet

2 cups strong brewed espresso
1 teaspoon ground cinnamon
¼ cup sugar
2 tablespoons unsweetened cocoa powder
2 tablespoons coffee-flavored liqueur
1 cup water
½ cup half-and-half

In a small saucepan, simmer espresso, cinnamon, sugar, and cocoa for 5 minutes. Combine with remaining ingredients and chill. Place in ice-cream maker and follow manufacturer's directions.

Yield: 1 quart

Coriander Seed

LORE AND LINEAGE

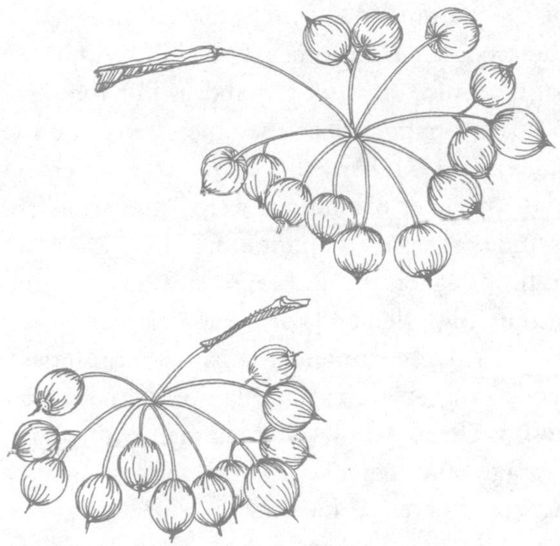

Many people report that the first time they taste a coriander seed, it seems strangely familiar. If this has happened to you, perhaps you lived too close to the corner candy store as a kid. There on the magical glass shelves lurked white- or pink-sugar balls to be chewed or sucked on until you got to a little seed in the center. Called candy marbles or Scotch candies, they have been childhood favorites since colonial times, when they were known as coriander comfits.

The musty, aromatic coriander seed has always been an essential ingredient in traditional grown-up food as well, like English black puddings and gingerbreads. The latter became naturalized by American settlers into Connecticut's ginger cake with stewed apples or colonial Virginia's ginger spice shortcake; into the spicy ginger cakes of North Carolina or the whipped-cream–crowned Alabama hot ginger loaf. Coriander seeds eventually made their way into everything, from New England oyster pies and the first Pennsylvania Dutch sausages to the various meat and chile dishes of the Southwest's Zuni Indians. Planted by early colonists before 1670, the seeds have an unusual and multidimensional flavor: lemon, caraway, sage, cumin, or all of the above. But their popularity may also have been partly economic, since they were once the most inexpensive of almost all spices. In 1771, coriander seeds were advertised in the *Boston Evening Post,* and coriander plantations were being established in this country. Kentucky is today's largest domestic supplier. Even so, the United States imports millions of tons of seeds annually, and the number keeps rising each year.

The high demand for coriander seed comes from many quarters: California's Armenian and Russian communities, who use the creamy brown seeds in eggplant caviars, lamb and coriander stews, kidney bean salads, and garlicky lentil soups; Italian Americans who like it in *mortadella* sausage and polenta; Danish pastry shops; and restaurants and spice houses, where it is included in chutneys, curries, *garam masala,* in anything à la Grecque, and in *taklia,* a Middle Eastern blend of garlic, salt, and seeds which is a delicious seasoning for ground lamb and beef. Coriander goes well with cooked fruits, rice puddings, creamy cheeses, and pickles. One impromptu recipe calls for a single seed, toasted and placed in a cup of steaming hot coffee.

SIGNATURE DISH: PICKLING SPICES

Always included in the mix of spices used for pickling, coriander is also a mainstay in anything à la Grecque, in sausages, and in most people's favorite interpretation of gingerbread.

The oil distilled from the seed is used in many cakes, breads, and confections. Toasted ground seeds, which make a magnificent last-minute sprinkle on pea soup, are sometimes mixed into cocoa powder. In fact, there seems no end to coriander's versatility. In *Early American Gardens* (1970), Ann Leighton describes dried coriander seeds as "convenient to sundry purposes" such as aiding digestion, preventing gout, and taking away "sounds in the ears."

Finally, it should be admitted that coriander seeds are not seeds at all but the dried spherical fruit of the plant *Coriandrum sativum*. A light toasting enhances their flavor and makes them easier to grind. They keep longer than any other seed—over two years or more—but once ground they should be used within a few months.

VINTAGE RECIPE

This recipe is from Amelia Simmons's *American Cookery* (Hartford: Hudson & Goodwin, 1796).

Loaf Cakes

Rub 6 pound of sugar, 2 pound of lard, 3 pound of butter into 12 pound of flour, add 18 eggs, 1 quart of milk, 2 ounces of cinnamon, 2 small nutmegs, a tea cup of coriander seed, each pounded fine and sifted, add one pint of brandy, half a pint of wine, 6 pound of stoned raisins, 1 pint of emptins, first having dried your flour in the oven, dry and roll the sugar fine, rub your shortning and sugar half an hour, it will render the cake much whiter and lighter, heat the oven with dry wood, for 1 and a half hours, if large pans be used, it will then require 2 hours baking, and in proportion for smaller loaves. To frost it. Whip 6 whites, during the baking, add 3 pound of sifted loaf sugar and put on thick, as it comes hot from the oven. Some return the frosted loaf into the oven, it injures and yellows it, if the frosting be put on immediately it does best without being returned into the oven.

Consumer Guide

Also known as: Indian—dhania; Burmese—nannamzee; Thai—mellet pak chee; Spanish—cilantro.

LATIN: *Coriandrum sativum*

Selection: Look for round, pale yellow seeds. They are found on all supermarket spice shelves.

Storage: Coriander seed may be purchased in whole-seed form or ground. The whole seeds keep their intense flavor much longer than the ground variety. In its whole form, coriander seed may be stored on a pantry shelf for up to 2 years. The ground spice should be used within 2 months.

Compatible herbs and spices: Cumin, nutmeg, cinnamon, mint, parsley, fresh coriander.

RECIPE LIST

Sorrel and Sweet Pea Soup
Open-faced Sandwich with Coriandered Eggplant and Cheese
Green Beans à la Grecque
Purple Pasta and Green Peppers
Coriander Cornbread Shells
Fresh Peach Gratin

Sorrel and Sweet Pea Soup

2 tablespoons (1/4 stick) butter
1/2 mild onion, chopped
2 cups chopped sorrel
3 cups Chicken Stock (page 352)
1 1/2 pounds fresh peas, shelled, or 2 10-ounce packages frozen
1 teaspoon ground coriander
1/2 cup plain yogurt or dairy sour cream
Salt and pepper

In a medium saucepan, heat butter. Sauté onion and sorrel about 5 minutes, or until mixture liquifies. Add stock and bring to a boil. Add peas and coriander, partially cover, and simmer 10 minutes. Puree mixture in a blender or food processor, then stir in yogurt. Taste for salt and pepper. Delicious served hot, cold, or at room temperature.

Serves 4

Open-faced Sandwich with Coriandered Eggplant and Cheese

1/4 cup olive oil
1 small eggplant (about 1 pound), coarsely chopped
1 small onion, chopped
1 tomato, seeded and chopped
2 teaspoons ground coriander
1 teaspoon ground cumin
1/2 teaspoon salt
1/2 teaspoon freshly ground pepper
1 tablespoon lemon juice
1/4 cup chopped parsley
8 slices baguette (about 4 inches diameter and 1 inch thick), lightly toasted
1 clove garlic, cut in half
8 slices Monterey Jack cheese or other mild cheese

In a large skillet, heat oil. Sauté eggplant, onion, and tomato over medium heat for about 6 minutes, or until eggplant is tender. Stir in coriander, cumin, salt, pepper, lemon juice, and parsley. Cook another 3 minutes.

Preheat broiler. Rub toasted bread slices with cut side of garlic. Spread eggplant mixture on bread and top each with a cheese slice. Place under broiler just until cheese begins to melt. Serve with knife and fork.

Yield: 8 sandwiches

Green Beans à la Grecque

5 cups water
2 pounds young green beans, topped and tailed
2 cups Chicken Stock (page 352)
1 tablespoon salt
½ cup white wine vinegar
¼ cup dry white wine
1 tablespoon coriander seed
1 bay leaf
1 teaspoon black peppercorns
2 cloves garlic, halved
½ teaspoon dried thyme
½ teaspoon sugar

In a large pot, bring water to a boil. Add beans and cook in gently boiling water for 3 minutes. Drain. Place stock and remaining ingredients in a noncorrosive cooking pot. Bring to a boil, add beans, and cook another 5 minutes. Allow beans to cool in cooking liquid, then place in jar. Pour liquid over them and refrigerate at least 24 hours before serving, shaking jar every so often. This will keep several weeks refrigerated.

Yield: about 1 quart

Purple Pasta and Green Peppers

2 green bell peppers, seeded and cut into eighths
2 cloves garlic
1 cup olive oil
¼ cup white-wine vinegar
1 tablespoon coriander seed
2 beets, scrubbed
1 cup melon seed pasta (also called orzo)
½ cup grated Parmesan cheese
Salt and pepper

In a small saucepan, place peppers, garlic, oil, vinegar, and coriander seed. Cook over low heat for 15 minutes. Remove and reserve. In a medium saucepan, cover beets with water and cook 10 to 15 minutes, or until beets can be pierced easily with a fork. With a slotted spoon remove beets and let cool a few minutes. Peel and cut into bite-size cubes.

In the same cooking water, cook pasta about 8 minutes, or until tender. Drain. Remove peppers from oil mixture with slotted spoon, reserving liquid, and place in serving bowl with beets, pasta, cheese, and salt and pepper to taste. Toss well to combine, and drizzle with reserved oil mixture. Delicious hot or at room temperature.

Serves 6

Coriander Cornbread Shells

1/4 cup yellow cornmeal
1/4 cup all-purpose flour
1/2 teaspoon baking powder
1/2 teaspoon baking soda
1/2 teaspoon ground coriander
1 teaspoon sugar
1/2 teaspoon salt
1 teaspoon grated lemon zest (page 363)
1 egg, lightly beaten
1/3 cup dairy sour cream or plain yogurt

Preheat oven to 450 degrees. Grease 12 madeleine molds.

In a large bowl, combine dry ingredients. Add zest and stir in egg and sour cream until well blended. Fill prepared molds two-thirds full. Bake for 12 to 15 minutes, or until golden. Allow to cool about 5 minutes before turning out.

Serves 6–8

Note: This batter may also be baked in a 9-inch square pan and cut into squares when cool.

Fresh Peach Gratin

3 tablespoons butter
6 large freestone peaches, cleaned and sliced into eighths
1 tablespoon lemon juice
¼ teaspoon ground cinnamon
1 tablespoon sugar
1 teaspoon ground coriander
1 cup dairy sour cream
1 cup dark-brown sugar

Preheat broiler to hottest setting. In a large skillet, melt butter. Add peaches and toss with lemon juice, cinnamon, sugar, and ½ teaspoon coriander. Sauté over medium heat for about 5 minutes.

Place peach mixture into a 9-inch round ovenproof dish (a porcelain quiche dish is perfect). Spread with sour cream. Sift brown sugar and remaining coriander over cream in an even layer. Place about 5 inches from heat and cook just until sugar melts, turning dish around if necessary.

Serves 6

Cumin

LORE AND LINEAGE

Cumin can be confusing. In appearance and taste, the oval, slightly bitter seeds closely resemble caraway and can be used in much the same way. Once toasted and ground, however, cumin develops its own alluring qualities. Its strong influence in the cooking of New Mexico, Arizona, and California can be traced to its presence in Mexican dishes, many of which contain cumin, or *comino,* in abundance. Cumin has become the spice sweetheart of many of today's eclectic-minded chefs, especially those who dabble in "new" ethnic cuisines. They are attracted by its versatility: cumin abounds in curry blends, chutneys, *garam masala;* it flavors East Indian cucumber *raitas,* Moroccan carrot salads, lentil and legume dishes like the Lebanese, fava-based *ful moudammes.* It permeates the rich flavorings of Greek *soutzoukakia* sausage and the Peruvian marinade for *anticuchos,* or beef heart.

Ground cumin seems natural enough in chili con carnes and other savory Tex-Mex dishes. But the crunchy little crescents are also found in hearty Texas breads and sugar cookies, the legacy of German families who settled in the Lone Star State, bringing their cumin traditions along with them. These include cumin-scented pickled vegetables, cheeses, and of course sauerkraut, often laced with fennel and juniper berries. The German Texans introduced cumin to barbecued javelina (a hundred-pound-plus beast feast), to Texas *cabrito con salsa* (roasted goat seasoned with cumin and marjoram), and to their distinctive Pedernales style "hoppin' John." Another regional favorite, fricassée of armadillo, is probably destined to remain a regional favorite, cumin or no cumin.

SIGNATURE DISH: CURRY

Cumin is ubiquitous in curry mixes which were once less welcome on our shores than they are today. The following description is from an 1867 American cookbook, *The Handbook of Practical Cookery, for Ladies and Professional Cooks: Containing the Whole science and art of preparing human food,* by Pierre Blot, founder of the New York Cooking Academy and Professor of Gastronomy (New York: D. Appleton and Company, 1867).

CURRY

We think that curry is very good and necessary on the borders of the Ganges River, and for that very reason we think also that it ought to be eschewed on the borders of the Hudson, Delaware, Ohio, and thereabouts.

We cannot describe curry better than by giving here the answer (*verbatim et literarim)* of a gentleman who has lived a few years in Java, to a question on the properties and qualities of curry. He said that he thought it good and even necessary to use some there on account of the climate, but every time he had eaten it he thought he was swallowing boiling alcohol or live coals.

In Florida, strong Hispanic influences continue in such specialties as cumin-fragrant pigeon pea stew, rich with tomatoes, onion, and garlic; avocado–chick-pea salad, with cumin vinaigrette; and *bolichi,* a sausage stuffed eye-of-round, redolent of lime and cumin.

Ironically, one of the earliest New World references to cumin comes from much farther north. In 1653, Adriaen van der Donck noted in *A Description of the New Netherlands* that "cummin seed . . . and the like succeed well but are not sought after." Nevertheless, one Dutch specialty, a cumin-flavored Edam cheese, remains popular today.

A member of the parsley family, cumin (*Cuminum cyminum*) is also valued for its oil, which is used as a stimulant. Also for "medicinal purposes" (as grandmother used to say) are two cumin-laced liqueurs: kümmel and crème de menthe.

Cumin seeds are actually the dried fruits of the plant. Asian white cumin seed can be substituted for the more common yellow-brown. Black cumin seeds, from a separate species entirely, are more peppery, aromatic, and complex. They mingle well with each other and with a diversity of herbs and spices.

VINTAGE RECIPE

This recipe is adapted from *The Pedernales Country Cookbook* by Lillian Fehrenbach (New York: Macmillan, 1968), page 23.

Barbecued Javelina

1 12-pound javelina, preferably female (see Note)

MARINADE

1 cup vinegar
2 tablespoons salt
½ gallon water

REMAINING INGREDIENTS

1 teaspoon salt
1 teaspoon fresh pepper
1 teaspoon oregano
1 large can tomato juice
2 tablespoons minced garlic
Juice and grated zest of 1 lemon
½ cup (1 stick) margarine
2 tablespoons Worcestershire sauce
1 tablespoon Tabasco
2 tablespoons mild mustard
½ teaspoon ground cumin
3 tablespoons cider vinegar
Salt and pepper to taste

Mix marinade ingredients and let javelina marinate for 1 hour. Remove, reserving marinade, and rub generously with salt, pepper, and oregano. In medium saucepan, combine remaining ingredients, bring to a boil, and simmer 20 minutes. Cook javelina on covered barbecue grill for 4 or 5 hours, basting often with reserved marinade.

Note: Also known as the peccary, the javelina (Spanish for "javelin") is a wild pig which is a favorite game animal in Texas. For culinary purposes, the boars are considered a bit strong, but the mama javelinas are just right, especially when feeding a large, adventurous crowd.

Consumer Guide

Also known as: Arabic—kammūn; Chinese—ma-ch'in; Dutch—komijn; French—cumin; German—Kreuzkümmel; Italian—cumino; Spanish—comino.

LATIN: *Cuminum cyminum*

Selection and storage: Cumin seed resembles caraway seed, but is lighter in color. Both whole and ground cumin seed are available in tins or jars on all supermarket spice shelves. Keeps well, tightly sealed, for about 3 months.

Whole vs. ground: For optimum flavor use freshly ground cumin. Toasting the seed before grinding enhances the flavor even more.

Compatible herbs and spices: Coriander, parsley, mint.

RECIPE LIST

Carrot and Split Pea Soup with Toasted Cumin and Coriander
Corn and Cumin Soup with Red Pepper
Spicy Lamb and Red Pepper Pizza
Eggplant in Cumin-scented Tomato Sauce
Chicken and Lentil Chili
Orange–Cumin Biscuits
Cumin Cornmeal Scones
Three-Pea Salad with Cumin Vinaigrette

Carrot and Split Pea Soup with Toasted Cumin and Coriander

3 tablespoons vegetable oil
1 small onion, chopped
1 clove garlic, minced
2 celery stalks and leaves, chopped
2 teaspoons cumin seed, toasted (page 360) and ground
1 pound carrots, cleaned and sliced 1/8 inch thick
6 cups Chicken or Beef Stock (pages 352, 353)
1 cup green split peas
Salt and pepper
1/2 cup chopped fresh coriander

In a large saucepan, heat oil. Sauté onion, garlic, and celery about 5 minutes, or until wilted. Add cumin and carrots and cook about 2 minutes. Add stock, bring to a boil, and add split peas. Simmer, partially covered, for about 45 minutes, or until peas are very tender. In a food processor or blender, puree about 2 cups of soup mixture, leaving about half the vegetables in the pot. Return puree to pot, taste for salt and pepper, and stir in coriander.

Serves 6

Note: If soup has thickened too much during cooking, add stock or water.

Corn and Cumin Soup with Red Pepper

2 tablespoons (1/4 stick) butter
1 small onion, chopped
1 tablespoon cumin seed, toasted (page 360) and ground
2 cups Chicken Stock (page 352)
2 10-ounce packages frozen corn kernels
1/2 teaspoon dried oregano
2 cups milk
Salt and pepper
1 red bell pepper, seeded and cut into very small dice

In a large saucepan, heat butter. Sauté onion with cumin until onion is tender (about 5 minutes). Add stock and bring to a boil. Add corn and oregano and simmer, partially covered, for 15 minutes. Puree with milk in blender or food processor, taste for salt and pepper, and reheat gently with red pepper.

Serves 6

Spicy Lamb and Red Pepper Pizza

2 tablespoons olive oil
2 cloves garlic, minced
1 jalapeño pepper, seeded and minced (page 361)
1 small onion, chopped
1 pound ground lamb
2 teaspoons cumin seed, toasted (page 360) and ground
2 tablespoons tomato paste
¼ cup dry red wine
¼ cup chopped parsley
¼ cup chopped fresh coriander
¼ cup whole-milk ricotta cheese
Salt and pepper
1 large red bell pepper, seeded and cut into strips
Cornmeal for dusting
1 recipe Spiced Pizza Dough (page 355)
Olive oil
4 ounces Havarti cheese, grated

In a medium skillet, heat oil. Sauté garlic, jalapeño, onion, and lamb about 5 minutes, or until lamb loses its pink color. Add cumin, tomato paste, wine, parsley, and coriander. Cook, stirring, for another 3 minutes. Remove to bowl. Stir in ricotta and salt and pepper to taste. Cool.

In same skillet, sauté red pepper about 3 minutes, until slightly wilted. Remove and reserve. Sprinkle a 13- to 15-inch pizza pan with cornmeal. Roll out dough to fit pan and brush edges with olive oil. Place pepper strips around edge, forming a ring. Fill in center with lamb mixture. Sprinkle cheese on top. Bake for 12 to 15 minutes, or until cheese is completely melted.

Serves 6

Eggplant in Cumin-scented Tomato Sauce

¼ cup olive oil
1 large eggplant, cut into 1-inch cubes
Flour for dredging
1 large onion, chopped
1 clove garlic, minced
1 tablespoon cumin seed, toasted (page 360) and ground
½ teaspoon ground coriander
3 large tomatoes, seeded and chopped
½ cup plain yogurt
¼ cup chopped parsley
Salt and pepper

In a large skillet, heat oil. Dredge eggplant in flour and lightly brown on all sides. Remove and reserve. Add onion, garlic, cumin, and coriander to same pan. Cook about 5 minutes, until onion is soft. Add tomatoes and simmer about 10 minutes. Return eggplant to pan and cook, covered, for about 10 minutes or until tender. Stir in yogurt and parsley. Taste for salt and pepper. Delicious hot or at room temperature as an accompaniment to grilled fish or chicken.

Serves 6

Chicken and Lentil Chili

1/4 cup oil
2 pounds skinned and boned chicken breasts, cut into strips
1 large onion, chopped
1–2 jalapeño peppers, seeded and chopped (page 361)
1 clove garlic, minced
2 tablespoons cumin seed, toasted (page 360) and ground
1/2 teaspoon dried oregano
1 28-ounce can imported Italian tomatoes, drained and coarsely chopped
1/2 cup Chicken Stock (page 352)
1 cup lentils
Salt and pepper
1/4 cup chopped fresh coriander
1/4 cup chopped mint

In a large saucepan or stockpot, heat oil. Briefly sauté chicken just until it loses its pink color and turns opaque. Remove and reserve. In same pot, add onion, peppers, garlic, cumin, and oregano. Cook about 10 minutes, until soft. Add tomatoes and stock and bring to a boil. Add lentils, cover, and simmer about 30 minutes, or until lentils are barely tender.

Add chicken to pot and cook, uncovered, for another 10 minutes. Taste for salt and pepper. Sprinkle with coriander and mint just before serving. May be served alongside of or over buttered rice.

Serves 8

Orange–Cumin Biscuits

2 cups all-purpose flour
1 tablespoon sugar
2 tablespoons cumin seed, toasted (page 360)
1 tablespoon grated orange zest (page 363)
1 tablespoon baking powder
1 teaspoon baking soda
Pinch of salt
½ cup (1 stick) cold butter, cut into pieces
½ cup buttermilk
2 tablespoons heavy cream

Preheat oven to 450 degrees; grease a baking sheet.

In a large bowl, combine flour, sugar, cumin, zest, baking powder, baking soda, and salt. Cut in butter until mixture is crumbly. Add buttermilk and stir until mixture comes together to form a dough.

On a floured surface, knead 1 minute. Roll out dough to ½-inch thickness, then cut biscuits with a 2-inch round cutter. Reroll scraps gently and cut again. Place on baking sheet and brush tops with cream. Bake for 12 to 15 minutes, or until golden.

Yield: 1 dozen

Cumin Cornmeal Scones

1½ cups all-purpose flour
½ cup yellow cornmeal
2 teaspoons baking powder
2 tablespoons sugar
2 teaspoons ground cumin, plus 2 tablespoons cumin seed
½ teaspoon salt
¼ cup (½ stick) cold butter, cut into pieces
½ cup heavy cream, plus 2 tablespoons for glaze
1 egg, lightly beaten

Preheat oven to 450 degrees. In a large bowl, combine flour, cornmeal, baking powder, sugar, ground cumin, and salt. Cut in butter until mixture is crumbly. Stir in ½ cup cream and egg until mixture holds together. Turn dough out onto a lightly floured surface and knead gently about 10 times. Roll out to ½-inch thickness and cut with a 3-inch round cutter. Place on ungreased baking sheet. Brush each scone with remaining cream and sprinkle with a few cumin seeds. Bake about 12 minutes, or until tops are golden.

Yield: about 1 dozen

Three-Pea Salad with Cumin Vinaigrette

2 cups cooked chick-peas
2 cups cooked green peas
1 cup snow peas, blanched (page 361)
1 large tomato, peeled, seeded, and coarsely chopped
1 clove garlic, minced
1 teaspoon cumin seed, toasted (page 360) and ground
1 teaspoon honey
1 teaspoon mild mustard
3 tablespoons lemon juice
½ cup olive oil
¼ cup chopped fresh coriander (optional)

In a large salad bowl, combine chick-peas, green peas, snow peas, and tomato. In a food processor, combine remaining ingredients except coriander. Pour over pea mixture and toss well to combine. Garnish with coriander if desired.

Serves 6

Ginger

LORE AND LINEAGE

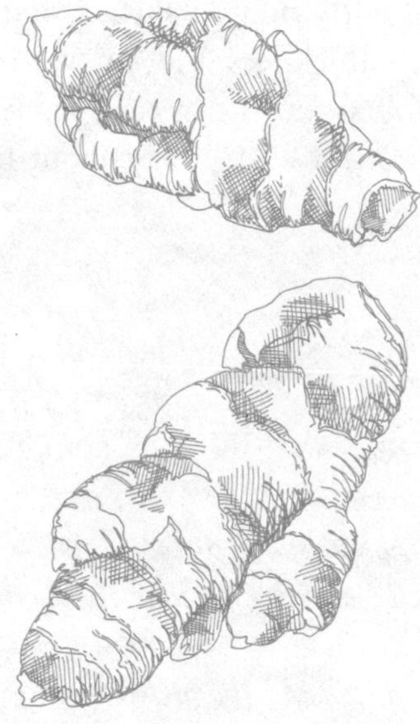

Bevridge. As one early American cookery book defined it, the word ***bevridge*** meant a drink made of ginger and spring water, sweetened with molasses. One such beverage, haymakers' switchel (page 266), became a staple in the hayfields of Vermont, where it was kept in a stoneware jug submerged in cool well water. When farmers had their "nooning," or midday meal, switchel was what they washed it down with. People enjoyed it for its refreshing ginger taste, or so they said; but most haymakers enhanced their switchel with a healthy dash of hard cider or rum.

Even outside the hayfields, Americans developed a taste for ginger drinks, such as ginger punch, gingerade (a Shaker creation), and ginger beer. In an 1820s recipe for the latter, one cup of ginger was scalded in half a pail of water and then dumped, ever so ceremoniously, into another pail of water, along with a pint of molasses. The popularity of ginger was not impaired by the old saloonkeepers' custom of putting out a bowl of ground ginger which customers could sprinkle into their ale. Today's gingerale is probably the nonalcoholic descendent of this concoction.

Ginger was always a kitchen staple in this country, with the obvious and well-appreciated results. Already by 1711, according to one historian, the wealthy Virginia planter William Byrd was eating "gingerbread all day long" in Virginia. In New England, Muster Day gingerbread signaled the coming of summer. It was baked on the first Tuesday in June, a day that started with military training for men and turned into a picinic for all by evening. As Sheila Hibben (*A Kitchen Manual,* 1941) puts it: "New England housewives have a way with ginger that surpasses anything ever produced in Dijon or anywhere else." Everywhere, at Christmas there were gingerbread men. *Miss Parloa's New Cook Book* (1880) included four gingerbread recipes: soft, hard, Canadian, and fairy. Thirty years later, Fannie Farmer reinforced the American identity by calling her gingerbreads "Cambridge" and "New York." And gingerbread even entered the literary realm in the form of the American Minnehaha cake at Hiawatha's wedding, immortalized by Longfellow.

SIGNATURE DISH: GINGERBREAD

However you make it, you may want to serve gingerbread according to the following suggestions from the cookbook *Suppers: Novel Suggestions for Social Occasions,* compiled by Paul Pierce (New York: Barse & Hopkins, 1907).

A QUILTING SUPPER

Build a little log cabin of twigs for the center of the supper table and arrange stick candy, bread sticks, celery, cheesesticks and other viands, log-cabin style, on pretty plates. Light the table by candles in old fashioned candlesticks. Serve a hot course, oyster patties, sandwiches, potato salad, hot gingerbread, apple sauce, tea and coffee.

Another ginger-spiked dish, Indian pudding, was popular partly because if it were left in a warm oven, it would cook, unattended, overnight. Made with cornmeal (or "Indian" meal), it was sweetened with molasses or maple syrup, according to the region, and was useful for any meal or course, from breakfast to dessert; it was sometimes served before the meat course or even instead of the meat course, depending on circumstances. Dutch settlers enjoyed ox tongue in ginger broth, a recipe from one of their early cookbooks.

The taste of ginger wasn't foreign to American Indians, who were well acquainted with North American wild ginger (*Asarum canadense*). They used it to flavor hominy and to disguise the taste of tainted meat, mudfish, and other foods. Similar in taste and aroma to true ginger (*Zingiber officinale*), wild ginger is from an entirely different family of plants.

Early on, Americans discovered an affinity between ginger and pumpkin, a relationship recorded by John Josselyn in his seventeenth-century notes on board ship. He referred to pumpkin as that "ancient New England Standing Dish," especially good when stewed with ginger. In the first American cookbook (1796), Amelia Simmons's pumpkin pie recipe has ginger in both the crust and the filling. She must have liked it inordinately; another of her recipes—for Gingerbread no. 4—calls for no less than one-quarter pound of the spice.

One way or another, ginger seemed destined to become a part of the American kitchen. In the mid 1800s, when Chinese immigrants came to work the gold mines and railroads, they were permitted to bring into California, for their personal use only, two jars of ginger. Those who worked as cooks introduced this, along with other flavorings like fresh coriander, through such "Chinese" approximations as chow mein, egg foo yung, and chop suey (Cantonese for "miscellaneous fragments").

Although ginger is now grown in southern Florida, the only climate in the United States favorable to its cultivation, the best-quality ginger is still from Jamaica. High in vitamin C, it can be delicious in many different forms. When grated, the knobby, brown root brings a fresh taste to cooked carrots, yams, and greens or to dressings for fruit and salads. Ginger juice

—obtained by slicing, peeling, and putting the root in a garlic press—adds a nippy dimension to soups, tomato purees, and peanut sauces. For a special touch, ground dried ginger can be dusted on meats before grilling or stirred into chutneys and relishes. The crystallized root, dried and sugared, makes an unusual addition to salads, ice creams, trifles, and other confections.

Ginger root is available, preserved in syrup, in specialty shops, and from herb dealers. The fresh root, well wrapped, will keep for a week in the refrigerator and for several months if frozen.

Of all recipes, from East Indian curries to German sauerbraten (which uses gingersnaps as a thickener), Fannie Farmer has perhaps the world's most straightforward. In her 1906 ginger sandwiches, she says simply: "Cut preserved Canton ginger in very thin slices. Prepare as other sandwiches."

VINTAGE RECIPE

The following is adapted from an old recipe in *Yankee Hill-Country Cooking* by Beatrice Vaughn (Brattleboro, Vermont: The Stephen Greene Press, 1963), page 197.

Haymakers' Switchel

1 cup light brown sugar
1 cup cider vinegar
3/4 cup dark molasses
1 tablespoon ground ginger
2 quarts cold water

In a large stone jug, combine ingredients and stir well. Place jug in spring water to cool, or use refrigerator. In by-gone days on the farms, the switchel was made from "water pumped from deep in the well and was considered quite cold enough for any man. There are many variations of this drink, some using maple sugar and boiled cider. My grandfather always said that nothing quenched a man's thirst or cooled his dusty throat in haying time so well as this homely drink."

Consumer Guide

Also known as: Chinese—jeung or sang keong; French—gingembre; German—Ingwer; Italian—zenzero; Spanish—jengibre.

LATIN: *Zingiber officinale*

Common varieties: Jamaican ginger is the fresh type most frequently found in supermarkets. It is more pungent than Asian ginger, which can usually be found in Oriental markets. Other forms include candied ginger, preserved ginger, and ground ginger.

Selection: Skin should be smooth and entire root should be firm to the touch.

Storage: Wrap fresh ginger in paper towel and then in plastic; store in refrigerator up to about 10 days. An alternative method is to peel and submerge root in a jar of sherry and store in refrigerator. To freeze root, wrap securly in plastic and place in freezer. Ground ginger should be stored in an air-tight container in a cool, dry, place.

Fresh vs. dried: Except for baked goods, fresh ginger is preferable. If fresh ginger is not available, substitute the candied variety, rinsing off the sugar before using.

Compatible herbs and spices: Fresh coriander, nutmeg, cumin, coriander seed, black pepper, red pepper, chives.

RECIPE LIST

Marinated Fish Crisps
Gingered Tomato Soup with Mint
Sautéed Snapper Sandwich with Ginger Mayonnaise
Ginger Monkfish with Apples and Leeks
Sea Bass in Filo with Ginger and Green Onions
Sauté of Snow Peas and Shiitake Mushrooms
Carrots and Snow Peas with Walnuts in Ginger Cream
Gingered Pear Sorbet
Lemon–Ginger Sponge Cake
Ginger Almond Shortbread

Marinated Fish Crisps

1½ pounds sole filets, cut into ½-inch strips
½ cup all-purpose flour mixed with ¼ teaspoon each salt and pepper
Vegetable oil for frying
1 small red onion, thinly sliced and separated into rings
Lettuce leaves or crackers

MARINADE
½ cup lime juice
2 cloves garlic, minced
1 tablespoon minced fresh ginger
¼ teaspoon sugar
½ teaspoon salt
⅛ teaspoon ground red pepper
2 tablespoons olive oil

In a small bowl, combine marinade ingredients until well blended. Set aside.

Blot fish dry with paper towels. Dredge in flour mixture. In a medium skillet, heat about ½ inch of oil until hot, about 350 degrees. Fry fish strips until golden on both sides (about 2 minutes). Remove and drain on paper towels. Place fish in noncorrosive dish. Put onion rings on top and pour marinade over all. Cover with plastic wrap and refrigerate for at least 12 hours (but not more than 36) before serving. Drain marinade from fish and serve on lettuce cups as first course or with crackers as an hors d'oeuvre.

Serves 6 as a first course or 12 as hors d'oeuvre

Gingered Tomato Soup with Mint

3 tablespoons olive oil
3 leeks (white part only), chopped
1 clove garlic, minced
2 nickel-sized slices fresh or rinsed candied ginger, chopped
4 large, ripe tomatoes, seeded and chopped
1 tablespoon light-brown sugar
1 cup tomato juice
1 cup Chicken Stock (page 352)
Salt and pepper
¼ cup chopped mint

In a medium saucepan, heat oil. Cook leeks, garlic, and ginger about 8 minutes, until soft. Add tomatoes and brown sugar and cook over medium heat for about 5 minutes. Add tomato juice and stock, bring to a boil, and simmer, partially covered, for 15 minutes. Taste for salt and pepper. Put soup through food mill, pressing down on vegetables to extract all their flavor. Or, puree in food processor (texture will not be silky-smooth). Sprinkle with mint. Delicious hot or chilled.

Serves 4

Sautéed Snapper Sandwich with Ginger Mayonnaise

2 snapper filets (4 ounces each)
¼ cup all-purpose flour
½ teaspoon salt
½ teaspoon ground ginger
2 tablespoons vegetable or olive oil
2 rolls or 4 slices bread, lightly toasted
¼ cup chopped green onions
Red leaf lettuce leaves

GINGER MAYONNAISE
1 tablespoon grated fresh ginger
2 tablespoons sherry wine vinegar
1 teaspoon mild mustard
1 egg
1 cup olive oil
Salt and pepper

Make mayonnaise first. In a food processor or blender, place ginger, vinegar, mustard, and egg. Process until combined. With machine running, pour oil in very slowly until mayonnaise is thick. Taste for salt and pepper. Set aside.

Blot fish dry with paper towels. On a flat plate, combine flour, salt, and ginger. Dredge fish in this mixture. In a medium skillet, heat oil. Sauté fish for 4 minutes on each side. Remove to paper towels. Spread rolls or bread with mayonnaise, top with fish filet, sprinkle with green onions, add lettuce, and serve.

Yield: 2 sandwiches

Ginger Monkfish with Apples and Leeks

1 pound monkfish filets, sliced ½ inch thick
½ cup all-purpose flour mixed with ½ teaspoon ground ginger
6 tablespoons (¾ stick) butter
1 tablespoon minced fresh ginger
2 leeks (white part only), thinly sliced
1 large Red Delicious apple, cored, quartered, and thinly sliced
¼ cup dry white wine
¼ cup Chicken or Fish Stock (pages 352, 353)
Salt and pepper
3 tablespoons chopped parsley

Blot fish dry with paper towels. Lightly dredge slices in flour mixture. In a large skillet, heat 3 tablespoons butter. Sauté fish over medium-high heat for about 2 minutes on each side. Remove and set aside. Add remaining 3 tablespoons butter to skillet and heat. Sauté ginger, leeks, and apple for about 2 minutes. Add wine and stock; bring to a boil while stirring and scraping bottom of pan. Simmer, covered, for 5 minutes. Return fish to skillet and cook, uncovered, for 3 minutes. Taste for salt and pepper. Sprinkle with chopped parsley.

Serves 4

Sea Bass in Filo wth Ginger and Green Onions

4 sea bass filets (about 6 ounces each), halved
Salt and pepper
Flour for dusting
4 teaspoons hot mustard
2 teaspoons soy sauce
1 teaspoon dry sherry
8 sheets filo dough
6 tablespoons (¾ stick) melted butter
4 green onions, julienned (page 362)
2 tablespoons julienned fresh ginger (page 362)

Preheat oven to 400 degrees. Grease a baking sheet.

Blot sea bass dry with paper towels. Sprinkle both sides with salt, pepper, and flour. Combine mustard, soy sauce, and sherry and spread on both sides of fish.

Place a sheet of filo on a clean surface. Spread lightly with butter. Fold in half like a book and brush with butter again. Place fish in center; sprinkle with one-fourth of the green onions and ginger. Fold top and bottom edges of dough over fish, brush lightly with butter, then fold left and right sides of dough over fish, creating a package. Brush with butter, place seam side down on baking sheet, and brush top with butter. Continue with remaining fish and filo dough in same manner. Bake for 12 minutes, or until golden brown.

Serves 4 as a main course or 8 as a first course

Sauté of Snow Peas and Shiitake Mushrooms

2 tablespoons (1/4 stick) butter
2 tablespoons vegetable or peanut oil
1 clove garlic, minced
2 teaspoons minced fresh ginger
1/2 pound fresh shiitake mushrooms, stemmed and caps sliced
1/4 cup Chicken Stock (page 352)
1 tablespoon soy sauce
1 tablespoon dry sherry
1/2 pound snow peas, strings removed
Salt and pepper
1/4 cup toasted pine nuts (page 360)
2 green onions, sliced into rings

In a large skillet, heat butter and oil. Sauté garlic, ginger, and mushrooms for 5 minutes, or until mushrooms become soft. Add stock, soy sauce, and sherry. Bring to a boil and add snow peas. Simmer, covered, for 1 minute. Uncover and cook about 1 minute, or until some of the liquid evaporates.

Taste for salt and pepper. Sprinkle with pine nuts and green onions and serve.

Serves 4

Carrots and Snow Peas with Walnuts in Ginger Cream

1 cup heavy cream
2 nickel-sized slices fresh ginger
¼ cup (½ stick) butter
1 cup walnut pieces
4 large carrots, peeled, sliced ¼ inch thick, and blanched (page 361)
½ pound snow peas, strings removed and blanched (page 361)
Salt and pepper

In a small saucepan, boil cream and ginger until reduced to ½ cup. Discard ginger and set aside cream.

In a large skillet, heat butter. Sauté walnuts about 5 minutes, or until golden. Add carrots and snow peas and sauté over medium heat for about 4 minutes, stirring frequently. Pour cream over vegetables and cook over high heat just until bubbly at edges. Taste for salt and pepper and serve.

Serves 6

Gingered Pear Sorbet

6 ripe Comice pears, peeled, cored, and quartered
1 nickel-sized slice fresh ginger
1 lemon
½ cup sugar, approximately
½ teaspoon ground ginger

Place pears, fresh ginger, and juice of half a lemon in a large saucepan with enough water to cover. Bring to a boil and cook for 2 minutes. Allow pears to cool in water. Place cooled pears, juice of other half of lemon, sugar, and ground ginger in a blender or food processor and puree. Pour into ice-cream maker and freeze according to manufacturer's directions.

Serves 6

Lemon–Ginger Sponge Cake

8 eggs, separated
1 cup sugar
2 tablespoons lemon juice
Grated zest of ½ lemon (page 363)
¾ cup all-purpose flour
Pinch of salt
1 teaspoon baking powder
½ teaspoon ground ginger

Preheat oven to 375 degrees. Grease and flour a 9-inch tube pan.

In a large bowl, beat yolks with half the sugar about 5 minutes, or until thick and pale. Stir in lemon juice and zest. In a medium bowl, beat egg whites until thick and foamy. Gradually add remaining sugar and beat until stiff and shiny. Combine flour, salt, baking powder, and ginger and add to yolks. Place whites over yolk mixture and fold gently until blended. Bake for 50 minutes, or until top springs back when pressed. Cool upside down on a cake rack for at least 30 minutes. To remove cake from pan, run a sharp knife along edge and release. Delicious with your favorite ice cream or all by itself.

Serves 12

Ginger Almond Shortbread

1 cup (2 sticks) butter, room temperature
⅔ cup sifted confectioner's sugar
1 teaspoon almond extract
1¾ cups all-purpose flour
2 teaspoons ground ginger
¼ cup finely ground almonds
24 whole almonds

Preheat oven to 350 degrees. In a large mixing bowl, cream butter with sugar and almond extract until smooth. Add flour, ginger, and ground almonds and beat until mixture is well combined. On a floured surface, roll out dough to ½-inch thickness. Cut into 2-inch rounds and place 1 inch apart on an ungreased baking sheet. Press an almond into the center of each cookie and bake about 20 minutes, or until very lightly colored. Remove to rack and cool.

Yield: about 2 dozen

Mustard

LORE AND LINEAGE

The Chinese . . . transformed the mustard weeds which grew wild throughout the Monterey Bay region into agricultural gold.

—SANDY LYDON
Chinese Gold: The Chinese in the Monterey Bay Region, 1985

The story of mustard in America is reminiscent of the tale of Johnny Appleseed, but with exactly the opposite intention. To the California farmers of the Monterey area, about a hundred years ago mustard was nothing but a pest. So when a man named Jim Jack came along offering to get rid of the bothersome plants in exchange for the seeds, he was hired by one and all. He contracted with a number of fellow Chinese, harvested and sold some of the seed, and stored the rest. Shortly thereafter, mustard crops everywhere failed, resulting in a worldwide demand for Jack's seeds. The magnitude of his profits motivated farmers of the Monterey region to cultivate mustard, using Chinese farm labor for the harvest. Although that area no longer produces a commercial crop, California remains the largest mustard-growing state. Current U.S. production amounts to about 73 million pounds of seed a year. And in California's honey-productive Lompoc Valley, fields of flowering mustard have a special purpose: to attract bees.

Called the "spice of nations," mustard appears in every culinary tradition. American Indians dried its seeds to use as flavoring and ate the tender raw shoots and lavender flowers of pink mustard. Later, the Franciscan padres planted mustard seeds to link the missions they were establishing along the California coast. In their wake they left long, golden "mustard trails."

On the Eastern Seaboard, meanwhile, the arrival of mustard in 1735 was advertised in the *South Carolina Gazette*: "Just imported from London by John Watson . . . mustard seed." Mustard was probably the most commonly used condiment, its presence assumed, even when not specified. The most primordial Boston baked beans depended on mustard, and its aroma filled the streets in the days when families brought their beans to the village bakery to have them slow-cooked all night in the great, hot ovens. Throughout New England, corned beef and cabbage was served with mustard or mustard pickles. It was popular even before the 1840s Irish immigration, when the *de rigueur* potato was added to the pot. Kennebunk pickle, another New England dish, combined tomatoes, cabbage, peppers, and celery preserved in cloves, cinnamon, sugar, vinegar, and mustard. Sausage recipes often ended with strict instructions like "theyr sauce is mustard." The Pennsylvania German sausages, especially blander types like *Weisswurst,* were accompanied by hot German mustards.

SIGNATURE DISH: BOSTON BAKED BEANS

No matter what the recipe, the real clue to this old favorite's popularity lies in its appeal to the American sweet tooth, from its maple syrup, brown sugar, molasses, shaved maple sugar, or all four ingredients. Everything else is negotiable, including the type of bean, which might be anything from New England soldier beans and Swedish brown beans to Southwestern Hopi beans.

Norwegian immigrants of the nineteenth century settled in towns like Grand Forks, North Dakota, and Decorah, Iowa, bringing their *lefse* flat bread and lye-cured cod dish called *lutefisk,* "whose failure to enter into the general American cuisine," according to Waverley Root in *Eating in America* (1976), "is easily understandable." In any case, they served it with mustard sauce, possibly for the same reason that there was always a big mustard pot in the western stagecoach stations of the 1860s. Although the food was often less than appetizing, all complaints were countered with the suggestion, "Well, then, help yourself to the mustard." Mustard was a big help also in the Pacific Northwest, where it spiced the regional meatballs made from elk meat. And in Texas, both mustard and paprika are used in a dish that seems to have something for everybody: argyle ham with baked bananas.

Mustard can be confusing, especially when you consider that French's mustard is based on the old English Colman mustard but is actually American, with headquarters in Rochester, New York (on Mustard Street, to be exact). Mustard comes in three forms. Powdered dry mustard, also called ground mustard or mustard flour, refers to the hot English type or the Chinese *gai lat.* The powder can be added directly to the cooking pot, but should be done with an eye on the clock because water or liquid releases the volatile oils within ten or fifteen minutes of mixing. After about an hour, however, the oils evaporate along with all their desirable piquancy. Prepared mustard, or mustard paste, is a mix of seed, salt, vinegar, or some other liquid and often some additional spices. This type includes everything from Dijon-type mustard to hot dog mustard, a bland concoction tinted with turmeric or vegetable coloring. Last, there is mustard seed, which comes in three colors: Black (*Brassica nigra*), the preferred choice for East Indian dishes, is the most potent and most expensive because it must be hand harvested; Brown (*B. juncea*) is slightly less pungent and often substituted for Black; and White (*Sinapis alba*) is sometimes called Yellow Mustard and often is mixed with starch and coloring.

Mustard oil is pressed from the seed and used as an odorless cooking medium in India and many Third World countries. In comparison with other warming spices, mustard is the all-time champion. Chile pepper affects the back of the throat, and black pepper affects the top of the tongue. But mustard causes sensations throughout the whole mouth.

VINTAGE RECIPE

This recipe is excerpted from *The Army Cook,* a technical manual (April 24, 1942), p. 185.

126. Sauce, barbecue

1 gallon catsup
1 gallon vinegar
2 to 3 cups dry mustard
2 tablespoons red pepper
3 tablespoons black pepper
¾ cup chili powder
2 medium size pieces garlic
½ cup salt

Bring to boil and let boil 2 hours or until it begins to thicken. Mix well and keep it stirred.

Consumer Guide

Also known as: Arabic—khardal; Chinese—chieh; Dutch—mosterd; French—moutarde; German—Serf; Italian—senape; Spanish—mostaza.

LATIN: *Brassica nigra (Black mustard)*
B. juncea (Brown mustard)
Sinapis alba (White mustard)

Common varieties: The 2 most common varieties are white (or yellow) and brown mustard seeds. The former is milder and is found in most domestic prepared mustards. Brown mustard seed is used in Dijon-type mustard and is stronger in flavor. A third, less common variety is black mustard seed, primarily used in Asian and Indian cuisines.

Storage: Whole mustard seed has a long shelf life when kept in a cool, dry place. Ground and prepared mustard loses some of its potency after 3 months.

Compatible herbs and spices: All herbs and spices are compatible with mustard.

RECIPE LIST

Mustard-soaked Ripe Olives
Two Celeries with Mustard
Lamb in Mustard Cream
Salmon in Dill and Dijon Mustard
Asparagus with Mustard Butter

Mustard-soaked Ripe Olives

2 cups water
½ cup white wine vinegar
1 bay leaf
1 tablespoon mustard seed
½ teaspoon salt
½ teaspoon black peppercorns
1 tablespoon sugar
2 16 ounce cans pitted large black olives, drained
2 tablespoons chopped parsley

In a medium saucepan, bring all ingredients except olives and parsley to a boil. Simmer, covered, for 10 minutes. Remove from heat and place olives in mixture. Allow to cool and then transfer to a jar and place in refrigerator for 24 hours. Drain olives and sprinkle with parsley. These will keep, covered, in refrigerator for about 2 weeks.

Yield: 4 cups

Two Celeries with Mustard

¼ cup (½ stick) butter
1 leek (white part only), thinly sliced
6 celery stalks, strings removed and sliced ¼-inch thick
1 small celery root, peeled and cut into ¼-inch sticks
½ cup dry white wine
½ cup Chicken Stock (page 352)
2 tablespoons heavy cream
1 tablespoon strong mustard
Salt and pepper
¼ cup celery leaves

In a large skillet, heat butter. Sauté leek, celery, and celery root about 5 minutes, or until barely tender. Add wine and stock and bring to a boil. Simmer, partially covered, for 5 minutes. Remove cover and stir in cream mixed with mustard. Cook over low heat for another 3 minutes. Taste for salt and pepper and sprinkle with celery leaves.

Serves 6

Lamb in Mustard Cream

1/4 cup (1/2 stick) butter
1 shallot, minced
6 loin lamb chops or steaks (about 8 ounces each)
Flour for dredging
Salt and pepper
1 cup dry white wine
1/2 cup heavy cream
2 tablespoons Dijon-type mustard

In a small skillet, heat 2 tablespoons butter. Sauté shallot about 5 minutes, or until wilted. Set aside.

Blot chops with paper towels. Dredge in flour mixed with salt and pepper. In a large skillet, heat remaining butter. Cook chops over medium-high heat for about 5 minutes on each side, or until golden brown. Remove chops to a large baking dish.

Preheat oven to 400 degrees. Add wine to skillet and cook over medium heat until syrupy (about 5 to 8 minutes). Pour over chops and sprinkle with shallot. Cover with foil and bake about 30 minutes, or until tender. Mix cream with mustard. Pour over chops and bake, uncovered, for about 8 minutes more.

Serves 6

Salmon in Dill and Dijon Mustard

6 salmon steaks (6 to 8 ounces each), about 1-inch thick
Salt and pepper
Flour for dredging
½ cup Dijon mustard
1 egg, lightly beaten
2 teaspoons chopped fresh dill, or ½ teaspoon dried
2 cups dry bread crumbs
6 tablespoons (¾ stick) butter, melted

Preheat oven to 400 degrees. Blot salmon dry with paper towels. Sprinkle with salt and pepper and lightly dredge in flour.

In a small bowl, combine mustard, egg, and dill. Spread mixture on salmon and coat with bread crumbs. Spread 2 tablespoons melted butter in a large baking dish and place salmon in dish. Drizzle remaining butter over salmon and bake for 25 minutes, turning steaks once.

Serves 6

Asparagus with Mustard Butter

6 tablespoons (¾ stick) butter
½ teaspoon salt
½ teaspoon freshly ground black pepper
1 tablespoon strong mustard
1 teaspoon chopped parsley
1 teaspoon chopped chives
1½ cups water
1 pound asparagus, cut diagonally into 2-inch pieces

In a food processor or a blender, combine butter, salt, pepper, mustard, parsley, and chives until smooth. Chill in freezer or refrigerator until fairly firm (1 to 2 hours).

In a medium skillet, bring water to a boil. Add asparagus and cook 3 minutes, or until barely tender. Remove asparagus with a slotted spoon and run under cold water. Bring water in which asparagus cooked to a boil again over high heat and add mustard butter, 2 tablespoons at a time. Sauce will foam and thicken slightly. Pour over asparagus and serve immediately.

Serves 4

Nutmeg and Mace

LORE AND LINEAGE

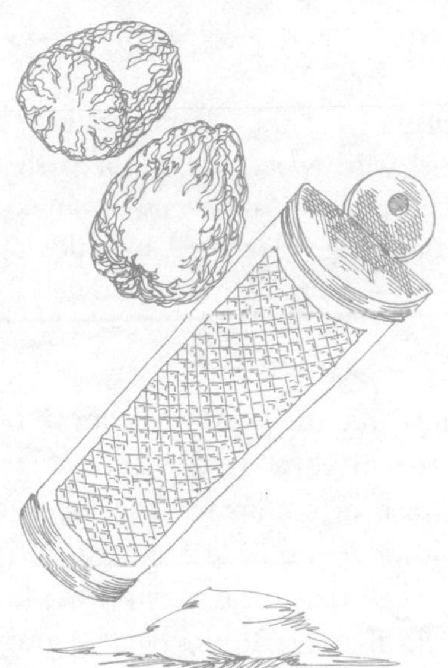

Sack posset was a drink that every bride in colonial New York was supposed to know how to make. Consisting of milk, sugar, Spanish sack, nutmeg, and no less than twenty eggs, the rhythmic recipe was easy to remember:

> Stir them with steady hand and conscience prickin'
> To see the untimely fate of twenty chickens.

Over the years, nutmeg has contributed more than its share of poetry to our culture. Another example comes from the Vieux Carré section of New Orleans. There, on Sunday mornings, vendors of deep-fried, nutmeg-spiced rice cakes (called *calas*) would attract the after-church trade by chanting "*Belle cala, tout chaud.*"

In Concord, Massachusetts, Louisa May Alcott was so fond of steamed pudding with nutmeg sauce that she named her home after it: Apple Slump. And mace—which is the outer covering of nutmeg with a similar though somewhat stronger taste—has also inspired a few ditties:

To make a good chowder and have it quite nice,
Dispense with sweet marjoram, parsley and spice;
Mace, pepper and salt are now wanted alone
To make the stew eat well and stick to the bone . . .

—from Chowder, An Old Recipe, 1834, in Jessup Whitehead, *The Steward's Handbook, 1899*

Nutmeg and mace come from a fruit that resembles a peach. Once opened, the mace is visible as a bright, red-orange lacy coating, called blades, attached to a brown kernel, inside of which is the nutmeg. It takes four hundred pounds of nutmeg kernels to produce a pound of mace. Freshly grated mace and nutmeg are far superior to powdered because the volatile oils disappear quickly after grating. Once grated, both nutmeg and mace should be refrigerated.

SIGNATURE DISH: PUMPKIN PIE

A victim of its own universal popularity, this pie can be made with a can of pumpkin pie mix, a shake of the mysteriously named pumpkin pie spice, and piled into a frozen shell. But it is one American original that truly benefits from the "from scratch" approach, especially freshly grated nutmeg.

Nutmeg was once so prohibitively expensive that it had a certain snob appeal. Nutmeg owners kept the little jewels in silver boxes with a separate compartment for the grater. Counterfeit nutmeg, made of wood, was sold by the proverbial sly Yankee peddler, earning Connecticut the name (Wooden) Nutmeg State. As evidence of its high cost, an early American recipe for fritters concludes, "Excepting for company the nutmeg can be well dispensed with."

Once it became widely available, after the break-up of the Dutch trade monopoly, nutmeg became popular in all types of dishes and for a variety of reasons. According to the *Hartford Courant,* August 18, 1788, Benjamin Franklin's favorite breakfast was a "bowl of porridge sweetened with honey and spiced with nutmeg." Nutmeg was the essential spice of an 1820s fast-food dessert called rennet pudding, which could be whipped up in five minutes, according to one popular recipe, whenever "your husband brings home company when you are unprepared." A nineteenth-century formula for syllabub, which must have aroused attention, concluded with the directions "grate nutmeg into it, milk your cow into the mixture very fast. . . . This is very good for evening entertainments. . . ."

Nutmeg and mace permeated the cookery of all regions. In the Tidewater area of Virginia, traditional English pound cake was literally a pound each of butter, sugar, eggs, and flour flavored with brandy and mace. Also originating in Virginia was tansy pudding, an omelet-type dish seasoned with spinach juice, tansy, and nutmeg. The American doughnut had a direct ancestor in the nutmeg-flavored *oliekoeken,* which the Pilgrims learned to make from the Dutch in Amsterdam *before* they sailed to the New World. The Pennsylvania Germans still make their nutmeg-tasty doughnuts called *fastnachts,* a special for Shrove Tuesday. In Czech communities in Cedar Rapids, Iowa, and in Wilber, Nebraska, the smell of nutmeg and mace fills the air during Christmas week as loaves of the Czech braided holiday bread called *houska* emerge from the ovens.

Nutmeg is the main flavor of gumbo lamb, a Dakota Sunday dinner dish having nothing to do with New Orleans. "Dakota gumbo" refers to the loamy dark soil near the Black Hills, on which graze the sheep that end up in the recipe. Mace was important in an interstate dessert that affected many regions and certainly "traveled" well: the Northern Pacific Railroad's fruit cake. The recipe originated at the Paris International Exposition of 1900, was adapted by two of the railroad's bakers, and became a mainstay among the elaborate offerings in their luxurious dining cars.

Finally, nutmeg and mace are essential to at least three other old American standbys—sausages, bologna, and Worcestershire sauce—and, we hope, to some new American standbys below.

VINTAGE RECIPE

This recipe is from *Modern Domestic Cookery and Useful Receipt Book: Adapted for Families,* by W. A. Henderson (New York: Leavitt & Allen, circa 1875).

Citron Pudding

Take a spoonful of fine flour, two ounces of sugar, a little nutmeg, and half a pint of cream. Mix them well together, with the yolks of three eggs. Put it into tea-cups, and divide among them two ounces of citron cut very thin. Bake them in a pretty quick oven, and turn them out upon a china dish.

Nutmeg: Consumer Guide

Also known as: Arabic—basbāsa; French—muscade; Italian—noce moscata; Swedish—muskot.

LATIN: *Myristica fragrans*

Storage: Ground or grated nutmeg should be stored in the refrigerator to keep aroma fresh. Whole nutmeg can be stored in the pantry.

Whole vs. packaged ground: The difference between freshly grated nutmeg and pre-ground is astonishing. If you use nutmeg even only once a year, we urge you to buy a nutmeg grater; you will become a fresh-nutmeg convert instantly.

Compatible herbs and spices: Cinnamon, cloves, cumin, coriander seed.

Mace: Consumer Guide

Also known as: French—macis; German—Muskatblute; Indian—javatri; Spanish—macia or macis.

LATIN: *Myristica fragrans*

Selection: Mace, the outer covering of nutmeg, is found in ground form on the spice shelf of supermarkets. In blade form it is not widely available.

Storage: Mace is one of the more perishable spices; therefore it is best kept in a tightly sealed jar in the refrigerator.

Compatible herbs and spices: Cinnamon, black and red pepper, parsley, fresh coriander.

RECIPE LIST

Buttermilk French Toast
Calzone with Spinach, Apples, and Ricotta
Mushroom Macaroni Gratin
Cheese Popovers with Nutmeg
Chocolate Cake with Eggnog Custard
Iced Cherry Soup with Mace
Pumpkin Soup with Corn and Green Onions
Ricotta Rice Muffins

NUTMEG

Buttermilk French Toast

$\frac{1}{2}$ cup buttermilk
2 eggs
$\frac{1}{4}$ teaspoon salt
$\frac{1}{4}$ teaspoon grated nutmeg
4 slices egg bread, challah, or French bread, 1 inch thick and crusts removed
2 tablespoons ($\frac{1}{4}$ stick) butter
2 tablespoons vegetable oil
Confectioner's sugar
Syrup or jam

In a small bowl, combine buttermilk, eggs, salt, and nutmeg until well blended. Pour into shallow dish that will hold bread slices in 1 layer. Place bread slices in dish, pushing down slightly on bread to absorb egg mixture, and then turn bread over. Allow to rest at room temperature for 1 to 2 hours.

In a large skillet, heat butter and oil until foamy. Cook bread slices over medium heat for 2 to 3 minutes, or until golden brown on each side. Serve sprinkled with confectioner's sugar and pass the jam or syrup.

Serves 4 for light breakfast or 2 for heartier ones

Calzone with Spinach, Apples, and Ricotta

¼ cup (½ stick) butter
2 cloves garlic, minced
1 large bunch spinach, or 1 10-ounce package frozen, thawed
2 Golden Delicious apples, cored and cut into 1-inch chunks
¼ pound prosciutto, diced
8 ounces whole-milk ricotta cheese
2 ounces Parmesan cheese, grated
1 teaspoon grated nutmeg
½ teaspoon salt
½ teaspoon freshly ground black pepper
1 recipe Basic Pizza Dough (page 355)
2 tablespoons olive oil
Cornmeal for dusting

In a medium skillet, heat 2 tablespoons butter. Sauté garlic and spinach about 2 minutes, until wilted. Remove and reserve. In same skillet, heat remaining 2 tablespoons butter. Sauté apples about 2 minutes, or just until slightly softened. Remove and reserve with spinach mixture. In a large bowl, combine prosciutto, ricotta, Parmesan, nutmeg, salt, and pepper with reserved ingredients.

Preheat oven to 450 degrees. Divide dough in half and roll out each half into an 8-inch circle. Place half the filling on half of each of the circles, leaving a 1-inch margin around edge. Fold untopped half over the filling and seal edges by folding over. Brush tops with olive oil and place on baking sheet sprinkled with cornmeal. Bake 15 minutes, or until golden brown and puffed.

Serves 2–4

Mushroom Macaroni Gratin

½ cup (1 stick) butter
1 small red onion, thinly sliced
½ pound fresh mushrooms, thinly sliced
¼ cup chopped parsley
½ cup cornichons, drained and coarsely chopped (measured before chopping)
½ pound elbow macaroni, cooked
1 cup grated Monterey Jack cheese
¼ cup all-purpose flour
2 cups hot milk
½ teaspoon salt
½ teaspoon white pepper
¼ teaspoon grated nutmeg

Preheat oven to 375 degrees. Grease a 10-inch baking dish.

In a medium skillet, heat 4 tablespoons butter. Sauté onion and mushrooms about 5 minutes, or until soft. Toss with parsley, cornichons, macaroni, and ½ cup cheese. Set aside. In a medium saucepan, melt remaining 4 tablespoons butter. Stir in flour and cook, stirring, for about 3 minutes. Gradually whisk in hot milk over medium heat and bring to a boil. Cook, stirring, about 7 minutes, or until sauce thickens. Remove from heat and add seasonings. Stir ¾ cup of sauce into macaroni. Place macaroni in prepared baking dish and spread remaining sauce on top. Sprinkle with remaining cheese. Bake for about 30 minutes, or until golden and bubbly.

Serves 6

Cheese Popovers with Nutmeg

2 cups all-purpose flour
Pinch of salt
½ teaspoon grated nutmeg
½ cup finely grated Gruyère cheese
4 eggs, room temperature
2 cups milk, room temperature

Preheat oven to 450 degrees. Grease 8 popover or muffin molds.

In a large bowl, combine flour, salt, nutmeg, and cheese. Whisk eggs and milk until smooth and add to flour mixture, stirring until well blended. Allow mixture to rest about 15 minutes.

Heat popover pans for 5 to 10 minutes. Remove from oven and fill two-thirds full with batter, then return to oven. Bake 15 minutes, lower temperature to 375 degrees, and bake another 15 minutes, or until golden brown and crisp. Allow to cool a few minutes before removing from tins.

Yield: about 1 dozen

Chocolate Cake with Eggnog Custard

8 ounces semisweet chocolate, cut into pieces
10 tablespoons (1¼ sticks) butter
4 eggs, separated
1 cup sugar
2 tablespoons strong brewed coffee
2 tablespoons brandy
⅔ cup all-purpose flour
¼ teaspoon grated nutmeg

EGGNOG CUSTARD
⅓ cup sugar
5 egg yolks
1 tablespoon cornstarch

Pinch of salt
1/4 teaspoon grated nutmeg
1 1/2 cups milk
2 tablespoons brandy or bourbon

Preheat oven to 350 degres. Butter and flour an 8-inch springform pan.

In a medium saucepan, melt chocolate and butter over low heat. Remove from heat when smooth and glossy. Beat yolks until thick, adding sugar in 3 batches. After last addition, continue to beat about 5 minutes, or until very thick and light in color. Pour in reserved chocolate mixture, coffee, and brandy and mix just until well combined. Stir in flour and nutmeg. Beat whites until almost stiff, then fold into chocolate mixture. Pour into prepared pan and bake for 50 to 60 minutes, or until top appears crusty and slightly cracked. Cool on wire rack for at least 20 minutes before removing from pan.

In a small bowl, whisk sugar, yolks, cornstarch, salt, and nutmeg until thick. In a medium saucepan, heat milk just until small bubbles appear at edge. Pour milk into yolk mixture slowly, whisking until blended. Pour mixture back into saucepan and heat about 5 minutes, or until thickened and mixture coats the back of a spoon. Remove from heat and stir in brandy. Pour into bowl and allow to cool. Serve cake with eggnog custard.

Serves 8

MACE

Iced Cherry Soup with Mace

4 cups ripe sweet cherries, pitted
1 cup water
½ cup dry sherry
¼–½ cup sugar
2 tablespoons lime juice
¼ cup dairy sour cream
¼ teaspoon mace

In a medium saucepan, cook cherries with water, sherry, and sugar about 8 minutes, or until sugar is completely dissolved and cherries are soft. Place mixture in food processor or blender with remaining ingredients and puree until smooth. Taste and add additional sugar if necessary. Refrigerate until well chilled. Garnish with additional sour cream and an additional pinch of mace if desired.

Serves 4–6 as a soup course

Pumpkin Soup with Corn and Green Onions

1 pound pumpkin puree, fresh or canned
½ teaspoon mace
2 cups Chicken Stock (page 352)
1 cup corn kernels, fresh, frozen, or canned
3 green onions, sliced
Salt and pepper

In a medium saucepan, bring pumpkin, mace, and stock to a boil. Simmer, covered, for 10 minutes over low heat. Add corn and green onions and cook another minute. Taste for salt and pepper.

Serves 4

Ricotta Rice Muffins

1 cup all-purpose flour
1 teaspoon baking powder
½ teaspoon baking soda
¼ teaspoon salt
½ teaspoon mace
2 eggs
½ cup whole-milk ricotta cheese
¼ cup milk
¼ cup packed light-brown sugar
½ teaspoon vanilla extract
2 tablespoons vegetable oil
1 cup cooked white rice, either long or short grain

Preheat oven to 400 degrees. Grease 16 muffin tins.

In a small bowl, combine flour, baking powder and soda, salt, and mace. In a large bowl, beat eggs with ricotta, milk, brown sugar, vanilla, and oil for about 2 minutes. Add rice and the flour mixture and stir until well blended. Pour into muffin tins and bake about 30 minutes, or until a cake tester comes out clean.

Yield: 16

Pepper (Black, White, and Green)

LORE AND LINEAGE

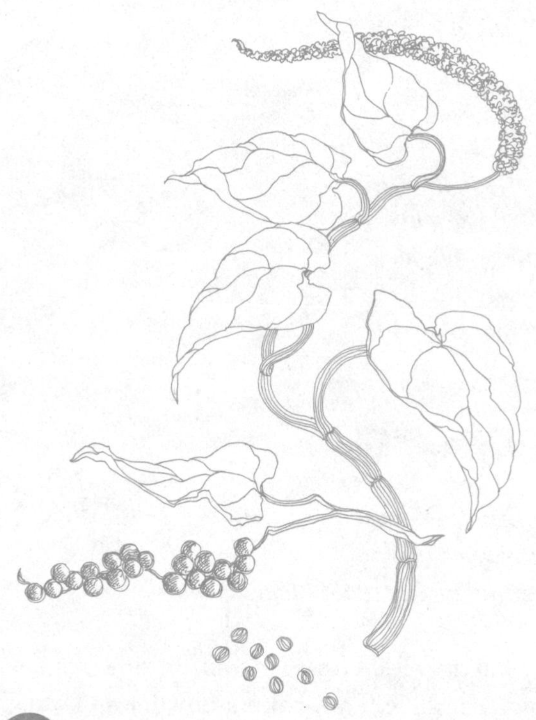

Of the many American dishes that feature pepper as their only spice, perhaps the most famous was inaugurated by George Washington himself. As the story goes, the general ordered his chef to prepare something particularly hearty for his starving Continental Army at Valley Forge. Having nothing on hand but tripe and black peppercorns, the chef combined them into a thick, satisfying ragout which so pleased the general that he named the dish after the chef's hometown. Philadelphia pepper pot soon became a cold-weather tradition in its namesake city, where black women sold it from pushcarts to the accompanying street cry, "Peppery pot, smokin' hot; makes backs strong, makes lives long."

SIGNATURE DISH: PHILADELPHIA PEPPER POT

Many cultures have their foods of the gods, and Philadelphia pepper pot is the closest we get in America. The dish has won its mythic dimensions not because of its ambrosial qualities but because of when, where, and for whom it was supposedly first prepared: during the War for Independence, at Valley Forge, for General George Washington. Or so they say.

Poetic though it may be, this culinary tale may warrant a grain of salt, especially since there already existed at the time a Pennsylvania German tripe dish called Dutch goose. Virginia pepper pot is a southern variation which has such added luxuries as veal knuckles and butter balls.

The New England boiled dinner evolved when the price of peppercorns, along with sugar, salt, and spices became reasonable enough to allow for the corning of beef. Vermont cooks like Beatrice Vaughan in *Yankee Hill-Country Cooking,* 1963, swear that, with just a bit of pepper for seasoning, "there's no better eating than a young coon properly baked."

In the mid-1800s another peppercorned regional dish became famous. It started with the Germans, Swiss, and Alsatians who settled near Cedar Rapids, Iowa. There they formed the Amana Colonies and began producing Westphalian-style cured hams covered in black peppercorns. These now widely acclaimed Amana hams are still served today in private homes and restaurants of the region, often with a swig or two of *piestengel,* the Amana rhubarb wine. From Mountain Home, Idaho, to Bakersfield, California, the Basques began to settle near pastures and mountains where they could work as sheepherders. Their cooking was as rugged as the Pyrenees from which they came; the men were often the main cooks, and peppercorns were their principal seasoning. They crushed them into lamb stews called *chilindron,* rich with red wine, garlic, and ham. They made peppery *tortilla de patatas* in black cast-iron skillets and cut it in thick, hot wedges. The American cowboy preferred simple, rib-sticking food, such as fort-style beef tongue spiced with crushed peppercorns and served with onions. Perhaps the simplest pepper recipe of all comes (via M. F. K. Fisher's *A Cordiall Water,* 1981) from up in the Kentucky mountains, where peppercorns were ground up and boiled with milk. Though it doesn't sound like a great drink, people made it so they could inhale its steamy vapors, which were supposed to cure sore throats; and they probably still do.

It was pepper that got this country involved in the international spice trade when, in 1797, Captain Jonathan Carnes brought back to Salem, Massachusetts, the first large pepper cargo from Sumatra. In short time the thriving pepper trade furnished enough revenues from import duties to pay 5 percent of all government expenses!

In this country there was another reason, besides availability, that pepper was often the only kitchen spice. At one point, cooking with spices was considered too fancy, if not downright scandalous. Simplicity advised that "nice" cooks confine themselves to "natural" flavors with a little help from butter, molasses, salt, catsup, and pepper. Even with these constrictions, some Victorian-era cookbooks managed a bit of flair, such as Mrs. (Sarah Tyson) Rorer's 1886 cookbook recipe for fried frogs. Eventually culinary style took another direction, however, and presentation and appearance became prime considerations. Consumption of white pepper increased as cookbooks began counseling its use in light-colored dishes to avoid those offensive old-fashioned black specks.

White pepper is usually less pungent than black and has a warmer, sweeter aroma. White, black, and green peppercorns are all from the same plant *(Piper nigrum)*. Peppercorns are picked when red, then dried until they shrivel and turn black. White pepper results from soaking the dried berry and removing the outer coating. Green peppercorns are immature fresh berries, freeze dried or packed in brine. Pink peppercorns, a separate plant, have a fresh tartness best preserved in water or vinegar. The following recipes focus on pepper, not as part of the ubiquitous duo of shakers on every tabletop but as one of the world's most profoundly satisfying tastes.

VINTAGE RECIPE

This recipe is from *Handbook of Practical Cookery for Ladies and Professional Cooks,* by Pierre Blot (New York: Appleton & Co., 1867).

Frogs

The hind-legs of frogs only are used as food; formerly they were eaten by the French only, but now, frog-eating has become general, and the Americans are not behind any others in relishing that kind of food.

Stewed—Skin, boil five minutes, throw in cold water, and drain. . . . Put in a stewpan two ounces of butter (for two dozen frogs); set it on the fire, and when melted, lay the legs in, fry two minutes, tossing now and then; then sprinkle on them a teaspoonful of flour, stir with a wooden spoon, add two sprigs of parsley, one of thyme, a bay-leaf, two cloves, one of garlic, salt, white pepper, and half a pint of white wine; boil gently till done, dish the legs, reduce the sauce on the fire, strain it, mix in two yolks of eggs, pour on the legs, and serve them.

Consumer Guide

Also known as: Arabic—filfil aswad; Dutch—peper; French—poivre; German—Pfeffer; Italian—pepe; Indian—kali mirich.

LATIN: *Piper nigrum*

Common varieties: Black peppercorns are picked when red and underripe, and during the drying process will turn black. White peppercorns are allowed to mature longer and then hulled to reveal their white color. The white peppercorn is less pungent than the black. Green peppercorns are young undried berries with a fresh and very pungent flavor. (Pink peppercorns, with their blend of sweet and pungent, are from a different plant.)

Selection: Black and white pepper may be found on spice shelves in whole or ground form. Freshly ground pepper is preferred for most dishes. Green and pink peppercorns are packed in water or vinegar. Freeze-dried green peppercorns are also available.

Storage: Whole peppercorns should be stored in a cool, dark place and will last about a year without loss of flavor.

Compatible herbs and spices: All herbs and spices are compatible with black pepper.

RECIPE LIST

Mixed Greens and Mandarins in Pepper–Honey Vinaigrette
Pepper and Potato Omelet
Lamburgers with Green Peppercorn Sauce
Baked Brie in Pepper–Nut Crust
Bread with Two Peppercorns

Mixed Greens and Mandarins in Pepper–Honey Vinaigrette

1 small head romaine, torn in bite-size pieces
2 Belgian endives, sliced
1 bunch watercress, stemmed
3 mandarin oranges or tangerines, peeled and sectioned
1 tablespoon coarsely ground black pepper
1 tablespoon honey
½ teaspoon salt
1 small shallot, minced
1 egg yolk
3 tablespoons white wine vinegar
2 teaspoons lemon juice
½ cup olive oil

In a large salad bowl, combine greens with orange sections. In a small bowl, whisk pepper, honey, salt, shallot, egg yolk, vinegar, and lemon juice. Pour in oil while continuously whisking. Toss greens with dressing just before serving.

Serves 8

Pepper and Potato Omelet

2 tablespoons (¼ stick) butter
1 tablespoon olive oil
1 small onion, chopped
1 small red bell pepper, diced
4 small red potatoes, scrubbed and diced
1 teaspoon freshly ground black pepper
Pinch of ground red pepper
6 eggs
2 tablespoons water
Salt

In a 10-inch skillet, heat butter and oil. Sauté onion, bell pepper, and potatoes over medium-high heat for about 4 minutes. Stir in black and red pepper and cook, covered, over low heat for about 5 minutes, or until potatoes are tender. Beat eggs with water and pour into skillet. Cook over medium heat for about 5 minutes, lifting edges of omelet to let uncooked egg run into bottom of skillet. Cover and cook another 3 to 4 minutes, or until entire omelet is cooked. Sprinkle with salt and cut into wedges.

Serves 6

Lamburgers with Green Peppercorn Sauce

1 pound ground lamb
½ pound ground beef
1 tablespoon minced shallot
1 tablespoon Dijon-type mustard
2 tablespoons dry red wine
½ teaspoon salt
½ teaspoon freshly ground black pepper
¼ teaspoon dried oregano
2 tablespoons (¼ stick) butter
¼ cup Beef Stock (page 353)
2 tablespoons dry vermouth
2 tablespoons green peppercorns (packed in brine), drained and lightly smashed
½ cup heavy cream

In a large mixing bowl, combine first 8 ingredients. Form into 6 equal patties. In a large skillet, heat butter. Cook burgers on both sides until done according to taste (rare, medium, well). Remove and cover with foil to keep warm. Deglaze (page 361) skillet with stock and vermouth. Add peppercorns and cream and cook about 3 minutes, until thickened. Pour some sauce over each burger and serve.

Serves 6

Baked Brie in Pepper–Nut Crust

1 6-inch wheel brie cheese
1 egg white, lightly beaten
1 cup chopped pecans
2 tablespoons coarsely ground black pepper
3 tablespoons dark-brown sugar
Toast or vegetable rounds

Preheat oven to 375 degrees. Butter a 10-inch round ovenproof serving dish. (A ceramic quiche dish works well.)

Brush entire surface of brie with egg white. Combine pecans, pepper, and brown sugar on a piece of wax paper. Dredge brie in pepper mixture, making sure that entire surface is covered. Place in baking dish and bake for 20 minutes. Serve with toasted bread slices or vegetable rounds.

Serves 12

Bread with Two Peppercorns

6 cups all-purpose flour
2 teaspoons salt
1 tablespoon green peppercorns (packed in brine), rinsed and coarsely chopped
1 tablespoon coarsely ground black pepper
2 packages active dry yeast, proofed (page 362) in 2 cups warm water with 1 tablespoon honey
2 tablespoons olive oil
Cornmeal for dusting

In a large bowl, combine flour, salt, green peppercorns, and black pepper. Pour in yeast mixture and oil and mix well until dough comes together. Turn out onto a floured surface and knead about 7 minutes, until smooth and elastic, adding more flour as needed. Place dough in a greased bowl, and cover with plastic wrap. Let rise in a warm spot about 1 hour, until doubled.

Punch dough down and knead on floured surface for 1 minute. Shape into 2 round loaves and place on baking sheet sprinkled with cornmeal. Cover with towel and let rise about 1 hour.

Preheat oven to 400 degrees. With a sharp knife or razor, make 3 slashes on surface of each loaf. Bake about 35 minutes, or until bottom of loaf sounds hollow when tapped.

Yield: 2 loaves

Poppyseed

LORE AND LINEAGE

Eating contests are one of the things people in the Czech community of Montgomery, Minnesota, look forward to all year. These contests are a high point of Kolachy Day, named after the sweet turnovers filled with citron or fruit and topped with poppyseeds. *Kolaches* and other Czech pastries have one thing in common: lots of poppyseeds. In fact, they say you can tell you're in the Czech part of town when you see poppy plants growing in the gardens. And you can probably recognize the winners of the eating contests by the number of little blue-black seeds stuck in their teeth.

The Czechs brought more than poppyseeds when they started emigrating a hundred years ago to the farmlands of Wisconsin and Iowa, and to towns like Taberville, Ohio, and Wilber, Nebraska, whose populations soon became virtually all Czech. They brought their holiday food customs, like boar's head on New Year's Eve, boiled carp on Christmas Eve, and roast goose on St. Wenceslaus Day (September 28). And with all these dishes they serve lots of *makovy chleb* (poppyseed bread) and crackling patties sprinkled with poppyseeds. For dessert there is *makovy dort* (a poppyseed cake with raisins and lemon rind) and other poppyseed pastries, like *pecivalky* (poppyseed pockets), *ceske makovy* (fried poppyseed cakes), and poppyseed strudels and pies, now made with canned poppyseed filling. Actually the cooking of Bohemia, so rich in the culinary traditions of the Austro–Hungarian Empire, was itself a melting-pot cuisine. Once settled in the American Midwest, the Czechs melded one melting pot into another. When Hungarians immigrated to the Midwest, they added such poppyseed pastries as babka, their traditional coffee cake.

The Russo–German Mennonites who began arriving in Kansas and South Dakota in the late nineteenth century also brought *their* melting pot with them. After fleeing from Germany for religious reasons, they lived in several different areas, adopting culinary customs wherever they went. Once here, they revealed the wonders of Slavic poppyseed pies, cooked red cabbage, and fruit salads topped with poppyseed vinaigrette. They used poppyseeds on *piroshki*; on raised rolls called *bubbat,* with smoked-sausage filling; and sometimes even on zwieback, a tradition for *faspa,* or Sunday lunch. For all these baked goods they used the hard winter wheat they had managed to cultivate on the Russian Steppes. It was this very wheat which transformed Kansas into the nation's breadbasket.

SIGNATURE DISH: ANY KIND OF SANDWICH ON A POPPYSEED ROLL

Many people come to know poppyseeds the first time they eschew the everyday sandwich and elect instead to have their ham, turkey, or burger put into something with strange little black pebbles on top. Poppyseeds are baked atop golden-brown woven biscuits, braided egg breads, hamburger buns, and crusty "bakery" rolls; and almost any sandwich is the better for it.

There are two hundred species of poppyseed, all belonging to the Papaveraceae family. This family of plants has always fascinated people because of its opium connections, even though no narcotic properties reside in the seed itself. The shell of the seed pod contains the opium and that only in one species, *Papaver somniferum.* Nevertheless, according to custom, early English colonists sprinkled seeds of whatever poppy species they had over their children's food in the (probably vain) hope that it would "help them sleep."

Oil pressed from the seeds, which can be used like olive oil for cooking, is called olivette. A light toasting in a dry frypan helps bring out the nutty flavor of the seeds, making them all the more delicious in egg breads, fruit salads and dressings, or on rice and fresh greens. They are one of the main ingredients in commercial bird seed. For a "seedy" effect in muffins and on rolls or breads, try using equal portions of poppy, caraway, and sesame seeds. To grind poppyseeds, soak them first for several hours, drain, and process in a poppyseed grinder or crush with a mortar and pestle.

Poppyseeds come in all colors, from slate blue to white, the latter being the choice of East Indian cooks. Incredibly, the white seeds are sometimes dyed blue to satisfy the whims of the commercial market. Presumably the birds have no preference, and any color will suffice in the following recipes.

VINTAGE RECIPE

This recipe is adapted from *Favorite Recipes of the Nebraska Czechs* (published by the Nebraska Czechs of Wilber, Nebraska, 1968), page 38.

Poppy Seed Crown Cake

1½ cups milk
1 cup ground poppyseed
½ cup (1 stick) butter
1½ cups sugar
2 eggs, separated
2 cups all-purpose flour
2 teaspoons baking powder
1 teaspoon vanilla extract
Confectioner's sugar

Mix ¾ cup of milk with the poppyseed and cook in a small saucepan 5 to 7 minutes. Let stand overnight. Cream butter and sugar; add egg yolks and poppyseed. Add sifted flour and baking powder alternately with the remaining ¾ cup milk. Beat egg whites and fold into the batter. Pour into a greased and floured tube pan. Bake at 375 degrees for 45 minutes. Turn out onto cake rack to cool. Sprinkle with confectioner's sugar.

Consumer Guide

Also known as: Arabic—khashkhash; Chinese—ying-shu; Dutch—slaap-bol; French—pavot; German—mohn; Hungarian—makos; Polish—makom; Indian—khas khas.

LATIN: *Papaver somniferum (and species of Papaver)*

Selection and storage: Blue-black variety may be found on spice shelves of all supermarkets, packed in jars or cans. White poppyseeds are carried by stores specializing in Indian foods. Both varieties can get rancid at room temperature and should be stored airtight in the refrigerator, where they will keep for 6 months.

Compatible herbs and spices: Poppyseeds have a nutlike flavor and may be used with parsley, dill, fresh coriander, red and black pepper, ground coriander, and cumin.

RECIPE LIST

Noodles with Cabbage and Poppyseeds
Melon Salad with Poppyseed Dressing
Fresh and Dried Apple Poppyseed Bread
Polenta and Poppyseed Cake

Noodles with Cabbage and Poppyseeds

6 tablespoons (3/4 stick) butter
1 small head savoy cabbage, coarsely shredded
1/4 cup poppyseed
Salt and pepper
1 pound broad egg noodles, freshly cooked

In a large skillet, heat butter. Sauté cabbage about 4 minutes, or until tender. Add poppyseed and cook another 2 minutes. In a large bowl, toss noodles with cabbage mixture. Taste for salt and pepper.

Serves 6–8

Melon Salad with Poppyseed Dressing

1 head romaine lettuce, coarsely shredded
2 cups cantaloupe balls or chunks
2 cups honeydew melon balls or chunks
2 cups crenshaw melon balls or chunks
2 cups green seedless grapes
1/4 cup plain yogurt
1/4 cup cottage cheese
Grated zest of 1/2 lemon (page 363)
1 tablespoon lemon juice
1 tablespoon honey
1 tablespoon toasted poppyseeds (page 360)
Chopped mint (optional)

In a large bowl, combine lettuce and fruits. In a food processor or a blender, combine yogurt, cottage cheese, lemon zest and juice, and honey until smooth. Stir in poppyseed. Pour over fruits just before serving and sprinkle with mint.

Serves 8

Fresh and Dried Apple Poppyseed Bread

½ cup (1 stick) butter, room temperature
½ cup light-brown sugar
1 cup granulated sugar
3 tablespoons applejack or cider
2 teaspoons vanilla extract
4 eggs
1 cup dried currants
1 cup chopped dried apples
1½ cups grated green apples (peeled or not, as you wish)
½ cup poppyseed
2 cups all-purpose flour
1 teaspoon baking soda
1 teaspoon baking powder
Pinch of ground cinnamon and grated nutmeg
½ teaspoon salt

Preheat oven to 350 degrees. Grease and flour two 8- x 4-inch loaf pans.

In a medium mixing bowl, cream butter and sugars until light. Add applejack, vanilla, and eggs, 1 at a time, beating well after each addition. In a separate bowl, combine currants, dried and fresh apples, and poppyseed and add to egg mixture. In a separate bowl, mix remaining ingredients and add to egg mixture, beating just enough to combine. Pour into prepared pans and bake 1 hour. Cool.

Yield: 2 loaves

Polenta and Poppyseed Cake

½ cup poppyseed, soaked in milk to cover for 1 hour
⅔ cup butter, room temperature
2⅓ cups confectioner's sugar
1 teaspoon almond extract
2 whole eggs plus 2 yolks
1¼ cups sifted cake flour
⅓ cup polenta or yellow cornmeal

Preheat oven to 325 degrees. Grease an 8-by-10-inch loaf pan.

Drain poppyseed thoroughly and set aside. In a mixing bowl, cream butter and confectioner's sugar until light and fluffy. Add extract, whole eggs, and yolks and beat well. Stir in poppyseed. Combine flour and cornmeal and add to butter mixture, beating just until well combined. Pour batter into prepared pan and bake 1½ hours. Cool 10 minutes and unmold. Sprinkle with additional confectioner's sugar if desired.

Serves 8–10

Red Pepper (Paprika, Cayenne, and Chile)

LORE AND LINEAGE

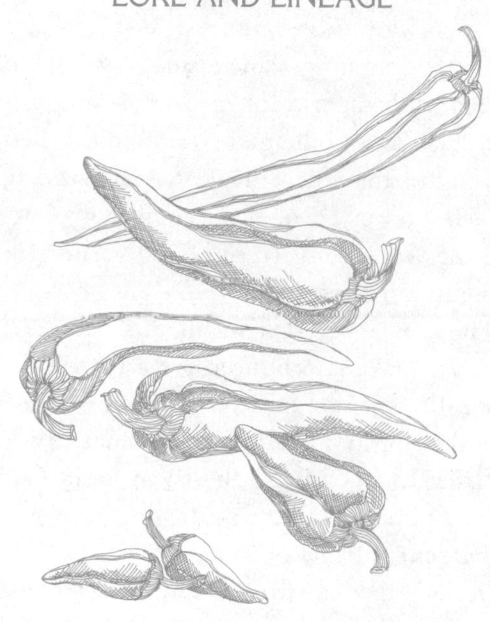

According to a 1969 Gallup Poll of American food preferences, goulash rated among the top five favorite meat dishes. Interpretations of what goulash actually is, however, varied across the country (most of them would not be recognized as goulash by citizens of Budapest), but all versions contained that one essential Hungarian ingredient: paprika. Americans consume 8 million pounds of paprika a year, an astounding amount considering the spice was virtually unknown when Hungarians first began emigrating here in the late 1800s. In cities like Cleveland, which soon had one of the largest Hungarian populations outside of Budapest, the fragrance of chicken and veal paprikash suggested the many appealing possibilities of the spice, which was soon naturalized into catsup, sauces, and condiments.

In New Jersey, Hungarians still celebrate the Feast of the Pig's Wake *(diszno-tor)* on butchering day. Paprika figures prominently in the resulting garlicky *kolbász* sausages; in *gulyásleves,* a goulash soup with caraway and little dumplings called *galuska*; and in *töltött káposzta,* a whole cabbage stuffed with sauerkraut, pepper, rice, and pork. In South Bend, Indiana, paprikash and homemade dumplings called *csipetke* mark the feast of the blessing of the wheat seed on March 24. In Texas, paprika is rubbed on roasted ears of corn, *elote,* along with butter and lime; and Texans can face the world with rose-colored garlic grits thanks to the strong tinge of Hungarian paprika.

There is a paradox in all this because the peppers *(Capsicums)* from which paprika is produced are a New World plant. Peppers were enthusiastically received all over Europe where tamer, less fiery varieties were soon developed, including the aromatic sweet peppers from which paprika is made. In 1937, Dr. Albert von Szent-Gyorgyi won the Nobel Prize for his research on ascorbic acid, which proved that paprika has more vitamin C than citrus fruits.

In the American Southwest, however, even the most incendiary peppers became part of the region's food. In New Mexico and Arizona, the pulp of red chile peppers is mixed with hominy, pork, and oregano to produce *posole*; chiles and garlic flavor the marinade that is the essence of *carne adobado,* as well as the stock for *puchero,* a boiled dinner with chick-peas and vegetables. Chicken *mole,* deviled raisins, and fried lamb's quarters—actually one of the native greens—get their intrinsic warmth from chile peppers and seeds.

Creole cooks use hot peppers with tomatoes to enliven rice and beans, okra stews, and crawfish étouffées. Some insist that the bright, red Louisiana Sport Pepper is the only choice for regional dishes. In the Mississippi Delta, Cajun social gatherings such as *piodheries* (hoeing bees) or *ecosseries* (hulling bees) have always been good excuses for accompanying feasts of shrimp gumbos and other peppery fare.

From the Louisiana bayou country comes another regional specialty, the now-world-famous Tabasco sauce, a patented formula first produced on

Avery Island by the Edward McIlhenny family. This sauce has inspired a repertoire of its own, including the Alabama catfish sandwich, a scooped-out, crusty roll slathered with mustard, catsup, and Tabasco, on which is piled hot, deep-fried catfish. Of more universal consequence is the Tabasco-laced Bloody Mary, invented in 1920 by Ferdinand Petiot, a bartender at Harry's New York Bar in Paris.

SIGNATURE DISH: BLOODY MARY

It makes sense that the all-American Bloody Mary—rich and tomatoey and vibrating from more than a dash of Tabasco—was born in the twenties at a place called Harry's New York Bar. It must be admitted, however, that the bartender-inventor (Ferdinand Petiot) was French and the bar was in Paris.

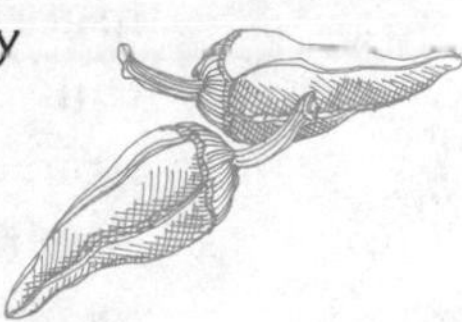

Cayenne (often sold as "ground red pepper") is another form of hot pepper spicing. It is a mix of *Capsicum* peppers from just about everywhere—except Cayenne, French Guiana, which only contributed its name. From cayenne peppers, early pioneers made what must have been a bracing tea which was supposed to cure cholera.

Cayenne is the zip in many Appalachian dishes with such personalized names as Daisy Justus's souse meat and Lizzie Moore's raccoon; as for Mrs. Vergil Lovell's turtles, she herself advises "you can put a little pod of pepper in. It won't hurt them a bit." You need quite a big pod, however, to flavor Texas pâté, made from either half a deer's liver or a whole goat's liver, whichever your butcher can supply. A more well-known American creation, lobster Newburg, also revolves around cayenne. The story of its creation—in 1876 in New York's Delmonico's restaurant for one Captain Ben Wenberg—is probably just a story.

Possibly the most famous American *Capsicum* dish is chili. The chili powder on which it is based usually consists of a mixture of several types of dried ground chile peppers plus seasonings like cumin and oregano.

Among the most famous is Gebhardt's, named by its creator and originally packaged in Texas. The controversy over the best possible chili recipe still rages nationwide; it includes such elaborate old contenders as Cincinnati five-way chili (made with chocolate and served on spaghetti!) and some new competition like Brendlinger's California vegetarian chili (made with roasted whole spices, fresh fava beans and shucked corn). Even the most devoted chile pepper lover might have trouble with a Gold Rush holiday dish called Sutter's meal: five courses, all made with beef and hot red peppers, including the Christmas plum pudding! The dispute has deep historical roots: some say the Aztecs taught the Spanish the art of making chili con carne when Cortez entered Mexico in 1519. (The word *chile* is from an ancient Mexican language, Nahuetl.) Others contend that North American Indians used chiles to preserve meat, a practice that was imitated by chuck-wagon cooks who mixed powdered chile peppers with meat for their hungry cowpokes. More recently, at New Mexico State University's horticultural department, Dr. Roy Nakayama proved conclusively that chile powder not only preserves meat, but makes tough meat palatable by breaking down fiber.

There are more than two hundred species of *Capsicum,* ranging from the milder California, poblano, and ancho to the hot serranos, jalapeños, and pequins. According to some Black American folk tales, the best ones are grown by bad-tempered people. Perhaps the heat is transferred? For safety's sake, handle them all (even the grumpy gardener) with gloves.

VINTAGE RECIPE

This recipe is adapted from a 1930s American cookbook using, if not actually abusing, paprika: Berolzheimer, Ruth, ed., *The Prudence Penny Binding of the United States Regional Cookbook,* p. 658. First published 1939.

Bunny Salad

Dissolve a package of lime gelatin in 2 cups of warm water. Pour into 8 x 8 x 2 pan and let firm up. For each salad, fill a pear half with cottage cheese mixed with mayonnaise and chopped almonds. Force firm gelatin through a ricer to make a "bed" of "leaves." Place pear on leaves and decorate pear thusly: using some whole almonds, make bunny's ears, mouth, and tail. Make eyes by dipping the pointed end of knife in paprika. Garnish with small carrot shaped from cheese and a sprig of parsley.

Makes 6 bunnies.

Consumer Guide

Common varieties: Ground red pepper (cayenne) is the red ground chile powder made from the pods of ripe, pungent chiles. Paprika is made from grinding chile pods in varying intensities, from sweet to hot; "Hungarian" paprika usually refers to the sweet variety. (Commercially packaged chili powder is not always pure ground chiles. It contains sugar, salt, cumin and other ingredients.)

LATIN: *Capsicum annum (paprika)* *C. frutescens (cayenne, chili peppers)* *(and species of Capsicum)*

Selection: Both varieties should have bright red-orange color and are found on spice shelves of supermarkets.

Storage: To prevent bug infestation, red pepper should be stored tightly sealed in the refrigerator. It will keep, refrigerated, for about 6 months.

Compatible herbs and spices: All herbs and spices are compatible with all red peppers.

RECIPE LIST

Chicken Liver Potato Salad with Tarragon and Oranges
Black Bean Ragout with Fried Polenta
Corn on the Cob with Cajun Butter
Chicken Paillard in Pepper-pod Marinade
Avocado–Bacon Sandwich with Red Pepper Mayonnaise

Chicken Liver Potato Salad with Tarragon and Oranges

3/4 pound chicken livers, cleaned and halved
1/4 cup all-purpose flour mixed with 1/4 teaspoon ground red pepper
2 tablespoons (1/4 stick) butter
1/2 pound new potatoes, cleaned, cubed, cooked, and cooled

1 large seedless orange, peel and pith removed, then sectioned
½ head romaine lettuce, torn into bite-size pieces

DRESSING
1 teaspoon Dijon-type mustard
⅛ teaspoon ground red pepper
2 cloves garlic, minced
1 tablespoon chopped fresh tarragon, or 1 teaspoon dried
2 tablespoons red wine vinegar
6 tablespoons olive oil
Salt

Blot livers dry with paper towels and dredge in flour–red pepper mixture. In a medium skillet, heat butter. Sauté livers over medium heat for about 3 minutes on each side, or until done. In a large salad bowl, combine livers with potatoes, orange sections, and lettuce and toss well. To make dressing, combine ingredients then pour over liver-potato mixture and taste for salt.

Serves 6 as a first course

Black Bean Ragout with Fried Polenta

1 pound black beans, soaked overnight in cold water to cover
3 tablespoons olive oil
½ pound prosciutto, diced
4 cloves garlic, minced
1 jalapeño pepper, seeded and chopped (page 361)
3 leeks (white part only), sliced
2 carrots, peeled and sliced
2 large ripe tomatoes, seeded and coarsely chopped
1 teaspoon ground cumin
1 teaspoon ground red pepper
½ teaspoon freshly ground black pepper
6 cups Beef Stock (page 353)
Salt

FRIED POLENTA

2½ cups water
1 cup polenta or yellow cornmeal
2 cloves garlic, pushed through press
Salt and pepper
2 tablespoons olive oil
2 tablespoons (¼ stick) butter

Drain beans and rinse. In a large saucepan, heat oil. Sauté prosciutto, garlic, jalapeño, and leeks until prosciutto browns lightly and vegetables are soft (about 8 minutes). Add carrots, tomatoes, cumin, and red and black peppers. Cook about 3 minutes over medium-high heat. Add beans and broth. Bring to a boil, then simmer, partially covered, about 1¼ hours, or until beans are tender.

Meanwhile, in a medium saucepan, bring water to a rolling boil. Gradually pour in cornmeal, stirring continuously. Stir in garlic. When all the cornmeal has been added, turn down heat and cook, stirring, about 10 minutes, or until thick and mixture pulls away from sides of the pan. Taste for salt and pepper.

Spread polenta in a greased 9- x 9-inch pan. Allow to cool and get firm. In a skillet, heat oil and butter. Cut polenta into squares and fry until golden brown on each side (about 3 minutes).

Taste bean ragout for salt and pepper and serve over or alongside fried polenta.

Serves 8

Corn on the Cob with Cajun Butter

¼ cup (½ stick) butter, cut into pieces
1 small clove garlic
⅛ teaspoon ground red pepper
½ teaspoon paprika
⅛ teaspoon salt
½ teaspoon dried thyme
6 ears corn, freshly cooked or grilled

In a food processor, combine all ingredients except corn until smooth. Spread on hot corn or refrigerate for future use.

Serves 6

Chicken Paillard in Pepper-pod Marinade

½ cup olive oil
3 dried whole red jalapeño chiles
Juice of medium lemon
¼ teaspoon ground white pepper
Pinch of salt
3 skinned and boned whole chicken breasts, split
¼ cup chopped parsley

In a small skillet, heat oil. Sauté chile pods for about 4 minutes, or until they turn dark brown; discard. Allow oil to cool, then stir in lemon juice, white pepper, and salt. Pound chicken breasts to a ⅛-inch thickness and place in noncorrosive flat dish. Pour seasoned oil over chicken and allow to marinate about 2 hours, turning several times.

Preheat grill or broiler to highest setting. Remove chicken from marinade and place about 4 inches from source of heat. Cook about 4 minutes on each side, basting with marinade from time to time. Remove to serving dish and sprinkle with parsley.

Serves 6

Avocado–Bacon Sandwich with Red Pepper Mayonnaise

4 slices whole-grain bread
½ pound thick-sliced bacon, cooked until crisp
1 small avocado, peeled and sliced
1 large ripe tomato, sliced
¼ cup fresh coriander
2 Boston lettuce leaves, cut into shreds

RED PEPPER MAYONNAISE
1 1½-ounce jar chopped pimientos, rinsed and drained
½–1 teaspoon ground red pepper or to taste
1 tablespoon lemon juice
1 teaspoon mild mustard
1 egg, room temperature
1 cup vegetable oil
Salt

Make mayonnaise first. Place pimientos, red pepper, lemon juice, mustard, and egg in bowl of food processor or blender and puree. With machine running, very slowly add oil, processing until thickened. Taste for salt.

Spread 2 slices of bread with mayonnaise. Layer bacon, avocado, and tomato on each slice. Top with a mixture of coriander and lettuce, and add remaining slice of bread.

Yield: 2 sandwiches

Saffron

LORE AND LINEAGE

You can tell at a glance that Mrs. Chancey's Spanish Bean Soup is an old recipe: it calls for ten cents' worth of saffron! At today's prices, such an amount would be undetectable in this spicy Tampa, Florida, soup, preserved in the pages of Marjorie Kinnan Rawlings's *Cross Creek Cookery* (1942). Mrs. Chancey drew upon a heritage that began when the Spanish arrived in St. Augustine in 1565. Saffron dishes weren't far behind, one of the earliest being garbanzo soup with *chorizo* and saffron. Within a hundred years, saffron started showing up in such unlikely places as the Hudson River Valley, where Dutch cooks prepared partridges in saffron sauce. Their recipes came from the most popular culinary guide of its time in that area, a 1683 Dutch cookbook called *The Wise Cook and Housekeeper.*

Even more surprising, at first glance, is the lavish way the Pennsylvania Dutch use this luxury spice in many of their otherwise homey dishes. Their familiarity with saffron begins with the Schwenkfelders, a Protestant sect which left Silesia in 1734 because of religious persecution and moved to Pennsylvania. Once there, they continued their specialty as cultivators of saffron and soon transformed Lancaster County into a saffron center. They were able to use what would otherwise be a prohibitively expensive spice for pot pies, soups, and noodle dishes; in Pennsylvania Dutch chicken *stoltzfus,* in saffron breads, and in the traditional Schwenkfelder wedding cake.

At about the same time, saffron was included in the food supplies for the de Anza expedition that came to establish the presidio in San Francisco. There, however, it was a luxury item reserved only for the commander, Juan Bautiste de Anza, and the chaplin, Father Pedro Font.

Both French and Spanish influences are responsible for saffron's importance in Creole and Cajun cookery. But it was an English poet who gave saffron a permanent place in literature as well. In his "Ballad of Bouillabaisse," William Thackeray praises the combination of herbs, saffron, and "hotchpotch of all sort of fishes" that he enjoyed in his favorite Louisiana restaurants, like Terre's Tavern.

SIGNATURE DISH: FISH STEWS

Louisiana *bouillabaisse,* San Francisco *cioppino,* southwestern *sopa de mariscos,* and other "American regional" fish stews are all transported out of the ordinary by a few thin threads of saffron.

The most unlikely place to find saffron-scented dishes would seem to be the American Midwest. And yet they are there, in Wisconsin and throughout Michigan's Upper Peninsula, where saffron flavors little meat and potato cakes called *pasties,* introduced by the Cornish who worked the mines. Today in the midwestern melting pot, the Finnish, Italians, Germans, Poles, and Swedish all claim credit for the only authentic version of the *pasty.* Swedes also use saffron in their Easter *saffronsbröd* and in St. Lucia buns for Christmas. There, and everywhere else Italians settled, saffron perfumes rice dishes like *risotto Milanese* and the intriguingly named *suppli al telefono* (croquettes on the telephone). These deep-fried, saffron-seasoned rice balls are formed around a lump of mozzarella; when you eat them, the cheese pulls out into strings that look like telephone wires.

To get a pound of saffron, you need half a million stigmas removed carefully, by hand, from 100,000 crocus flowers. Derived from the Arab word for yellow, saffron (*Crocus sativus*) has an elusive bittersweet flavor and fragrance. It has been described as having a taste "most resembling sunlight." Try to buy the threads, since powdered saffron is easy to adulterate. Beware of Mexican saffron, or bastard saffron (*Carthamus tinctorius*), which is really from safflower and does not compare in flavor.

Outside the kitchen, saffron has been used as a dye, a tea, and a medicine. The Pennsylvania Dutch once made a drink for children to help bring on measles; it was part of an American Indian treatment for gout. An Irish custom dictates that washing sheets in saffron strengthens the limbs. As an opiate, it is reputed to subdue hysteria; but there are also claims that it is a stimulant which makes people imitate animals. American cookbooks have also added to its nonculinary lore. The eighteenth-century manuscript, *Martha Washington's Booke of Cookery,* counseled that "it is good for women in travell." A bit later, Lydia Maria Child's 1829 edition of *The American Frugal Housewife* recommended it "when the digestive powers are out of order." However, Sheila Hibben's *A Kitchen Manual* (1941) finally gets to the point. She says, "Spanish saffron . . . is known by too few cooks for the agreeable seasoning it is."

VINTAGE RECIPE

This recipe is from *Cross Creek Cookery* by Marjorie Kinnan Rawlings (New York: Charles Scribner's Sons, 1942), page 7.

Mrs. Chancey's Spanish Bean Soup

1 pound Spanish beans
½ teaspoon soda
2-pound ham hock
4 large onions
4 buttons garlic
½ bell pepper
4 Spanish sausages
4 pig's feet (fresh)
4 medium-sized potatoes
1 small head cabbage
½ teaspoon saffron (or about 10¢ worth)
Salt to taste
Black pepper to taste
2 bay leaves

Add soda to water and soak beans overnight. Wash beans well the next morning. Cover ham hock well with cold water, add beans and start cooking slowly. Cut up onions, garlic, bell pepper, and in about twenty minutes add to soup together with bay leaves and saffron. Cut sausages in pieces of four each and add to soup. Cut pig's feet in half, lengthwise, and cook separately until tender; then add to soup and cook slowly. Cut up potatoes and add to soup, and when beans are about done, cut up cabbage as for slaw and add to soup. Season to taste with salt and black pepper.

Be sure to cook slowly always. More water may be needed at end, but soup is supposed to be very thick. Imported sausage cannot be bought now but domestic will do. Serves eight to ten.

Consumer Guide

Also known as: Arabic—za'farān; Dutch—saffraan; French—safran; German—Safrangewurz; Italian—zafferano; Spanish—azafrán.

LATIN: *Crocus sativus*

Selection: Saffron can be found in dried form, since it is only made by drying crocus stigmas. It is usually found in powdered and whole thread form, the latter more desirable because it keeps its flavor longer. If you cannot find saffron on your market spice shelf, ask for it because it may be kept in a dark place or under lock and key.

Storage: Saffron should be kept in a cool, dark place because it loses its flavor when exposed to light. Keeps well for up to 4 months.

Compatible herbs and spices: Fresh coriander, cumin, mint, parsley, chives.

RECIPE LIST

Saffron Stars and Snow Pea Soup
Paella Pasta
Poached Salmon with Saffron Beurre Blanc
Lettuce and Saffron Rice Soup
Saffroned Vegetable Flan
Rice Pudding with Saffron and Golden Raisins

Saffron Stars and Snow Pea Soup

1 quart Chicken Stock (page 352)
½ cup stellini *(tiny, star-shaped pasta)*
¼ pound snow peas, strings removed and cut into strips
½ teaspoon saffron threads
¼ cup lemon juice
4 eggs
Salt and pepper

In a medium saucepan, bring stock to a boil. Add pasta and cook another 10 minutes. Add snow peas and cook 3 minutes. In a small bowl, whisk saffron, lemon juice, and eggs until light. Remove about 1 cup of the stock from the pot and gradually whisk into egg mixture. Pour egg mixture back into soup and cook over low heat, stirring, until mixture is thickened (about 5 minutes). Taste for salt and pepper.

Serves 6

Paella Pasta

¼ cup olive oil
1 onion, chopped
2 cloves garlic, chopped
1 red bell pepper, seeded and chopped
1 pound skinned and boned chicken breast, cut into ½-inch cubes
½ pound chorizo *(Spanish sausage), sliced*
½ cup dry white wine
½ teaspoon dried oregano
½ teaspoon saffron threads
½ cup Chicken Stock (page 352)
2 tablespoons tomato paste
1 10-ounce package frozen peas
½ pound shrimp, shelled and deveined
12 mussels, scrubbed
1 pound pasta, freshly cooked
¼ cup (½ stick) butter
2 teaspoons capers, rinsed and drained

In a large skillet, heat oil. Sauté onion, garlic, bell pepper, chicken, and sausage over medium heat for about 10 minutes. Add wine and oregano and bring to a boil, stirring and scraping the bottom of the pan. Dissolve saffron in stock and add to skillet along with tomato paste. Simmer about 5 minutes, then add peas, shrimp, and mussels. Cook, covered, until mussels open (3 to 5 minutes). Toss hot pasta with butter, top with paella mixture, and garnish with capers. Serve in pasta bowls or soup plates, making sure that each portion contains some of each of the ingredients.

Serves 6

Poached Salmon with Saffron Beurre Blanc

2 cups dry white wine
1/4 cup white wine vinegar
3/4 cup water
1/4 cup chopped shallots
1/2 teaspoon salt
1/2 teaspoon freshly ground black pepper
1/2 teaspoon saffron threads
6 salmon filets (about 6 ounces each), skinned
1/2 cup (1 stick) butter, cut into tablespoon-size pieces
Red or golden caviar (optional)

In a skillet large enough to accommodate salmon, place wine, vinegar, water, shallots, salt, pepper, and saffron and simmer, covered, for 10 minutes. Place salmon in liquid in 1 layer, cover, and cook for 7 minutes. Remove salmon and cover with foil.

Boil poaching liquid rapidly until only 1/2 cup remains. Strain into small saucepan. Bring to a boil and whisk in butter, 1 piece at a time. After all butter has been incorporated, cook only until creamy (about 2 minutes). Serve sauce over salmon and garnish with caviar.

Serves 6

Lettuce and Saffron Rice Soup

3 tablespoons butter
2 tablespoons chopped shallots
1 large head romaine lettuce, shredded
1 large head Boston lettuce, shredded
1 quart Chicken Stock (page 352)
1/2 teaspoon saffron threads
2/3 cup long-grain white rice
Salt and pepper

In a 4-quart saucepan, heat butter. Cook shallots and lettuces (save some shreds for garnish) about 5 minutes, until wilted. Add stock and saffron and bring to a boil. Add rice and simmer, covered, for 15 minutes, or until rice is tender. Puree in blender or food processor. Taste for salt and pepper and garnish with reserved lettuce shreds. May be served hot or cold.

Serves 6

Saffroned Vegetable Flan

3 tablespoons butter
2 large leeks, white part only, thinly sliced
1 small red bell pepper, seeded and thinly sliced
½ pound fresh mushrooms, sliced
1 small head green cabbage, coarsely shredded
¼ teaspoon saffron threads dissolved in ¼ cup warm water or Chicken Stock (page 352)
2 eggs plus 2 yolks
½ cup milk
½ cup heavy cream
Salt and pepper
Pinch of grated nutmeg

Preheat oven to 350 degrees. Grease a 9-inch round baking dish.

In a 12-inch skillet, heat butter. Sauté leeks and pepper about 5 minutes, until wilted. Add mushrooms and cabbage and cook another 5 minutes. (Skillet may appear to be overflowing, but contents will cook down quickly.) Add saffron mixture and cook over medium-high heat until most of the liquid has evaporated (about 8 minutes). Remove from heat and allow to cool about 10 minutes. Drain any liquid that may have accumulated while cooling.

Combine remaining ingredients until well blended. Place vegetables in prepared baking dish and pour custard mixture over. Bake about 40 minutes, or until custard is set.

Serves 6

Rice Pudding with Saffron and Golden Raisins

1½ cups long-grain white rice
1 quart water
½ teaspoon saffron threads
½ teaspoon salt
6 eggs
½ cup sugar
½ cup golden raisins
¼ cup (½ stick) butter, melted

In a medium saucepan, bring rice, water, saffron, and salt to a boil. Cover and cook 10 minutes. Drain off any remaining liquid.

Preheat oven to 375 degrees. Grease a 10-inch baking dish.

Beat eggs and sugar until light. Add rice and raisins and mix well to combine. Pour into prepared dish and bake about 30 minutes, or until set and golden brown. Cut into wedges and serve.

Serves 8

Sesame Seed

LORE AND LINEAGE

One day, a friend served us halvah, the Middle Eastern sesame-seed candy. Eating our way through various flavors—chocolate, orange, and a kind of streaked mocha—we paused only long enough to mumble an appreciative "*mmMMm*" at appropriate intervals.

"Yes, it is delicious," came the unwanted news from our host, "and it has tons of calories." We slowed down a bit, pacing ourselves in deference to this new information.

"'Well, what do you expect?" our relentlessly informative host continued. "It tastes better than celery, doesn't it?"

That it does, as do other sesame-sprinkled specialties like sesame-crowned bagels and yeasty, pizzalike bialys (named for Poland's city of Bialystok). The Fresno sandwich, named for a California town in the San Joaquin Valley, is a sesame-topped pita bread, split open and stuffed with various fillings. Each August when the sizable Armenian community there celebrates the blessing of the grapes, the air is filled with the sweet nuttiness of sesame in many traditional dishes. These include Armenian *choerek* (sweet buns); *simit* (bread twists); *baba ganooj* (an eggplant dip); *hummus* (a chick-pea–*tahini* spread) and that nondietetic but still delectable confection, halvah.

Greek dishes are also well endowed with sesame seeds. At the big Greek fairs, called *glendi,* held in spring and autumn in Oakland, Pennsylvania, near Pittsburgh, colorfully decorated tables spill over with such holiday sesame breads and cakes as *lambropsomo, koulouria,* and *vasilopeta.*

But for sheer quantity of sesame-seed recipes, no region in this country can compare to the South, where the seeds first appeared in the late 1600s. Called benne seeds, they were originally brought by slaves into Carolina's Low Country. Afro-American cooks ground them into a paste with hominy, mashed them into broth or soup as a thickener, or used them as a coating for other foods. A contemporary Charleston dish of chicken coated with sesame seeds and orange seems to be a direct descendent from an old slave dish in which the chicken was coated with grape preserves, ground red pepper, and benne seeds. It was always served with hot cornbread.

SIGNATURE DISH: BENNE WAFERS

No single recipe for benne-seed wafers, which symbolize good luck in some parts of the South, can suffice for all the forms these traditional treats can take. They might be rolled cookies, thin wafers, crisp crackers, or a flourless Georgia version known as benne candy.

Other southern favorites include sesame-coated catfish and benne brittle; Savannah's sesame candies, once a common street food; and Charleston's benne-seed wafers, which are called good luck cookies. Blacks also considered sesame seeds good luck and sprinkled them on doorsteps to drive away the ants.

The American South today remains an important producer of sesame seeds, as are Arizona and California, all contributing to the world's 4 billion pounds annually. Much of this is made into sesame cooking oil, common in hot climates because it is highly stable and seldom turns rancid. Thomas Jefferson appreciated the advantages of sesame oil. In a letter to John Taylor dated January 6, 1808, he wrote: "All agree it is equal to the olive oil. . . . I propose to cultivate it for my own use at least." The light, tasteless sesame oil is distinct from the dark Chinese sesame oil; this flavorful oil is a condiment made from toasted sesame seeds. Also made from sesame is the malt-based confection *niu bi tang,* which is often covered with seeds, and is served in Chinese restaurants to close a meal.

Sesame seeds (*Sesamum indicum*) are actually 50 percent oil; they are usually white, but may be brown, red, or black. The seeds are high in protein; calcium; vitamins A, C, E, and B^2; and phosphorus. Unless they are cooked with food, they should be toasted to bring out their flavor. Just put a layer in a frying pan and take it off the heat when the seeds begin to jump. Their warming flavor is excellent as a garnish for fruit salads, noodles, cheese spreads, stuffings, and any recipe calling for nuts. Or try the following recipes; all of them, you will find, taste better than celery.

VINTAGE RECIPE

The following reflects several recipes and instructions for an old southern way with catfish.

Sautéed Sesame Catfish

4 small catfish, boned and skinned
1/4 cup sesame seed
1/2 cup all-purpose flour
Salt and pepper
1/4 cup (1/2 stick) butter or bacon fat

Dry fish on paper towels. Mix seeds, flour, and salt and pepper to taste. Roll fish in mixture. In a large skillet, heat butter or fat until sizzling; cook fish 3 to 5 minutes each side.

Consumer Guide

Also known as: Arabic—simsim; Chinese—jee-mah; Italian—sesamo; New Orleans and elsewhere in our South—benne.

LATIN: *Sesamum indicum*

Common varieties: White (hulled), tan (unhulled), black oval.

Selection: Pale-colored hulled or unhulled sesame seeds are suitable for most recipes unless otherwise specified. If possible, buy them at a shop where they are sold in bulk, since the turnover tends to be greater.

Storage: Sesame seeds will keep indefinitely in the freezer or refrigerator. Long-term storage at room temperature may turn them rancid.

Compatible herbs and spices: All herbs and spices are compatible with sesame seed.

RECIPE LIST

Baked Eggplant and Tomato Salad with Toasted Sesame Seeds

1 large eggplant (about 1½ pounds), baked, cooled, and cubed
2 ripe tomatoes, seeded and cubed
1 cup Greek olives, pitted and halved
1 bunch green onions, thinly sliced
½ head romaine lettuce, shredded
2 tablespoons red wine vinegar
1 tablespoon lemon juice
1 teaspoon honey
½ teaspoon dried oregano
1 clove garlic, minced
1 tablespoon Oriental sesame oil
⅓ cup vegetable oil
Salt and pepper to taste
⅓ cup sesame seed, toasted (page 360)

Preheat oven to 400 degrees. Pierce eggplant in several places with a fork. Place on baking sheet and bake for about 30 to 40 minutes, or until soft.

Remove flesh from skin of the eggplant and, in salad bowl, combine with tomatoes, olives, green onions, and lettuce. Mix remaining ingredients except sesame seed until well blended and toss with vegetables. Sprinkle with sesame seed.

Serves 4

Sour Cream Sesame Twists

1½ cups all-purpose flour
1 cup (2 sticks) butter, cut into pieces
½ cup dairy sour cream
1 egg, beaten with ½ teaspoon salt
½ cup sesame seed

In a medium bowl, combine flour and butter until crumbly. Stir in sour cream until dough forms. Knead on a lightly floured surface just until mixture holds together. Form into disc, wrap airtight, and refrigerate for at least 3 hours or overnight.

Preheat oven to 400 degrees. Line a baking sheet with foil or parchment paper.

Roll out dough on floured surface to an 8 x 12 rectangle about ⅛-inch thick. Brush entire surface with egg mixture. Sprinkle with sesame seeds and run rolling pin gently over them to make sure they stick. Cut rectangle in half so that both pieces measure 8 x 6 inches. Cut dough into strips 6-inches long and ¾-inch wide. Twist into spirals and place on prepared baking sheet. Bake for about 18 minutes, or until golden. Allow to cool on racks. A tasty accompaniment to soup and salads.

Yield: about 2 dozen

Stir-fried Mustard Greens with Sesame Seeds

2 bunches mustard greens
¼ cup vegetable oil
1 tablespoon sugar
1 teaspoon salt
¼ cup sesame seed
2 teaspoons Oriental sesame oil

Remove stems and cut mustard greens leaves into 1-inch shreds. In a wok or large skillet, heat oil until hot but not smoking. Add greens, sugar, salt, and sesame seed and stir-fry mixture about 1 minute, or until wilted. Drizzle with sesame oil and serve.

Serves 6

Note: If you do not have a large enough skillet, divide ingredients in half and cook in 2 batches.

Sesame Orange Chicken

1 cup plain yogurt
3 tablespoons fresh orange juice
3 skinned and boned chicken breasts, pounded lightly
2 eggs
⅔ cup bread crumbs
3 tablespoons chopped parsley
½ cup sesame seed
6 tablespoons vegetable oil
Salt and pepper

In a medium bowl, combine yogurt and 2 tablespoons of orange juice. Place chicken pieces in this mixture and marinate in refrigerator for about 4 hours, turning chicken occasionally. Drain chicken and blot dry with paper towels.

Beat eggs with remaining 1 tablespoon orange juice. Combine bread crumbs, parsley, and sesame seed. Dredge chicken first in egg mixture and then coat with crumb mixture. Place on a platter and chill about 30 minutes to 1 hour.

In a large skillet, heat oil. Cook chicken over medium heat for about 8 minutes on each side, or until golden and tender. Sprinkle with salt and pepper to taste. Delicious hot or at room temperature.

Serves 6

Benne Bourbon Buttons

2 cups all-purpose flour
1/3 cup sugar
2 tablespoons bourbon
1 cup (2 sticks) butter, room temperature
1/2 cup sesame seed, toasted (page 360)

Preheat oven to 350 degrees. Butter and flour a baking sheet.

Combine all ingredients except 1/4 cup sesame seed until a soft dough forms. Form into walnut-size balls and place on prepared sheet. Flatten slightly with the bottom of a glass dipped in flour. Sprinkle balls with remaining sesame seed. Bake about 15 minutes, or until lightly golden.

Yield: about 2 dozen

Herb and Spice Vinegars and Mustards

Celery Vinegar

Pound two gills of celery seed, put it into a bottle and fill it with strong vinegar; shake it every day for a fortnight, then strain it, and keep it for use.

—VIRGINIA HOUSEWIFE, 1856

Flavored vinegars and mustards have always been a mainstay in American kitchens. Early cookbooks are full of recipes and, it is our prediction, forthcoming American cookbooks will soon be also. These days, people are looking for good-tasting, natural ways to add or enhance flavor without increasing salt or caloric content. Making flavored vinegars and mustards is a great use for leftover fresh herbs or pulverized spices. They also are wonderful gifts. Almost any herbs and spices can be used, and the basic procedures are identical.

FLAVORED VINEGARS

Herb and spice vinegars are really infusions. The herbs or spices are usually put in a sterilized jar, covered with simmering vinegar, and left to steep for days. Because of their high oil content, fresh leaves of herbs make particularly successful infusions, but just about anything will work. This includes the aromatic seeds of spices, fresh or dried herbs and spices, flower tops and petals, or grated fresh roots.

Flavored vinegars are useful mixed with oil as salad dressings. They add zest to soups, stews, and bland vegetables and can be sprinkled on broiled fish or boiled shellfish just before serving.

For fresh leaves: To make 1 pint of vinegar, you need a good fistful of chopped fresh leaves. Gently bruise the leaves to help release oils, place in sterilized bottles, and cover with simmering vinegar. Cool. Cover tightly; shake the bottle occasionally for 1 to 2 weeks, and start tasting the vinegar after a week or so. When strong enough, remove the herbs or leaves. Strain, if desired, and cap or cork tightly.

For dried herbs, spices, or seeds: Put about 3 tablespoons of the dried herbs or spices in sterilized, wide-mouthed jars of 1-pint capacity. Add simmering vinegar and proceed as for fresh leaves. Vinegars may be made by using a combination of fresh herbs or a mix of herbs and spices. The following recipes are especially delicious.

Opal Basil Vinegar

2 cups white wine vinegar
1 cup opal basil, rinsed and dried

Heat vinegar in a saucepan until just to the simmering point. Place basil in a large sterilized, heatproof jar. Pour vinegar over basil and allow to cool. Place cap tightly on jar and allow to sit for about 10 days, shaking occasionally. Decant into sterilized bottles, straining out leaves if desired. Cork or cap bottle and store in cool dry place.

Yield: 1 pint

Note: Green basil may be substituted with very little difference in flavor, but indeed the majestic color that opal basil lends to this vinegar is very special.

Cinnamon Cider Vinegar

Try this unusually delicious vinegar on a green salad mixed with fruits.

1 quart cider vinegar
1 tablespoon honey
2 2-inch-long cinnamon sticks

In a medium saucepan, heat ingredients until simmering. Allow to cool. Place each cinnamon stick in a sterilized 1-pint bottle. Pour vinegar over each and cork or cap securely. Store in a cool, dark place about 3 days before using.

Yield: 2 pints

Rosemary Garlic Vinegar

1 cup white wine vinegar
1 cup red wine vinegar
2 large cloves garlic, peeled and cut in half
2 4-inch sprigs rosemary

Combine vinegars in a saucepan and heat until simmering. Place a garlic half at each end of a rosemary sprig and place in a large sterilized jar. Pour vinegars over, let cool, and tightly cap jar. Allow to sit about 10 days, shaking occasionally. Decant into half-pint bottles, placing 1 garlicked rosemary sprig in each. Cork or cap and store in cool dry place.

Yield: 2 half-pints

Ginger–Chive Sherry Vinegar

2 cups sherry wine vinegar
2 slices fresh ginger
1 cup chives, cut into 1-inch lengths

Heat vinegar and ginger in a saucepan until simmering. Cover and allow to sit 30 minutes. Remove ginger and discard. Place chives in a sterilized jar. Pour still-warm vinegar over chives, let cool completely, then cap jar. Allow to sit about 10 days, shaking occasionally. Strain and decant into a sterilized 1-pint bottle. Cork or cap and store in cool, dry place.

Yield: 1 pint

Varietal Vinegars

Using the steeping method described, you can make any number of tasty vinegars by varying the herb and/or spice blends. Here are some of our other favorites:

Honey–Mint Vinegar
Tarragon–Shallot Vinegar
Parsley–Red Pepper Vinegar
Sherry–Sage Vinegar
Oregano–Garlic Balsamic Vinegar

FLAVORED MUSTARDS

Herb and spice mustards can be made in two simple ways: either mix the fresh or dried herbs or spices into prepared mustard; or add dried herbs or spices to powdered mustard. For the latter, proceed by adding water, a drop of honey or some other sweetening, and vinegar, possibly flavored with the same herb or spice.

Flavored mustards are delicious with sausages and cheeses; they enliven any kind of sandwich; they add great interest to a simple salad dressing. Sage mustard is excellent with pork, duck, or goose, as is thyme mustard; chicken, lamb, and turkey are natural with tarragon; lamb goes well with rosemary; garlic or chive mustard are ideal with beef. The following are a few flavorful favorites.

Basic Homemade Mustard

¼ cup mustard seed
¼ cup dry mustard
½ cup hot water
½ cup white wine vinegar or flavored vinegar
1 teaspoon salt
1 teaspoon honey

In a small bowl, combine mustard seed, dry mustard, and water. Let sit, uncovered, for about 2 hours. Place in a food processor or blender with remaining ingredients and process to desired consistency (smooth to grainy). Pour into a clean jar, seal, and refrigerate. Mustard may be used at once, but a few days rest mellows the flavors.

Yield: about 1 cup

Honey–Dill Mustard
Using basic recipe, increase honey to 2 tablespoons and stir in 2 tablespoons fresh dill or 1 tablespoon dried.

Coriander–Mint Mustard
Using basic recipe, use mint vinegar and add 2 teaspoons freshly ground coriander seed.

Tarragon–Shallot Mustard
Using basic recipe, puree 1 tablespoon chopped shallots with mustard mixture and stir in 1 tablespoon fresh tarragon.

Parsley–Chive Mustard
Stir in 2 tablespoons chopped parsley and 1 tablespoon chopped chives to basic recipe.

Red Pepper–Honey Mustard
Using basic recipe, increase honey to 2 tablespoons and stir in 1 teaspoon red pepper flakes.

Note: A good-quality, store-bought Dijon-type mustard may be used as a base for any of these flavorful combinations; just stir the herb and/or spice mixture right in the jar.

Herb Bundles and Spice Blends

> Remember there is a difference between one bay leaf and two bay leaves; and the difference between one clove of garlic and two cloves of garlic is enough to disorganize a happy home.
>
> —NEW ORLEANS CITY GUIDE
> Federal Writers' Project, 1938

From the hill country farms of Vermont or the Greek fishing communities of Florida to the Basque restaurant owners in Nevada and California, America's cooks have always known what summer is: a time to revel in the fresh taste of herbs and to put some aside to dry for the cold days to come. Sometimes they tied a few herbs together and wrapped them in muslin. What they named these herb clusters depended on what country they had come from, where they settled in America, or what they intended to do with them. There were bouquets garnis, soup bunches, and vinegar blends; herb bundles, fines herbes, sweet bags, sausage mixes, herb peppers, or soup spirits. Whatever their names, they were basically shortcuts: ways of "storing" taste and releasing it instantly when needed.

Although the permutations and combinations approach the infinite, we find the following bundles particularly successful.

Bouquet Garni

Make a sandwich of two 2-inch lengths of celery stalk, 1 bay leaf, 3 sprigs fresh parsley, and 1 sprig fresh thyme (or ½ teaspoon dried). Tie with kitchen string. Immerse in soups and stews.

Quatre Epices

Combine thoroughly ¼ cup freshly ground black pepper, 1 tablespoon ground ginger, 3 teaspoons freshly grated nutmeg, and ¼ teaspoon ground cloves. Store in airtight jar. Enhances the flavor of pâtés and sausages.

Fines Herbes

This flavorful blend consists of 4 herbs: parsley, chives, tarragon, and chervil, blended in equal proportions. Fresh is best to make delicious egg, vegetable, and fish dishes.

Curry Powder Blend

Combine thoroughly 1 tablespoon ground cumin, 2 tablespoons ground coriander, ½ teaspoon ground cloves, ½ teaspoon ground cinnamon, 1 teaspoon ground cardamom, ¼ teaspoon mace, ¼ teaspoon freshly grated nutmeg, ½ teaspoon ground red pepper, 1 tablespoon turmeric. Store in airtight jar.

Five-Spice Powder

Combine thoroughly 1 tablespoon freshly ground Sichuan peppercorns, 1 tablespoon ground cinnamon, 1 tablespoon ground fennel seed, ¼ teaspoon ground cloves, and 4 star anise, ground. Store in airtight jar.

Dried herbs and spices may be used most successfully in many combinations by tying them in small squares of cheesecloth. In fact, these seasoning bundles may be prepared ahead and stored in an airtight jar in quantity for future use. Some combinations that are especially appealing to us are:

bay leaf, parsley, and tarragon—for poultry
bay leaf, fennel seed, dill—for fish
sage, parsley, garlic, rosemary—for lamb
basil, garlic, parsley, marjoram—for tomato-based soups or sauces
rosemary, oregano, thyme, bay leaf—for beef

Basic Recipes

Chicken Stock

1 leek, all white part and about 1 inch of green
2 carrots
2 celery stalks
1 onion, cut in half and stuck with 6 cloves
1 whole chicken or a mixture of necks, backs, and wings weighing about 5 pounds
6 peppercorns
½ teaspoon dried thyme
1 bay leaf
4 quarts water

Cut leek, carrots, and celery into 1-inch pieces. Place into a large stockpot with remaining ingredients and bring to a boil. Skim foam as it accumulates. Reduce to a simmer and cook, uncovered or partially covered, for about 2 hours. Add more water if more than 1 cup evaporates during cooking time. Strain into bowl or storage container and refrigerate or freeze.

Yield: about 4 quarts

Fish Stock

2 pounds fish bones from nonoily fish (not salmon)
1 carrot, sliced
1 leek (white part only), sliced
1 celery stalk, sliced
½ teaspoon dried thyme
1 bay leaf
1 sprig parsley
3 peppercorns
Pinch of salt
1 slice lemon
2 cups dry white wine
2 cups water

Place all ingredients in a large pot and bring to a boil. Reduce to a simmer and cook, uncovered, for 25 minutes. Strain and store in refrigerator or freezer.

Yield: about 1 quart

Note: An alternative method is possible when fish bones are difficult to obtain. A suitable substitute can be made using 2 cups bottled or canned clam juice, 1 cup dry white wine, 1 cup water, and specified herbs and spices, simmered for 5 minutes.

Beef or Veal Stock

8 pounds beef and/or veal bones, cut into 3-inch pieces
2 onions, sliced
2 carrots, sliced
2 celery stalks, sliced
2 tomatoes, quartered
1 Bouquet Garni (page 350)
4 quarts water

Preheat oven to 450 degrees. Arrange beef and onions in a large roasting pan and place in oven. Brown on all sides, turning as necessary. Transfer bones and onions to a large stockpot and add remaining ingredients. Discard fat from roasting pan and deglaze (page 361) with 1 cup water, scraping up all particles sticking to bottom of pan. (This will give your stock flavor and color.) Add pan juices to stockpot and bring contents to a boil. Reduce to a simmer and skim foam as it accumulates on surface. Simmer, partially covered, at least 4 hours, adding more water if more than 1 cup evaporates during cooking. Strain into bowl or storage container and refrigerate or freeze.

Yield: about 3½ quarts

Pâte Brisée

1½ cups all-purpose flour
Pinch of salt
½ cup (1 stick) cold butter, cut into 8 pieces
2 tablespoons cold vegetable shortening, cut into pieces
About 5 tablespoons ice water

In a bowl or food processor, mix flour and salt. Cut in butter and shortening until mixture is crumbly. Add half the water and mix or process just until dough holds together. If mixture seems too dry, add remaining water but do not overprocess. Form into a disc, wrap, and refrigerate at least 1 hour before using.

Yield: enough pastry for a 9- or 10-inch tart

Basic Pizza Dough

1 tablespoon active dry yeast
1 teaspoon honey or sugar
3/4 cup warm water
2 1/2 cups all-purpose flour
1 teaspoon salt
1 tablespoon olive oil

Mix yeast and honey or sugar with warm water in a small bowl; let proof (page 362) about 10 minutes. In a separate bowl, combine flour and salt. Pour in yeast mixture and olive oil and mix until well combined. Turn out onto a floured surface and knead until smooth and springy (approximately 5 minutes), adding more flour if necessary. Form into a ball and place in an oiled bowl. Turn dough around so that all surfaces are oiled. Cover with plastic wrap and place in a warm spot to rise until doubled in bulk (about 1 hour).

Punch down and allow to rest about 10 minutes before rolling out.

Yield: enough dough for one 14-inch pizza or two 8-inch calzones

Herbed Pizza Dough

Add 1/4 cup finely chopped fresh herbs to flour in basic recipe. Some of our favorite combinations are parsley and garlic; basil, garlic, and oregano; and rosemary and thyme.

Spiced Pizza Dough

Add 1 tablespoon ground cumin, 1/4 teaspoon ground red pepper, and 1/2 teaspoon paprika to flour in basic recipe.

Basic Pasta Dough

1¾ cups all-purpose flour plus ½ cup semolina, or
2¼ cups all-purpose flour
½ teaspoon salt
3 eggs
1 tablespoon olive oil

In a food processor or by hand, combine flour(s) and salt. Add eggs and oil and mix until dough forms. Form into a disc, place under a bowl, and let rest about 15 minutes before rolling out and cutting into desired shapes.

Yield: about 1½ pounds

Herbed Pasta Dough
Add 3 tablespoons chopped fresh herbs to flour in basic recipe. Delicious combinations are parsley and fresh coriander; basil and garlic; sage and parsley; or parsley, thyme, and oregano.

Spiced Pasta Dough
Add 1 tablespoon freshly ground black pepper, ¼ teaspoon grated nutmeg, and ½ teaspoon ground red pepper to flour in basic recipe.

Pesto

2 cups fresh basil leaves
4 cloves garlic
¼ cup toasted pine nuts (page 360)
½ cup grated Parmesan cheese
1 teaspoon dried oregano
Salt and pepper to taste
½–¾ cup olive oil

Combine ingredients in a food processor or blender to make a rough-textured puree. If storing for future use, cover surface with a layer of additional oil to prevent discoloration. May be refrigerated up to a week and frozen up to 4 months.

Yield: 1 cup

Mayonnaise (Food Processor Method)

1 egg, room temperature
1 teaspoon Dijon-type mustard
1 tablespoon lemon juice or vinegar
Salt and pepper to taste
1 cup oil (vegetable or olive, or a mixture)

Place ingredients in a food processor bowl fitted with the steel blade and process well to combine. With machine running, add oil very slowly through feed tube. As the mayonnaise thickens the oil can be added faster. Taste and correct seasonings.

Yield: 1¼ cups

Mayonnaise (Hand Method)

2 egg yolks
Pinch of salt
1 teaspoon Dijon-type mustard
1 cup oil (vegetable or olive, or a mixture)
1 tablespoon lemon juice or vinegar

In a small bowl, whisk yolks, salt, and mustard until thick. Begin adding the oil very slowly, almost drop by drop, beating well after each addition. When the mayonnaise has thickened, add the oil more quickly, making sure it has all been incorporated in the mixture. Stir in the lemon juice or vinegar. May be stored in refrigerator for up to 10 days. Do not freeze.

Yield: 1¼ cups

Herbed Mayonnaise
Using either method described, stir in tablespoons of finely chopped herbs of your choice. We like watercress, chives, dill, and basil in combination or each by itself. Allow mayonnaise to rest about 30 minutes before using to allow herbs to infuse.

Fresh Tomato Sauce

2 tablespoons olive oil
2 cloves garlic, minced
2 pounds fresh ripe tomatoes, seeded and coarsely chopped, or 28-ounce can imported Italian tomatoes, chopped
1 bay leaf
½ teaspoon dried oregano
Salt and pepper to taste
1 sprig parsley

Heat olive oil in a saucepan and add garlic. Cook over medium heat for 2 minutes, then add remaining ingredients. Simmer about 25 minutes or until sauce thickens slightly. Remove bay leaf. May be refrigerated for about 10 days or frozen for up to 6 months.

Yield: about 1 cup

Tomato Cream Sauce
Follow method described for fresh tomato sauce. After sauce has simmered 25 minutes, add ¼ cup heavy cream and cook another 5 minutes.

Crème Fraîche

Authentic crème fraîche is a naturally fermented cream that can now be found in the dairy cases of some specialty food shops. The price is very high, from $3 to $4 a pint. It has a wonderfully nutty flavor and reacts very favorably in sauces that are exposed to long and high heat because it does not curdle. The following is a most satisfactory and less costly substitute.

1 cup heavy cream, preferably not ultrapasteurized
½ cup dairy sour cream or 2 tablespoons buttermilk

Heat cream to approximately 80 degrees (very warm to the touch—but thermometer method is best). Pour into a clean jar and add sour cream or buttermilk. Stir gently and cover loosely. Allow to sit at room temperature until thickened, which may take anywhere from 8 to 24 hours. Cover tightly and store in refrigerator for up to 1 week. It will continue to thicken after refrigerated.

Yield: 1½ cups

Basic Methods

TOASTING NUTS AND SEEDS

Nuts: Spread desired amount of nuts on a baking sheet and place in preheated 350-degree oven for about 10 minutes, shaking pan once during that time. Nuts should be no darker than a light golden brown.

Seeds: Place desired amount of seeds in preheated skillet (preferably nonstick). Cook over low heat, shaking pan occasionally just until seeds turn golden brown.

COOKING ARTICHOKES

Cut off stem and small leaves around base. With a very sharp knife, slice about ½ inch off the prickly top, leaving a fairly flat surface. With sharp scissors, snip off prickly tips of remaining leaves. Boil, uncovered, in a large pot of salted water with half a lemon for 30 to 40 minutes. Artichoke is done when leaves pull out easily. Drain upside down on paper towels. To remove the inedible choke, spread leaves open from center. Pull out cone of light green leaves, and, with a small spoon, scrap out the fuzzy core, which is the choke.

PEELING TOMATOES

Place tomatoes in boiling water for 30 seconds. Remove, allow to cool, and peel with small paring knife.

ROASTING PEPPERS

Place peppers over a gas burner, under a broiler, or on a barbecue grill. Roast until skin blisters and blackens, turning peppers often. Place in a plastic bag until cool enough to handle, then scrape skin away with a small paring knife.

HANDLING HOT PEPPERS

Owing to the volatile oils in peppers, such as jalapeño or serrano, they require careful handling. Kitchen gloves should be worn when cutting them, especially if there are cuts or wounds on hands. If working without gloves, wash hands well after handling peppers because any remaining oils can cause painful and sometimes dangerous irritations, particularly to eyes.

DEGLAZING

To capture the flavors and precious pan juices and browned particles after the sautéeing or roasting process, first pour off fat. Add liquid (stock, wine, water, or cream) and cook over medium heat while scraping and stirring.

BLANCHING

Place vegetables or fruits briefly into boiling water (not more than a few minutes) to remove raw taste, set color, or facilitate the peeling of fruits and tomatoes.

CUTTING VEGETABLES

Julienne: Cut food into matchstick-size pieces.

Chiffonade: To cut greens in a chiffonade, stack the leaves (sorrel, basil, spinach, chard, etc.), roll them up like a cigarette, and cut shreds crosswise with a sharp knife.

REDUCING LIQUIDS

This technique is used to evaporate and thicken a liquid, such as a stock, soup, or sauce. Boil the liquid rapidly to concentrate its flavor and reduce its volume according to individual recipes.

PROOFING YEAST

To be activated, yeast must be dissolved in warm liquid, about 105–115 degrees. Stir yeast into warm liquid and allow to stand 5 to 10 minutes. If yeast is active and alive, a foam will form on surface. If yeast is no longer active, it will sink to bottom. If the latter happens, discard mixture and begin again with fresh yeast.

BAIN-MARIE OR WATER BATH

Most frequently used for delicate custard-based dishes, a bain-marie is simply a large pan filled with hot water in which the custard molds are placed to be cooked or kept warm.

ZEST

The outer, colored part of the rind (not the pith) of citrus fruits (lemon, orange, lime) contains flavorful oils. It is removed with a tool called a zester, or a grater or peeler, and added to various dishes for flavor.

DRIED BEANS—QUICK-SOAK METHOD

Place beans in a large pot with enough cold water to cover. Bring to a boil and cook 2 minutes. Remove from heat and let beans stand 1 hour. Drain and proceed with recipe.

PARCHMENT PAPER

Packaged in rolls like wax paper, this silicone-treated paper is excellent as a nonstick lining for baking pans. Wiped clean, the paper may be re-used. Food can be wrapped and baked in parchment for an effect very much like steaming, since the paper is nonporous and the food thus cooks in its own juices and vapors. This paper can usually be found in specialty cookware shops.

Suggested Seasonal Menus

SPRING

EAT YOUR VEGETABLES

Carrot and Sorrel Bisque
Asparagus with Mustard Butter
Braised Lentils and Leeks
Saffroned Vegetable Flan
Cheese Popovers with Nutmeg

SLOOP SALAD SUPPER

Chicken and Carrot Thread Salad
Greek Salad Pita Sandwich
Corn, Cress, and Potato Salad
Ricotta Rice Muffins

FISHERMAN'S CATCH

Shrimp in Fennel Mustard
Baby Trout with Yellow Tomatoes and Tarragon
Salmon and Sorrel Tart
Parsley Pasta with Clam Sauce
Ported Pineapple with Papaya Puree

WALKER'S REWARD

Melon Salad with Poppyseed Dressing
Buttermilk French Toast
Eggs Basildict
Cumin Cornmeal Scones

WINTER

APRÈS AEROBICS

Salubrious Soup
Winter Wheat Salad with Parsley and Mint
Rosemary–Raisin Whole Wheat Corn Muffins
Oranges and Black Grapes in Rosemary-scented Syrup

BIG GAME "BURGOO"

Watercress and Walnut Tartlets
Mustard-soaked Ripe Olives
Paella Pasta
Warm Carrot Salad with Cinnamon and Chives

NEW YEAR'S DAY "BLUNCH"

Tomato–Tarragon Soup with Vodka
Chive Omelet Wheels
Chick-peas, Sausage, and Sage
Savory Cabbage–Apple Strudel
Fennel and Honey Rye Muffins

VALENTINE'S DAY DINNER

Salmon Tartare in Cucumber Cups
Saffron Stars and Snow Pea Soup
Sea Bass in Filo with Ginger and Green Onions
Stir-fried Mustard Greens with Sesame Seeds
Cappuccino Sorbet

AUTUMN

BANNER YEAR BIRTHDAY PARTY

Sunchoke Vichyssoise
Lamb in Mustard Cream
Lemon Rice with Walnuts and Watercress
Two Lettuces with Basil Vinaigrette
Chocolate Cake with Eggnog Custard

COVERED DISH AU COURANT

Braised Lamb Shanks in Rosemary Mustard
Barley Pilaf with Pecans and Dill
Black Bean Ragout with Fried Polenta
Fennel Fricassée
Lemon–Ginger Sponge Cake

THANKSGIVING DAY LEFTOVERS LUNCH

Pumpkin Soup with Corn and Green Onions
Turkey Crepinettes
Glazed Carrots and Brussels Sprouts with Chives and Toasted Almonds
Cinnamon–Apple Noodle Soufflé

SPICY SWEET SIXTEEN PARTY

Spicy Lamb and Red Pepper Pizza
Ribs in Spicy Orange–Coriander Sauce
Pasta with Two Pestos
Green Beans à la Grecque
Bread with Two Peppercorns
Ginger Almond Shortbread

SUMMER

FOURTH OF JULY

Iced Cherry Soup with Mace
Grilled Skirt Steak with Tomato–Tarragon Relish
Corn on the Cob with Cajun Butter
Minted Potatoes with Sherry Vinegar
Grilled Chicken with Fennel Puree
Fresh Peach Gratin

FIRST HARVEST FROM THE VEGETABLE GARDEN

Cold Cucumber and Beet Soup with New Potatoes
Eggplant and Sausage Pasta
Corn Custards with Sorrel Sauce
Warm Yellow Squash in Tomato–Basil Vinaigrette
Fenneled Figs and Fresh Raspberries

EATING OUT OF HAND

Basil Cheese Toasts
Mozzarella Cakes with Thyme–Tomato Pesto
Sautéed Snapper Sandwich with Ginger Mayonnaise
Lamburgers with Green Peppercorn Sauce
Bay Shrimp and Watercress Sandwich
Benne Bourbon Buttons

SHAKER PLATE

Sister Abigails's Blue Chive Omelet
Fried Chicken Wings with Lemon–Mint Sauce
Shaker Spinach with Rosemary
Sage and Salt Cornmeal Flats

TOO HOT TO COOK NIGHT

Grape Gazpacho
Carrot and Zucchini Salad with Basil and Walnuts
Shrimp and Cucumber Rémoulade
Minted Berry Cream

TAPA-TERIA

Shrimp Pâté with Tarragon and Mustard
Mozzarella Cakes with Thyme–Tomato Pesto
Salmon Fritters with Watercress Sauce
Potato Pancakes with Chive Sauce
Basil Cheese Toasts

List of Recipes by Courses

APPETIZERS AND FIRST COURSES

SOUPS

SANDWICHES

PASTA, PIZZA, AND GRAINS

LITTLE MEALS

LITTLE MEALS (*cont.*)

SALADS

MAIN DISHES

MAIN DISHES (*cont.*)

VEGETABLES AND ACCOMPANIMENTS

DESSERTS

BREAD BOX

Selected Bibliography

Adams, Ramon F. *Come An' Get It: The Story of The Old Cowboy Cook.* Norman, Oklahoma, 1952.

Anderson, Frank J. *An Illustrated History of the Herbals.* New York, 1977.

Bartlett, Virginia K. *Pickles and Pretzels: Pennsylvania's World of Food.* Pittsburgh, 1980.

Belote, Julianne. *The Compleat American Housewife, 1776.* Concord, California, 1974.

Berolzheimer, Ruth, ed. *The American Woman's Cook Book.* Chicago, 1953; Prudence Penny Binding.

———. *The United States Regional Cook Book.* Chicago, 1953; Prudence Penny Binding.

Better Homes and Gardens. *Heritage Cook Book.* Des Moines, 1975.

Briggs, Desmond. *A Pinch of Spices.* London, 1978.

Brooks, Karen Gail, and Gideon Bosker, M. D. *The Global Kitchen.* New York, 1981.

Brown, Alice Cooke. *Early American Herb Recipes.* New York, 1966.

Brown, Dale, and the editors of Time-Life Books. *The Cooking of Scandinavia.* New York, 1968.

———. *American Cooking: The Northwest.* New York, 1970.

Carroll, Peter N., and David W. Noble. *The Free and the Unfree: A New History of the United States.* New York, 1977.

Child, Lydia Maria Francis. *The American Frugal Housewife.* Boston, 1836; 20th Edition, reprinted New York, 1972.

Dampney, Janet, and Elizabeth Pomeroy. *All About Herbs.* London, 1977.

David, Elizabeth. *Spices, Salt and Aromatics in the English Kitchen.* New York, 1970.

Day, Mahon. *New York Street Cries in Rhyme.* New York, 1825; reprinted New York, 1977.

Eckhardt, Linda West. *The Only Texas Cookbook.* Austin, 1981.

Edmonds, Andy. *Let the Good Times Roll! The Complete Cajun Handbook.* New York, 1984.

Elverson, Virginia T., and Mary Ann McLanahan. *A Cooking Legacy.* New York, 1975.

Farmer, Fannie Merritt. *The Boston Cooking-School Cook Book.* Boston, 1906; Boston, 1909.

Federal Writers' Project. *Almanac for Thirty-Niners.* [n. p.], California, 1938.

———. *California: A Guide to the Golden State.* [n. p.], New York, 1939.

———. *Festivals in San Francisco.* [n. p.], California, 1939.

———. *New Orleans City Guide.* [n. p.], Massachusetts, 1938.

Fehrenbach, Lillian. *The Pedernales Country Cookbook.* New York, 1968.

Feibleman, Peter S. *American Cooking: Creole and Acadian.* New York, 1971.

Field, Michael, and the editors of Time-Life Books. *A Quintet of Cuisines.* New York, 1970.

Fisher, M. F. K. *A Cordiall Water.* San Francisco, 1981.

Fox, Helen Morgenthau. *Gardening with Herbs for Flavor and Fragrance.* New York, 1970.

Garland, Linda Page, and Elliott Wiggonton, eds. *The Foxfire Book of Appalachian Cookery.* New York, 1984.

Gibbons, Euell. *Stalking the Healthful Herbs.* New York, 1970.

———. *Stalking the Wild Asparagus.* New York, 1962.

Greenberg, Sheldon, and Elizabeth Lambert Ortiz. *The Spice of Life.* New York, 1984.

Grieve, Maud. *Culinary Herbs and Condiments.* New York, 1971.

Hall, Dorothy. *The Book of Herbs.* New York, 1972.

Hampstead, Marilyn. *The Basil Book.* New York, 1984.

Hatfield, Audrey Wynne. *The Pleasures of Herbs.* New York, 1965.

Hayes, Elizabeth. *Spices and Herbs Around the World.* New York, 1961.

Heal, Carolyn, and Michael Allsop. *Cooking with Spices.* London, 1983.

Hersey, Jean. *Cooking with Herbs.* New York, 1972.

Hess, Karen, ed. *Martha Washington's Booke of Cookery.* New York, 1981.

Hibben, Sheila. *A Kitchen Manual.* New York, 1941.

———. *American Regional Cookery.* Boston, 1946.

Hillegass, Catherine J., ed. *Nebraska Centennial First Ladies Cookbook.* Lincoln, Nebraska, 1966.

Hogner, Dorothy Childs. *Herbs: From the Garden to the Table.* New York, 1953.

Hollister, Will C. *Dinner in the Diner: Great Railroad Recipes of All Time.* Corona del Mar, California, 1964.

Hooker, Richard J. *A History of Food and Drink in America.* New York, 1981.

Humphrey, Sylvia Windle. *A Matter of Taste.* New York, 1965.

Jones, Evan. *American Food: The Gastronomic Story.* New York, 1975.

Kavasch, Barrie. *Native Harvests: Recipes and Botanicals of the American Indian.* New York, 1977.

Kent, Louise Andrews. *The Vermont Year-Round Cookbook.* Boston, 1965.

Kimball, Yaffe, and Jean Anderson. *The Art of American Indian Cooking.* New York, 1965.

Koehler, Margaret H. *Recipes From the Russians of San Francisco.* Riverside, Connecticut, 1974.

Krutch, Joseph Wood. *Herbal.* New York, 1965.

Lamprey, L. *The Story of Cookery.* New York, 1945.

Lehner, Ernst. *Folklore and Odysseys of Food and Medicinal Plants.* New York, 1962.

———. *How They Saw the New World.* New York, 1966.

Leighton, Ann. *American Gardens in the 18th Century.* Boston, 1976.

———. *Early American Gardens.* Boston, 1970.

Leonard, Jonathan Norton. *American Cooking: The Great West.* New York, 1971.

Lestz, Gerald S. *The Pennsylvania Dutch Cookbook.* New York, 1970.

Lewis, Oscar. *Bay Window Bohemia.* New York, 1956.

———. *This Was San Francisco.* New York, 1962.

Liebman, Malvina W. *Jewish Cookery From Boston To Bagdhad.* Miami, Florida, 1975.

Linsenmeyer, Helen Walker. *From Fingers to Finger Bowls: A Sprightly History of California Cooking.* San Diego, 1976.

Ljungmark, Lars. *Swedish Exodus.* Carbondale, Illinois, 1979.

Lydon, Sandy. *Chinese Gold: The Chinese in the Monterey Bay Region.* Capitola, California, 1985.

MacDonald, Barbara, Carolyn Boisvert, and Peggy Miller, eds. *Fifty States Cookbook.* Secaucus, New Jersey, 1977.

Mawson, Monica. *Herb and Spice Cookery.* London, 1972.

Mazza, Irma Goodrich. *Herbs for the Kitchen.* Boston, 1939.

McBride, Mary Margaret. *Harvest of American Cooking.* New York, 1956.

McGee, Harold. *On Food and Cooking: The Science and Lore of the Kitchen.* New York, 1984.

Miller, Amy Bess Williams, and Persis Wellington Fuller, eds. *The Best of Shaker Cooking.* New York, 1970.

Miloradovich, Milo. *The Art of Cooking with Herbs and Spices.* New York, 1950.

Moskos, Charles C. *Greek Americans: Struggle and Success.* Englewood Cliffs, New Jersey, 1980.

Muenscher, Minne Worthen. *Minnie Muenscher's Herb Cookbook.* Ithaca, New York, 1978.

Nathan, Joan. *An American Folklife Cookbook.* New York, 1984.

Nebraska Czechs of Wilber. *Favorite Recipes of the Nebraska Czechs.* Wilber, Nebraska, 1968.

Parry, John W. *The Story of Spices.* New York, 1953.

Pellegrini, Angelo M. *The Food-Lover's Garden.* New York, 1970.

Perl, Lila. *Red-flannel Hash and Shoo-Fly Pie: American Regional Foods and Festivals.* New York, 1965.

Phipps, Frances. *Colonial Kitchens, Their Furnishings and Their Gardens.* New York, 1972.

Rawlings, Marjorie Kinnan. *Cross Creek Cookery.* New York, 1942.

Rodgers, Ann. *A Basque Story Cook Book.* New York, 1968.

Root, Waverley. *Food.* New York, 1980.

———, and Richard de Rochement. *Eating in America: A History.* New York, 1976.

Rutherford, Meg. *A Pattern of Herbs.* London, 1975.

Scully, Virginia. *A Treasury of American Indian Herbs.* New York, 1970.

Shenton, James P., et al. *American Cooking: The Melting Pot.* New York, 1971.

Simmons, Amelia. *American Cookery.* Hartford, 1796; reprinted New York, 1958.

Stern, Jane and Michael. *Goodfood.* New York, 1983.

Stobart, Tom. *The Cook's Encyclopedia.* New York, 1980.

———. *Herbs, Spices and Flavorings.* New York, 1970.

Thorne, John. *Simple Cooking.* New York, 1987.

Vaughan, Beatrice. *Yankee Hill-Country Cooking.* Brattleboro, Vermont, 1963.

Von Welanetz, Diana and Paul. *The Von Welanetz Guide to Ethnic Ingredients.* Los Angeles, 1982.

Webster, Helen Noyes. *Herbs: How to Grow Them and How to Use Them.* Newton, Massachusetts, 1939.

Williams, Susan. *Savory Suppers and Fashionable Feasts: Dining in Victorian America.* New York, 1985.

Wilson, Jose, and the editors of Time-Life Books. *American Cooking: The Eastern Heartland.* New York, 1971.

Wormser, Richard Edward. *Southwest Cookery: or at Home on the Range.* New York, 1969.

Index

About the Authors

Like her coauthor, Jeannette Ferrary was born in Brooklyn, New York, and began her career by teaching. Since then, she has worked as a bilingual researcher in Bogota, Colombia, an advertising director for her own firm in St. Paul, Minnesota, a tutor, copywriter, and consultant. A course with Simone Beck in Chateauneuf de Grasse, France, gave focus to her preoccupation with food and ultimately led to her present role as author, reviewer, and writer. Her articles and stories have appeared in *The New York Times Book Review, Harvard Magazine,* the *Journal of Gastronomy,* and *California Magazine.* She is a regular contributor to the *New York Times,* writing about California food and lifestyle. In the course of all this, she has lived in California at three separate times, the last time being in 1974. At that time she moved to Belmont, just south of San Francisco, where she has decided to live permanently with historian/author Peter Carroll and their young daughter, Natasha Carroll-Ferrary.

Louise Fiszer founded Louise's Pantry Cooking School and Cookware Shop, Menlo Park, California, in 1978 where she teaches and serves as director. She and the school have been featured in the *New York Times* and other publications for innovative contributions in the area of California and regional American cooking. She is the coauthor of *The California-American Cookbook* (Simon and Schuster). A former New Yorker, she now makes her home in Northern California with her husband Max (and her two sons, when they get hungry enough to come home for mother's cooking).